M000110806

SPIRIT

SPIRIT

SPIRIT

VOLUME 1

ENTER THE COURTS OF HEAVEN

By

NADIA JOHNSON

The Sale of this book without its cover is unauthorized. If you purchased this book without its cover, you should be aware that it was reported as "unsold and destroyed." Neither the author nor the publisher has received payment for the sale of this "stripped book."

Spirit Spirit Spirit

Copyright © 2021 by Nadia W. Johnson

All Rights Reserved. No portion of this book, in part or in full, may be reproduced, stored in a retrieval system, or transmitted in any form or by any means – electronic, mechanical, photocopying, scanning, recording, or otherwise – except for brief quotations in printed reviews, without the prior permission in written form by the author.

Unless otherwise noted, all Scripture quotations are taken from The New King James Version. Copyright © 1992 by Thomas Nelson, Inc. Used by permission. All rights reserved.

Scripture quotations taken from the Amplified (AMP) Bible, Copyright © 1954, 1958, 1962, 1964, 1965, 1987 by The Lockman Foundation. Used by permission. (www.Lockman.org). Scripture quotations taken from the Amplified Bible, Classic Edition (AMPC), Copyright © 1954, 1958, 1962, 1964, 1965, 1987 by The Lockman Foundation. Used by permission. (www.Lockman.org). Scripture quotations marked taken from the Expanded Bible (EXB), Copyright © 2011 by Thomas Nelson, Inc. Used by permission. All rights reserved. Scripture quotations taken from the Jubilee Bible 2000 (JUB), Copyright © 2013, 2020 by Ransom Press International. All rights reserved. Scripture quotations taken from the Mirror Bible, Copyright © 2021 Mirror Word. All rights reserved. Scripture quotations taken from the New International Version® (NIV) Bible, Copyright © 1973, 1978, 1984, 2011 by Biblica, Inc.™. Used by permission. All rights reserved. Scripture quotations taken from the New Living Translation (NLT) Bible, Copyright © 1996, 2004, 2007 by Tyndale House Foundation. Used by permission. All rights reserved. Scripture quotations taken from the King James Version (KJV) Bible. All rights reserved. Scripture quotations taken from the Passion Translation®, Copyright © 2017, 2018, 2020 by Passion & Fire Ministries, Inc. Used by permission. All rights reserved.

Illustrations: Monica Hart

Cover, Design: Segun Aluko.

ISBN-13: 978-0-578-96368-6

ISBN-10: 0-578-96368-6

CONTENTS

DEDICATION

This book is dedicated to the Eternal Spirit in Whom I live - God the Father, in Whom I move - God the Son, in Whom I have my being - God the Holy Spirit; for its through You, and for Your praise, I write.

Through You, "my tongue is the pen of a ready writer." (Psalm 45:1).

ACKNOWLEDGMENTS

To Ime, my love, you have always believed in me. Thank you for working overtime through birthing this book; For sharing in its passion, and for ensuring excellence. Indeed, God gave me you. Thank you for loving me to bits and unwaveringly through many journeys. And this being one of a multitude.

Thanks to my incredible daughters, Deborah & Aimee; Every night, I have listened as you take turns to pray over this book and for would-be readers year after year. Today, I rejoice in God for equipping you growing ladies to stand by me and to invest in everyone holding this book right now.

I specifically want to thank my beloved elder brother, Dr. Jeff Bajah & his wife Vera for their expert overseeing, review & generous contributions to this project.

Special thanks to my beloved brother Dr. Brian Bajah & his wife Ivy for standing with me and generously supporting me through this process.

To my beloved sister, Cindy Aluko, you have been my life partner and rock through every stage of this journey; special gratitude. And to my dearest in-law and the lead graphic designer for all *Spirit Talks with Nadia* projects and this book cover, thank you, Segun Aluko.

Thanks to my heart loves Isabel, Jayden, Raphael, Jason & Caren; filling my love tank through this journey.

Thanks to my dad, Isaiah Bajah, for being a God-honoring father; for setting an example of daily prayer altars using "Every day with Jesus" through my childhood.

Special thanks to Tony & Monica Hart, for your unwavering

support and dedication from the very conception of this book. Thank you, Monica, for the beautiful illustrations and as you work translating to Spanish.

I am beyond grateful for the love of my amazing friends, Rika & Joshua Noonan; thanks for every expert input and constant supervision to see this project come to light. Without you, this would still be a vision.

To Marie Bigirumwami, my friend and Kingdom partner, your consistent prayer support and encouragement to birth this book is beyond me. Thank you.

I am particularly grateful for my dear friends Kemi Folarin & Onyeche Cort; your input, love, prayers, and encouragement have sustained me on this journey.

Thanks for the love and immense support of our dear friend, Terry Foster. Your continued belief in this calling is precious.

I am thankful to you, my dear friend Lauren Trogdon for your excellent review of the manuscript and much-needed guidance through this process.

Special thanks to my fantastic prayer warrior team & partners who bring me so much grace & support in every way; Alan Ndibwami, Amanda G, Chantal Condo, Connie Mason, Cynthia Choi, Dvine Roman, Erika, Esther Kangebe, Fiona Kulubya, Jaynie Jackson, Jeanne Uwitonze, Jenelle Cunningham, June Kikumu-Aquil, Leatitia Rwiyegura, Linda Mamman, Matta Aderonmu, Rachel Hashweh, Sally Angeles, Sally Vasques, Solange Kassia, Solome Kalule, Tanisha Asihene, Valerie Robinson. Through your commitment, you held my hands in this process. And I cannot give adequate thanks to each one of you.

I want to especially appreciate the support of my lovely friends on this journey: Adaora Ajibo, Alma Estrada, Amanda & JP Leynes, Christopher Iyalla, Devorah Robinson, Dr. Enitan Ibrahim Akinsoyinu, Heidi Shumaker, Helen Kulungian, Jossy Katigi, Joy Kikumu, Joy Obande, Katherine Nash, Maribel Gonzales, Mikki Wade, Rebecca Inegbedion, Ruth Baba-Ochankpa, Ruth Najera, Segun Fagbohun, Shireen & Boris, Stuart & Yemi Balantyne, Unekwu Weston, Vera Yol.

Sincere gratitude to Bradley Grose for your on-going support with this project.

To Pastor Oluwatoyin Elizabeth Adefuye of Gate of Heaven Prayer Ministry: Thank you for being a mighty woman of God and covering my family and me in love and prayers. My spiritual journey in understanding my authority and moving forward in deliverance stems from your yes to God.

Special thanks to Brother Ian Clayton for being a true father and significant impact in bringing relevance to my heavenly encounters.

To brother Gabriel Ako: much gratitude for your selfless and thorough Spirit-led mentorship through my teenage years.

Special thanks to pastors; Jared Ming, Dr. James Rene, Mark Raymond, Moses Lawani, Paschal Udah, for your leadership and for providing me with opportunities to minister and fulfill my calling within the body.

To you, my dear reader, oh what joy I have had holding you in my heart through every word. You are so loved. Here's from me to you.

FOREWORD

I have had the honor and pleasure of getting to know Nadia Johnson for over a decade now. It is my belief Nadia's book, *Spirit Spirit Spirit*, is a critical contribution at this most important hour to the Body of Christ.

At a time when "Materialism" has triumphed in our age, Nadia has given Believers in the God of the Bible (and any true seeker) the powerful tools to help us understand how to live out our lives full of the power and authority in this age. She brings us back to that taproot in our faith as she reminds us that "God is Spirit" (John 4:24) and is the Father of all spirits (Hebrews 12:9). Only by understanding that God is Spirit and we human beings that He created a spirit, soul, and body can interact with our Creator and know why we exist and how we can live meaningful and purposeful lives in this age.

Materialism, simply put, is that thinking that human beings can only rely upon that which they can see, smell, touch, taste, or hear. The dominating materialist thinking of our age is that it is only by our five senses by which human beings can obtain knowledge and understanding for all of life.

We have been influenced to our core by this philosophy of materialism; It dominates the thinking of academia, the intelligentsia, the church, and all spheres of society and culture worldwide. Materialism has reduced human beings to think of us as a "package of molecules" that exists for a time and then is dissolved back into the universe without having had any meaning or purpose. Nadia tears off that mask of misunderstanding profoundly; With such clarity, she returns us to the understanding of our lives as Spirit Beings, even as we live out our earthly existence in the material natural realm.

In the first sentence of chapter one, Nadia introduces the core concept of her powerful book, stating, "The Kingdom of God and the kingdom in darkness all exist in the spirit realm." That is a radical thought for Believers as we have so absorbed the materialistic thinking of our time that we can miss the massive importance of this first sentence as it introduces the concept of "Spiritual Realm" as reality in which we must engage. The dominating materialist view of our age has so soundly rejected the concept that we humans are "Spirit Beings," Sadly, a philosophy that shouts out that "God is Dead" has been so thoroughly embraced by the intelligentsia, the elites, the movers, and shakers of the world system.

Nadia Johnson reminds us of the powerful truth throughout her book that as Believers in the Living God, we have the power to CHOOSE which spirit realm we engage. Nadia states it so eloquently and powerfully when she poses the question: "What sort of being do we become when we join ourselves with God?" Nadia puts forth the profound yet straightforward explanation that God "desires for us to reflect Him on earth and, by so doing, bring the earth into harmony in the manner that He holds Heaven." Adding that results in "Healings, love, joy, peace, and goodness will be seen on earth when we engage God and walk in his light."

Although human beings have made remarkable discoveries that have changed the way we live, it seems like we know less about ourselves than previous generations. Looking back in history, those who came before us didn't have all the modern conveniences we now have. But, they had a peace and strength that eludes most today. It seems as our knowledge of the natural world has increased, our understanding of spiritual things has decreased. Most human beings appear to believe that we only live in the realm where we can see, smell, taste, touch, and feel. Sadly, even many Christians have lost this spiritual point of view. As Nadia so eloquently describes in her book, most Christians do not know who they are in the Spirit.

Nadia points out that it is true that we were all born sinners (Psalm. 51:5) and had the nature of the devil working in us (Ephesians 2:2-3). But when we came to Christ and received salvation, we became a new person in the spirit. "If any man be in Christ, he is a new creature: old things are passed away; behold, all things are become new." (2 Corinthians 5:17). This Spirit realm is that which Nadia so powerfully points us to in her book. In the Spirit, you became a brand-new species of being. Your spirit is totally new. There isn't an old sin nature left in you.

Nadia brings us back to that understanding that it is in the spirit that we have been changed and made just like Jesus. Since God is a Spirit, and He deals with us based on who we are in the Spirit (John 4:24), this has changed everything. We can now worship God based on who we are in the Spirit and not on who we are in the flesh. She also introduces how we can access everything we are entitled to in Christ which are totally and completely available to us in the Spirit. We have His authority to walk in and with it experience the miraculous results.

I'm so excited about Nadia's helping us better engage with these truths as she helps us better understand how we can live powerfully and fully in the Spirit.

Anthony W. Hart, ESQ.
Family Law Attorney

PURPOSE

You know, I had some cool names when the Lord set me on the path to writing this book. However, I decided to ask the Lord what it should be. All I got was one word, "Spirit," three times. You can imagine. To feel better, I ran it by a few people, along with the other titles I had prior. Of course, they preferred those alternatives. Guess how I felt.

After a few years of sitting on it with the Lord, I let go of my shallow ways. And I must say that it has certainly grown on me.

Spirit, spirit, spirit is a resounding gong to intimate us on our spirit nature's relevance. It is emphasizing that you are a complete spirit being. It is re-echoing that your spiritual nature is superior to your physical body (James 2:26). That your spirit has more impact on what happens around you than your soul and body ever could. As a spirit being, you play an active role in the Spirit realm and on earth.

The Lord wanted me to draw our focus to the need for us to pay attention to the part of our being that dictates what happens in our physical space. It is crucial to appreciate the Spirit realm's existence. This realm dictates everything that happens in the physical world or realm. As unnatural as that may sound to some, we, as spirit beings, play a vital role in the Spirit realm.

Over the years in ministry, I have seen many promising Christians unable to settle into a meaningful relationship with God, the Father, Son, and Holy Spirit. Some have struggled more than others. Most, not knowing how and others due to a sense of being lost out of the union God invites us to partake in within His Spirit Realm. There is so much disconnect between our spirit and how to live out of it in reality.

Through the Holy Spirit, the believer in Christ has privileged access to live, move and have their being out of the abundance Jesus came to give us. It is essential to add that most of the sufferings facing many today, whether directly or not, can be traced to either the unresolved spiritual battles or agreements entered into through time.

For too long, the enemy has kept himself busy running a rampage off of people's ignorance and misinformation. All to the detriment of many lives, relationships, families, and even genealogies. It is high time someone said, "Enough is enough; I am holding ground and taking back the power to be all that the Lord, my God, has ordained for me to be."

INTRODUCTION

My beloved, I am so glad you took this step. I desire to take you along with me on our shared journey in Abba Father through these pages. My joy is that this book will draw you into a deeper relationship with God the Father. It will hold your hand and lead you to experience the enormous riches we can all have in the Lord Jesus and bring you into realizing your full potential in and through His Holy Spirit. Together, we will engage with Heaven, unlock truths, enter in by faith, and flesh out God's divine purpose for you.

There is so much more to the norm of being saved and waiting or struggling to make Heaven. This book will help articulate the deep spiritual longing within while also providing an opening to walking into a real relationship with God today, in Heaven.

> *"God is a Spirit: and they that worship him must worship him in Spirit and in truth. "*(John 4:24)

God's word has established that our God is a Spirit, and He calls us to a life of worshipping Him in that Spirit form and out of the Spirit realm of His Kingdom. Yet have we sought Him in all the physical ways and places.

So be prepared to embrace the invitation to step in and out through the *door* - Jesus Christ. Through Jesus, you can take your Spirit man into God's Spirit Realm and worship the God Who is Spirit, interact with Him in your original spirit nature and truthfully soar in your spiritual life.

According to the gospel of John, Jesus speaking of Himself maintains He is the only legitimate access to the pastures that lie within the Father:

> *"I am the door. If anyone enters by Me, he will be saved and will go in and out and find pasture." (John 10:9 NKJV)*

The Lord Jesus is *the door*, the access way to God's Kingdom. As the door, Jesus Christ is the only passageway out of bondage from the demonic realm. He is the only passage into Heaven. Jesus said we would "*go in and out and find pasture.*" He is the door to Heaven's reservoirs of endless pasture.

Our salvation is a spiritual transaction that translates us from death to life. As spirit beings, when we believe in Jesus Christ as Lord and Savior, what takes place in the Spirit realm is we exit death, its kingdom (hell), and into life through Christ Jesus.

Through Adam's sin and our sinful ways, each one of us was once in the realm of darkness. As we yield to Christ Jesus's redemption work in our lives, we can now find pasture in the Kingdom of God.

When we go to God's Kingdom through the access *door* (see John 10:9-16 NKJV), we have access to God's endless pastures. We find God's limitless heart desire for us. God desires that we come to know and experience the fullness of His nature. He wants us to experience the full provision of His extravagant love, joy, peace, mercy, grace, and power. He desires we come to enjoy fellowship with Him and walk in glorious light, as He intended from the beginning.

By coming into His Kingdom, we partake of sonship activities that impact our existence on the Earth. We can come out of God's Kingdom, bringing excellent pasture like justice, truth, deliverance, and divine provision into the earth realm for meeting all our needs.

Jesus is our access-way to stepping into the kingdom realm of God, to all of these pastures that enable us to live out God's desire. The faith to step into Heaven and step out freely is an inheritance available to all saved. The pastures that await us include an intimate, face-to-face relationship with God. Just like Moses had.

> "*9 Then Moses went up, also Aaron, Nadab, and Abihu, and seventy of the elders of Israel, 10 and they saw the God of Israel. And there was under His feet as it were a paved work of sapphire stone, and it was like the very heavens in its clarity. 11 But on the nobles of the children of Israel He did not lay His hand. So they saw God, and they ate and drank.*" (Exodus 24:9-11)

In the intimacy of a Father-Son relationship, we come close enough to see what the will of God is. In the Spirit of communion, we can witness what the Father is doing and, through the Holy Spirit, we do likewise on the Earth, just as Jesus did (see John 5:19).

Though these are available to us through Christ Jesus, just like we choose to accept Jesus Christ as Lord and Savior, the choice to go in and partake of Heavenly pastures is ours to make. We must be willing to go in and draw from God's pasture and bring it to the Earth. We must be ready to flesh out through our lives and unto the world around us; into the places of authority, justice, power, dominion, and relationship with God and people. We must be willing to partner with everything that proceeds from God's Kingdom realm today and not after we die.

The hosts of Heaven are eager to assist us as we pray and bring Heaven to Earth. People who willfully choose the devil, such as those in the occult, have free access to demonic pastures. They have free access to their master, Satan, and they receive powers to promote the devil's kingdom on Earth. If their spiritually evil lifestyle can negatively affect people and the Earth's realm, how much more positively can ours (the sons of God and light-bearers) be?

In essence, all spirit beings are impactful in their spirit-life operations. Hence the need for us as sons of God to be consciously operational in God's Kingdom.

The Father has laid up for us such great and precious promises. My earnest desire is that this book helps you realize how to go into the spirit realm of God as a spirit being and take hold of God's promises. Beyond that, I desire that you also come to realize the greater purpose for which God called you. To a relationship with the one true God Himself in all His varying facets; To know what it truly means to fellowship with Him in Spirit and truth.

My sincere prayer for you is that the Lord will create such a deep hunger and strong desire within as you read. I pray that this will be a gate for you to step in and experience what the Father's heart is concerning you and all that is yours. Through this union, live in an existence of rule and reign with Him this day rather than later.

I humbly offer you my first, my heart on this shared journey into the greater in Jesus!

~

Pray with me:

Lord, I pray that we present our lives as a living sacrifice upon Your altar even now. We offer every part of our being to You in total surrender. Now purify us. Lord, fill us up to overflowing with Your love. I thank you for those parts of my being that understand Your truth. However, some are yet to; I ask that You open up those parts of me that have been in darkness and, as a result, have not experienced Your light, power, and truth. I am asking for the parts of me shut down through unbelief or wrong belief systems I have cultured and nurtured. I also present to You the parts of me that I never gave You access to, whether it be due to the ways in my bloodline, choices, or spiritual blindness. As I come to You, let the power of Your love reach into all those areas. I ask to comprehend the depth of such love that would cause You to go to such lengths to save me, to call me Yours in every meaning of sonship, friend, king, and priest. Through every page, through every meditation, do this, I ask. Let my Spirit emerge in the knowledge of who You are in me and I in You.

Amen!

1

SPIRITUAL LATITUDE

~ An Investment in your Body is as Long as you have it; an Investment in your Spirit is Life within the Eternal Spirit ~

The Kingdom of God and the kingdom in darkness all exist in the Spirit realm. As spirit beings, we empower any of these realms to function on the Earth as we engage them. God the Father of all Spirits wants us to know how important our engagements with the spirit realm impact our world.

God is Spirit (see John 4:24). And (God) is the Father of all Spirits (see Hebrews 12:9). As our Heavenly Father, He wants us to bear His image. He has given us His name to operate under His authority upon the Earth He gave us. Why will we engage with a counterfeit?

WHY THE EMPHASIS ON THE SPIRIT

Now, not only is God our Father, but He also invites us to be in union with Him. "But the one who joins with the Lord [in spiritual union] is one spirit with the Lord." (1 Corinthians 6:17 EXB)

What sort of beings do we become when we join ourselves with God? You might be wondering. It is why the Lord is emphasizing the Spirit. God's desire is for us to come into union with Him. He desires for us to reflect Him on Earth and, by so doing, bring the Earth into harmony in the manner He holds Heaven. Healings, love, joy, peace, and goodness will be seen on Earth when we engage God and walk in His light. We can then bring all of His glory and will into our world.

Whether we realize it or not, we engage in the Spirit realm through our spirit. If it is not God's Kingdom, then it is most certainly the dark kingdom. It is sad to note that there is less awareness of our call to operate out of our spiritual existence.

The Apostle Paul throws light on placing value on our body's most essential parts through covering. He writes; "In fact, the weaker our parts, the more vital and essential they are. 23 The body parts we think are less honorable we treat with greater respect. And the body parts that need to be covered in public we treat with propriety and clothe them." (1 Corinthians 12:22-23 TPT).

Apostle Paul uses the symbolism of the body to talk about various spiritual gifts in the Body of Christ, but let us look at this as concerning our own body. It profits us to pay attention to the features of our entire being and, in particular, the hidden part of our existence – our spirit.

Let us liken the Spirit realm to the weaker parts. However, we call them *"weaker"* because of our limited understanding of it and how it appears honorable to keep it veiled. In God's grand scheme for the universe, the *"covered"* – Spirit realm – is the more vital part in Paul's speech.

In almost all known religions, covering the body is portrayed as a symbol of modesty. It is a picture of how the most valuable things are often concealed. It also depicts a pattern of that which is in reality.

A person has and places worth in their field of study based on their investment to get value out of that field. Without physically meeting their patient, a doctor can give a detailed medical history of who they are by blood sample analysis. Doctors can even go further to tell existing conditions with a patient and the outcome of that person's life if the issue goes unchecked. Doctors can advise on how to remedy the situation with a high level of accuracy.

If we begin to pay attention to the happenings around us, we can most certainly tell patterns and behaviors and predict our families' and other groups' outcomes. And just as doctors provide a remedy to hidden issues within the blood, we will find remedies to the problems undetected by physical sight as we step into the Spirit realm of our God.

On the bright side, the Father of Spirits has intentionally covered up these mysteries for us to find glory in seeking them out.

"It is the glory of God to conceal a matter,
But the glory of kings is to search out a matter."

— PROVERBS 25:2

We pay much attention to the things everyone can see. However, there is neither mystery nor glory in that. As spirit beings, we should interest ourselves in understanding how the spirit realm operates. As beings made in God's image, we have the highest priority in God's Kingdom.

Through Jesus, we have access to God and the power to pull down the kingdom of darkness and establish God's Kingdom reign. We can only be successful in this when we get training in the areas that appear seemingly invisible.

You can discover specific patterns that potentially impact the outcome of a person's life by identifying what spirit beings they have allowed and mingled with. Sadly, many are unaware that some engagements have led to different spirit beings having permitted access to them in the Spirit realm.

In the earlier example, doctors can see an invisible operation in my blood and predict my life's outcome on things I do not know because they have the training to see it. Statisticians can predict the result of a situation because it is similar to the one they once documented. Both can do what they do due to being trained in that area of seeming invisibility.

History has information about world leaders and their peculiar characteristics. Some show personality disorders like narcissism drawn through studies and research.

Powers and kingdoms are influencing most of what goes on around us. Some are notorious for the trends we see in places and traits in people, including world leaders or narcissists. There are also powers and kingdoms dictating the gene pool and what your health will look like in the next year or more.

We must ask ourselves what is behind the things that manifest around us in the physical realm. What is that thing within my blood that has strengthened its occupation in my genealogy? What is the thing within my demography that has linked me to the outcome of a statistic? How do these things dictate what happens to me or how I am in society? Finding answers to this and many other such questions should be our primary focus.

Statisticians make reasonable forecasts and predictions based on data and information collected in the past and compared with the present. We all tend to give weight to their predictions on similar issues based on their knowledge on a matter. Even when it is not always a particular group, the data they collect reflects what we expect to see when dealing with similar issues.

These natural people have a way of making conclusive opinions that we receive as truth. We must understand that such a system is believed accurate in areas we cannot see with the natural eyes. It requires a trained eye to see.

Just as the doctors and statisticians train to see things that the layman doesn't, as spirit beings, our primary training is to see what is in the spirit that may not be apparent in the natural. When we do, we can see the trajectory of where that situation is going and seek to change if negative or strengthen it if favorable to arrive at a reasonable and successful end.

A lack of training and deficiency in this knowledge will only hinder us from getting the best outcomes in life, leading to much suffering. In the same way, the word of The Lord came to Hosea, saying, "My people are destroyed for lack of knowledge." (Hosea 4:6a)

I believe that God, the Father, is bringing to light long-hidden parts of our existence. We always relegated the spirit portion, which is of utmost importance, to the background as though it is a thing to be wary of, something not to be spoken. To its muffled voice, God gives a resounding voice - spirit, spirit, spirit!

I am sure you would agree it is worth looking into a kingdom that will influence our lives' outcomes. Understanding this existence that appears to be so covered up will prove to be more beneficial to us. It will put within our reach the power to understand and partake in effecting the needed change to the course of our lives for good.

~

PERCEPTION

The secular world view on life does not include a spiritual realm, let alone its relevance. Therefore one almost comes off as a joke when they delve into spiritual matters in the marketplace. Let us realize that it takes a spirit being to function in the Spirit realm. Only as spiritual beings can we have access and latitude within God's Kingdom realm.

The Merriam-Webster Dictionary defines "latitude" as the freedom of action or choice.

As we continue to study and practice living as spirit beings in the Spirit realm, we will soon discover that real treasure is within these parts that are covered up. We will find the latitude that Christ gave His life to bring us into. Jesus gave us the liberty within Him to choose how to act or do as spiritual beings within the spiritual realm. Just as clothing serves as a covering to the body, our body is a cloth over our spirit. So let us then apply this understanding to the physical realm;

consider it a veil over the spiritual realm. Consider that veil torn. Jesus did.

Realize that our life's outcome happens as we engage with the Spirit realm. Our engagement with the Kingdom realm of our God will positively impact our lifestyles, relationships, and destiny. For too long, we have engaged with a kingdom that does not have the light of God within it. Therefore, we have reflected darkness in our daily operations. We have helplessly watched as darkness covers the Earth.

Many blame God for allowing suffering, sicknesses, sex trafficking, hatred, wars, racism, etc. But the truth is that we are the ones in charge of the Earth. God gave it to us. "The heaven, *even* the heavens, *are* the Lord's; But the earth He has given to the children of men" (Psalm 115:16). We are the ones who have engaged with a dark realm and have reflected it on the Earth.

"God is light" (1 John 1:5). Why do we engage with and study the darkness rather than the light? In seeking after Him, we allow His light in, which reveals us as spiritual beings. With the entrance of His light, we become more alert and aware of God's kingdom realm around us, as well.

The Unseen Realm Dictates What Happens in the Seeing Realm

The Earth and all the universe make up the physical world. We often refer to all that is visible or physically perceivable as the material or earthly realm. There is also the "unseen" world. We often refer to the unseen or invisible world as the spiritual realm. The latter (spiritual) exists pretty much the same as the former (physical). Whether we realize it or not, there is more interplay between both realms than is often acknowledged.

God calls us to learn how to operate out from God's Heaven, and we play a part in the positives that manifest in the seeing realm we call Earth. The opposing realm also engages in activities that display the troubles we face on Earth. Mainly passed through the bloodline are the manifestations of some of the things we battle daily on Earth.

The spiritual realm is vast, operational, and fully functional. Both realms have influenced and continue to impact the other in some way or another. Closer attention would show the one (spiritual) has pre-eminence over the other (physical).

Interestingly, we are at a point in history when there is more reference to the spiritual realm than ever before. A world intensely thirsty for spiritual encounters seek it out in all the wrong places when we have it at our fingertips in the right and most authentic way.

"I am the way, ..."

— JOHN 14:6 KJV

Jesus Christ is the only one who can lead you into God's Spirit Realm. People will travel across continents to go on spiritual journeys where they are starved and drugged to enter the spirit realm. However, those activities they partake in (using drugs, calling on demonic spirits, idols, demigods, making incantations, casting spells, hypnosis, etc.) lead them to the demonic spirit realm and not God's Spirit Realm.

We are in a time of increasing awareness of the spiritual realm *(See Acts 2:17-18)*. A point in time when this realm is more spoken about than ever: God's design for us is to be total participants with Him in caring for and governing the Earth. To fulfill such a mandate, we must first understand our make-up as God designed us to be.

Recently, a well known celebrity spoke about going to Peru and engaging in spiritual exercises involving taking a drug that I suppose is the ayahuasca drug. She even encouraged people to do it. If only they knew the demonic doors that their actions open up. If only they knew that is such a debased place to operate from as a spirit-being made in God's image. To stoop so low and give yourself over to demonic influence and believe that you are getting something good or deserving is just sad.

We are spirit beings capable of interacting with the spiritual realm. Pretty much the same way our physical bodies interact with the earthly realm.

We have lost much ground from not walking in this truth and reality. We have also missed out on many great relationships, health, and opportunities. Our hearts, minds, and promises made have easily broken for the lack of genuine appreciation of God's divine plan for humanity.

I have good news for you. You can begin to take back lost grounds. Wherever you may have failed, it is possible to regain and thrive. I want you to know that it is the Father's good pleasure to give you the kingdom. As sons and daughters of the kingdom, we do ourselves well by consciously turning our intent towards our Father's kingdom realm *(see Matthew 6:33, Col 3:2)*.

We should not sit out and allow whatever comes to us; when we should be active participants of the Father's kingdom world. We should be embarking on a journey of actively engaging with the Kingdom of God as spirit beings and living liberated and more victorious lives on this Earth.

∾

OF THE SPIRIT

"God is Spirit, and those who worship Him must worship in spirit and truth."

— JOHN 4:24

God is Spirit, and so is His breath. *Ruach*, the Hebrew word for breath means *Spirit*. Adam responded to the breath of God by coming to life (see Genesis 2:7). Thus Adam was in effect a spirit being. Within the context that God made man in His image, it does suggest Adam altogether resembled God. He, too, was a spirit - the only form that guaranteed Adam capable of worshipping and communing with God in spirit and truth.

PONDER POINT:

Let us pause for a moment and try to understand what Adam's appearance must have been. Consider the look, image, form, and make-up of Adam. Imagine Adam in existence to allow him to be one with God in Spirit and interact and tend to the garden of Eden – the mandate God gave him. Through the Spirit, Adam would fulfill his God-centered purpose, walk in the true spirit of worship. Above all, consider that the man, Adam, was not struggling to have a face-to-face fellowship with God.

God ordained it so that with the component of man termed the 'body,' Adam could interact with the physical world and provide direct care, order, and service to the Earth. Consider that Adam's interactions with both God and the Earth were second nature to him.

Just as God is Spirit, man is also a spirit. The spirit of man was the covering and dominant part of Adam. In the beginning, Adam's being was wrapped and held together by his spirit-man. That was the initial nature of the man, Adam, as a being, in the image of God.

Later on, it was sad to see Adam and Eve naked after they sinned. The glory of their spirit-man no longer clothed them. Their spirit-man had retracted—the loss of the glorious presence of God. Following the fall, their soul and body took over dominion because they reversed authority by their choices. By their disobedience to God, they gave prominence to their soul, to *self-reason*.

By design, the human soul is the part of man that bridges between spirit and body to allow both to function in their capacity. The soul was to be under the spirit's influence and transmit that spirit life to and through the body. The soul was not to come under the charge of the body. When it (the body/flesh) is in control, we become very physical beings, living to gratify fleshly desires, with little or no expression of God, who engages with our spirit.

You may wonder how our body can influence the soul, being the center of reasoning. *Have you ever felt you could look prettier, slimmer, or taller?* Suppose you thought your dressing did not fully express your mood as much as you wanted. Then you have experienced what it is when the soul is transmitting out of the body's desires.

The body (the flesh nature) has its desires and triggers. You react to what you see, feel, and hear. All of these are what your soul will take and reason into a mindset. Your mind will reason out those desires, and you will express that. That is how you are as a physical being.

Now consider a person born blind. This person, regardless of color, will probably not set their mind for a change of skin tone. Whichever is in control (spirit or flesh), your soul will transmit out of that. A spirit-led life will express life by the Spirit – perfection. So also, a flesh-led life will express life by the flesh – corruption.

Our soul gets empowered by either our flesh/body or spirit to reason out, exhibiting the most dominant parts of our being. Therefore, a person consumed with love and a constant desire to be present with God, especially one captivated with worshiping God, will begin to live their life out of a place of worship and prayer wherever they are. For such a one, their soul desires and reasons out opportunities to fulfill the desires put out by their spirit. In this case, the spirit is the dominant part.

On the other hand, when a person is ruled by the flesh and consumed by greed, the soul can reason out ways of getting more stuff to satisfy the flesh and its desires at any cost. And with no cognizance for how it gets what it wants. Apply that to uncontrolled sexual desires, and you will open up a can of worms as that list is endless to the degree of depravity possible.

Adam's spirit was to stay dominant and actively engage God at all times. Adam had full responsibility and authority to govern Eden's garden and all put there in creation. His spirit was supposed to remain engaged to fulfill his God-given mandate. But when Adam and Eve sinned, they lost this divine connection with God the Father. As a direct consequence of their disobedience, the spirit-man receded inwards. From that moment on, the body took over dominance, expressing the desire to gratify the flesh.

As Adam proceeded to tend the garden, they realized it was no longer business as usual; they could see they were now "naked." Self-reason took over dominance rather than spirit living. Death entered the stage with the body (flesh with all its desires) now in control, instead of the spirit.

Jesus, by His death and resurrection, brought us into a better existence as spirit beings. However, we nurture the external man with good nourishment, exercise, and discipline. We commit time, resources, and energy to groom the mental parts of our being with self-development programs/activities, education, training to enable us to acquire a better life on Earth. The *dustman* has enjoyed its perks of self-achievement and recognition. What have we done with our spirit-man?

The Apostle Paul charges us through his 1st letter to the Corinthians.

"47 *The first man [was] from out of Earth, made of dust (earthly-minded); the second Man [is] the Lord from out of Heaven.*

48 *Now those who are made of the dust are like him who was first made of the dust (earthly-minded); and as is [the Man] from Heaven, so also [are those] who are of Heaven (heavenly-minded).*

49 *And just as we have borne the image [of the man] of dust, so shall we and so let us also bear the image [of the Man] of Heaven."*

— 1 CORINTHIANS 15:47-49 AMPC

Adam enjoyed the depths of supernatural fellowship with God, then proceeded to disobey God. This choice pushed him out of that place of spiritual intimacy with God to earthly existence. Unlike him (Adam), who functioned fully in both spirit and body as a grown adult and made his choice for his physical body to have dominion, we have not.

We come via the birthing canal as babies, which is very different from how Adam and Eve did. We spend a lifetime on Earth, groomed in many physical ways to adapt to Earth until we hopefully recognize there is more to us than just a physical existence.

You and I were born into a worldly mindset. We have known great depths of interaction with the Earth. We have undergone varying degrees of training in earthly ways on several levels.

Take time and think of all the areas you have mastered in the ways of the flesh and world, compare them to your mastery of Heaven. The good news is, we are on the other side of Adam, where we choose Jesus. We choose to accept all He offers us in choosing to bear His divine image.

Similarly, we have borne the image of man; we can and should now take on the image of the *life-giving* Spirit. It is what Apostle Paul was conveying in writing to the Corinthian Believers of his time. We can start by growing our spirit-man to the fullness of what Jesus offers us.

Even though we existed in God (the Father of Spirits) long before our physical form were woven together in our mother's womb (Jeremiah 1:5), we hadn't yet carried on/worn a body. So, we tend to forget that spirit life we had once we come to Earth. Like Jeremiah, God knew us before He formed us in our mother's womb.

> "*Therefore, if anyone is in Christ, he is a new creation; old things have passed away; behold, all things have become new.*"
>
> — 2 CORINTHIANS 5:17

When we ask Jesus to save us from our sinful ways, we make a decision that alters our entire lives. When we come to Him, repenting of all the deeds done in our flesh and the lifestyle of pleasing ourselves, He forgives us. We become a new creation (completely changed people) with different desires too.

> "11 The *Spirit of God, who raised Jesus from the dead, lives in you. And just as God raised Christ Jesus from the dead, he will give life to your mortal bodies by this same Spirit living within you.*
>
> 12 Therefore, *dear brothers and sisters, you have no obligation to do what your sinful nature urges you to do.*"
>
> — ROMANS 8:11-12 NLT

His Holy Spirit comes and lives within us to empower us to connect to who we are in the Spirit as spirit beings. The Holy Spirit quickens our mortal bodies to rise above the flesh and operate as a spirit being, thus fulfilling God's call upon the Earth.

As one born of the Holy Spirit, I have to reiterate that you have no obligation to do what your sinful nature urges you to do!

Moses at the Beginning of Adam

Before the fall, Adam and Eve reflected God's glory. Their spirit reflected the nature of God. They governed the garden by reflecting God into all life and nature. It was the way to bring harmony and order to all of creation.

Later on, in Scripture, we are informed of Moses's out-of-the-ordinary encounters with God. On several occasions, when Moses would come down from tarrying long and intimately in God's presence, he would glow. Moses caught a glimpse of what Adam looked like initially through times of intimacy in God.

"*29 Now it was so, when Moses came down from Mount Sinai (and the two tablets of the Testimony were in Moses' hand when he came down from the mountain), that Moses did not know that the skin of his face shone while he talked with Him. 30 So when Aaron and all the children of Israel saw Moses, behold, the skin of his face shone, and they were afraid to come near him. 31 Then Moses called to them, and Aaron and all the rulers of the congregation returned to him; and Moses talked with them. 32 Afterward all the children of Israel came near, and he gave them as commandments all that the Lord had spoken with him on Mount Sinai. 33 And when Moses had finished speaking with them, he put a veil on his face. 34 But whenever Moses went in before the Lord to speak with Him, he would take the veil off until he came out; and he would come out and speak to the children of Israel whatever he had been commanded. 35 And whenever the children of Israel saw the face of Moses, that the skin of Moses' face shone, then Moses would put the veil on his face again, until he went in to speak with Him.*"

— EXODUS 34:29-35

The above text discloses what happened when Moses returned from going up into God's presence on Mount Sinai. His countenance glowed so brightly the Israelites could not look him in the face. They had to put a veil over his face for him to relate to others. Bible scholars agree that Moses' relationship with *YHVH* was unique and intimate. So much that God would allow him a glimpse of the record of creation. (As revealed in the Tanakh, YHVH is the personal and unutterable name of the God of Israel, composed from the four Hebrew letters Yod, Hey, Vav, Hey.)

Moses is credited with being the writer of Genesis and all the accounts of creation. Without a doubt, Moses stepped into the beginning. He was at the beginning to write all that transpired then, by stepping into the One who Himself is 'the beginning and the end' - 'the Alpha and Omega.'

Considering the degree to which he engaged with God as a spirit being, Moses could embrace life from a perspective we may never know. It is an actual and higher perspective than the limited lens through which we do.

When we choose a debased view on the kind of life we can have as God's sons and daughters, we sell ourselves short of the truth. We also hinder ourselves from desiring and pursuing this kind of spirit life available to us.

Consider that Moses did not start off being that way; he went all out for a life he knew was possible. We can read Moses's accounts and reach in to grow our spirit man like he did. Just as in the beginning, when Adam and Eve were wholly spirit beings in God. They had God's capabilities as long as they chose to remain in Him.

Moses and Elijah Submitted to God in the Spirit

Again, in Matthew 17, we see a repeat of that out-of-the-usual appearance. Jesus' three disciples, Peter, James, and John, would witness Jesus in a transfigured appearance on the Earth.

> "*1 Six days later, Jesus took Peter and the two brothers, James and John, and hiked up a high mountain to be alone. 2 Then, Jesus' appearance was dramatically altered. A radiant light as bright as the sun poured from his face. And his clothing became luminescent—dazzling like lightning. He was transfigured before their very eyes. 3 Then suddenly, Moses and Elijah appeared, and they spoke with Jesus.*"

> — MATTHEW 17:1-3 TPT

It was no coincidence that men (Moses and Elijah) who walked on Earth with similar encounters of living out of their spirit nature showed up lots of years later in bodily form, with the bodies they still had. Looking back at these two great servants of God, Moses and Elijah, appearing at the transfiguration of Jesus, we'll see more things they both had in common.

Both were in the Old Testament days. They immersed themselves in an extraordinary relationship with God the Father in Spirit. Both walked with God and were not surprised at who they became. Consider this:

> "*And Moses the servant of the Lord died there in Moab, as the Lord had said. 6 He buried him in Moab, in the valley opposite Beth Peor, but to this day, no one knows where his grave is. 7 Moses was a hundred and twenty years old when he died, yet his eyes were not weak nor his strength gone. 8 The Israelites grieved for Moses in the plains of Moab for thirty days until the time of weeping and mourning was over.*"

> — DEUTERONOMY 34:5-8

Moses died, yet his eyes were not weak, nor his strength gone. When I read that, I see it as Moses' spirit left his healthy body. I see an intact body, one not showing any signs of deterioration either before or after death. One that had not begun to show signs akin to bodily corruption but separated from its spirit and soul and put away by the All-knowing, Majestic Creator for reasons best known to Him.

God would choose this unique process for Moses without allowing him to follow the due aging process, a sickness (heart attack even), get shot by an arrow, get killed by an animal, or simply allowing Moses to fall off a cliff. The God of the living and not the dead (Matthew 22:32, Mark 12:27, Luke 20:38). And He would witness Moses die and organize the burial of Moses by Himself.

My assignment is to bring *you* out to begin to seek God in Spirit, enter His Word by your spirit, spend time meditating on His Word in the Spirit, and desire God more as He reveals His ways by the Spirit. God is calling you back to the original way He made for you to operate.

The Bible states that Moses died in Moab, but what happened to His body? God buried it. The question now is, will a body buried by God deteriorate? I believe that the body God buried did not decay. Unlike Elijah's departure, which Elisha (his prodigy prophet) witnessed (2 Kings 2:11-14), there was no human witness at Moses' departure point. No human could find it; no man precisely knew where God buried Moses' body. And many have searched for several years, found nothing.

Could it be that the hiddenness of this one man's body was done with intentionality so that no one could find it? Was Moses's body hid in a realm only *active* spirit beings could see?

We would need to consider that because while no human being has been able to locate the exact place God buried Moses, Satan, on the other hand, seemed to be aware and disputed for the body of Moses. Spirit beings like angel Michael and Satan could see where God planted it.

'Yet Michael *the archangel, in contending with the devil, when he disputed about the body of Moses, dared not bring against him a reviling accusation but said, "The Lord rebuke you!"'

— JUDE 9

Many commentaries claim that Satan wanted the body because Moses disobeyed God. Man is a three-part being, consisting of spirit that lives in a body and possesses a soul.

First, I must clarify that the body is dust and returns to the ground (see Genesis 3:19). Our spirits come from God, and all return to Him (see Ecclesiastes 12:7). God is called the Father of all Spirits (see Hebrews 12:9); therefore, He owns/takes back every spirit that came from Him. It is the soul that goes on to Heaven or hell.

"The soul who sins shall die."

— EZEKIEL 18:20A

The choices made by the soul determines where it goes. Body and spirit destinations are pretty much set. So if there was a dispute on who owned Moses, then it would have to be one concerning who owned his soul, which was not the case here. Notice that Jude 9 didn't say the dispute was Satan claiming his right to have Moses's body either. What **it does say** is Satan *"disputed about the body of Moses."* And I believe we now can also see how unusual the circumstances surrounding the body of Moses were.

Satan Will Never Comprehend God's Wisdom

Could it be that the dispute was the way Moses's body was archived? I believe the Lord wants us to break free from belief systems and reach into the superior multi-faceted ways of God.

So, could it be that Moses' body would not know decay because Moses would have use of it at a later time? It was for God's greater purposes; how amazing seeing that Moses shows up with Elijah at the transfiguration of Jesus Christ, in Matthew 17:1-6.

Two fully functional spirit beings with physical bodies would witness the Eternal Spirit (Hebrews 9:14) revealed through His (Jesus's) physical body, radiating and transfiguring it before His trusted disciples.

Satan never had a clue about God's intentions to go about saving us either. God's wisdom always trumps Satan's, and it bothers him. Scripture says Satan wouldn't have crucified the King of Glory (Jesus) if He knew God's plans (1 Corinthians 2:8). Therefore, Satan didn't know why God will uphold a human body for the very first time.

But why will God make a mystery of this man's body? It makes you wonder how the conversation went at Beth Peor. Suppose Moses is closing his eyes, leaving his body, and giving up his spirit. Suppose he is proceeding to Heaven, and God is going, "here, Moses, I'm going to bury this one (and probably the only) human body with My Own Hands, and it's going to be yours."

And maybe He would add, "see you on the other side." I mean, what a way to die, right? I must say, a burial that tops any in all of human history.

I believe the Lord, the Living God, took exception to bury Moses's body to give him legal access to the earth realm to come at the transfiguration of Jesus Christ (Matthew 17:1-6). Only spirit beings with bodies have access to operate on the Earth legally. Ultimately, this shows us what God can do with bodies whose spirit beings are present with him.

Well, while Moses would pick up his "buried-by-the-Hand-of-God body" to show up at the transfiguration, Elijah, who defied death (2 Kings 2:11) and took his own body into Heaven, came with his own body and both spoke with Jesus in the flesh.

The fact that they still had access to come to the Earth after many years of leaving, or one would say, fulfilling their assignment, speaks volumes. In a way, they still had unfinished business in the body that housed their spirit man while they lived on Earth. It would account for the unique way the Lord attended to their bodies during their earthly departure.

Their presence at the transfiguration of Jesus speaks to the possibility of our (body's) transfiguration if we can be in tune with God in the measure Jesus was. It speaks to an inheritance we can press in and aspire to reach into as the body of Christ. To a people locked down in a boxed-up mentality about God's ways, He now reveals and shows His exceedingly *superior* ways of operating and so much more.

Satan Takes Issue with God's Unique Acts

Early Christian writings indicate an account originally in a Jewish work entitled *"The Testament (or the Assumption) of Moses."* It states that "a likely explanation of the dispute about Moses's body is that the devil challenged Michael's right to bury Moses since Moses had murdered an Egyptian (see Exodus 2:11-15). One of the mightiest of the angels withholding accusation of the devil's blasphemy is contrasted with the presumptuous evil speaking of the false teachers against supernatural beings."

Again, let's ponder on this with the Lord; I agree with the latter on not speaking presumptuously to supernatural beings, which many have ignored to their detriment. But I would re-consider the former when I ask myself, "will Angel Michael attempt to bury a body God had buried?"

I am inclined to believe it was a matter that was unusual, and because the Angel Michael was guard over Moses's body, Satan confronted him. Satan questioned this act of God, one he had never seen before. God concealed from Satan His plans for the body of Moses; Satan had a fit and raised a dispute over it. He knew that it was something hidden from him and sought ways to have Michael reveal it.

Michael then rebukes Satan in God's authority. Michael follows protocol; He upholds God's people against Satan and his cohorts. Thus, Michael was on his job, faithful per usual.

"But I will tell you what is noted in the Scripture of Truth. No one upholds me against these, except Michael your prince."

— DANIEL 10:12

We see a common trait through Scripture; Satan takes issue with and shows up when God does something he has not seen before, especially concerning man. He became alert at creation. Satan showed up at the one tree (of the knowledge of good and evil) that stood out among all others shortly after God created man in His image and began disputing what God said to Adam and Eve about the tree.

Satan succeeded against Eve in *disputing* what God said to them. But years later, when He came to Angel Michael, he got nothing out of him; instead, the Angel Michael rebuked Satan in the name of The Lord, saying: "...The Lord rebuke you." (Jude 9 NKJV)

WHAT THIS MEANS FOR US

Take a pause and allow this to sink into your Spirit; what endless possibilities abound in God beyond the limits of an earth-bound mindset.

For Jude, it was no longer a possibility. Let's say he read about this encounter from one of the dead sea scrolls and went on to address the issue of speaking blasphemously to supernatural beings.

We can also consider that Jude could see and relay an argument between Satan and the Archangel Michael concerning an undecayed (Moses's) body. God preserved for the future the body of a spirit being (Moses) who fully expressed Him on Earth. The Archangel Michael would stand to uphold it for a latter-day – at the transfiguration of God-the-Son on Earth. Hallelujah!

Every time men have dared to walk with God in Spirit and Truth; we witness God's omnipotent and omniscient nature on the Earth. For men like Moses and Elijah to later show up at Christ's transfiguration proves that such an existence is available to us. We never really pause to recognize God's purpose for such an expression.

I attempt to convey a superior existence in the spiritual union (1 Corinthians 6:17) with God beyond our (usual) thinking along the lines of living in a body and dying with it. Getting people, myself included, to see how a life with God in the spirit can defy death and bodily decay;

and not that we need to go far to have to seek it, but that God reveals His ways afresh for any to grasp and run with it if they choose.

In the new testament era, and about a thousand years after these men last walked this Earth, God has them show up on Earth again. Except that this time not in the spirit form but with whole bodies that suffered no decay. These men lived beyond the sands of time, and it made them still relevant beyond their time. God's word is accurate to say that we become one Spirit with Him - the Alpha & Omega.

"He that is joined to the Lord is one spirit with Him."

— 1 CORINTHIANS 6:17

Satan has been the enemy who has sought to deter us from believing in our spirit nature. He deceived Eve, then Adam, into losing their belief in God, thereby losing their position in the garden of Eden (Genesis 3). That was a loss that we have to recoup through Jesus Christ (1 Corinthians 6:20).

Satan fights to keep us within a capsule of limitation. Satan seeks to inhibit us from the realities of who we can be in God. While many of us strive to finish well and end up in Heaven, these men did not seek an end to their earthly existence. These men lived on within the union they had with the living God.

The physical realm has a firm grip on us because we are more accustomed to our physical bodies and their operations on Earth than with our spirits and being present in Spirit with God in His Kingdom realm. We have records of our birth, growth, career, etc., that prove its reality. We have tangible experiences at different points of our life with people that cements our programming.

However, as spirit beings, there is a record of who we are in the unseen realm. When we get accustomed to this heavenly existence, our experiences in Heaven also become as tangible to us as our experiences in the natural. We can have records and time stamps of the moments we have actively walked in God's Kingdom realm with Him.

I can guarantee that no one can take those from you or even try to talk you out of the reality of your existing encounters within God. These are realities that we must aspire to live in because it was natural for Moses and Elijah. Though human, they will undoubtedly tell a different story about living as God's sons than many of us would.

2

WALKING IN THE LIFE OF CHRIST JESUS

~ Whenever the Kingdom of God is Displayed, the Kingdom of Darkness is Displaced ~

~

How would our lives be if we thought of ourselves as spiritual beings daily? What choices would you make if you rose every morning and went about your affairs as a spirit being existing in a spirit world?

How was it that Enoch could go in and out of God's presence while in human form? (See Genesis 5:24) What was it like for Enoch to live this way daily till he was no more, for God had taken him, defying death? (See Hebrew 11:5) This man could enjoy a relationship with the Godhead to the point God would stop Enoch from returning to earthly existence.

What would it be like if we read every passage of scripture, the lives the patriarchs lived, and the stories Jesus told through the lenses of nurturing our existence as spirit beings and not just improving on this earthly body alone? Take a moment and ponder on these questions.

Allow yourself to engage with your spirit. Let your whole being engage in this reality that you begin to experience a shift in your focus. With that, by faith, you take a step towards what it means to walk in the spirit with God.

The First Time I Stepped into Heaven

On September 9, 2001, just two days before 9/11, my friend Rosie came over to visit. At the time, I was an undergraduate at the University of Jos, Plateau State, Nigeria. Jos was a bustling city in the North Central State of Nigeria, West Africa.

Life in Jos City centered around the university. The people were very outgoing, from businesses at the modern multi-purpose shopping complex to its teaching hospital center.

Rosie and I go back years to our high school days. We had not seen each other for a while, so we had lots of catching up to do. We were chatting away when suddenly, I felt a nudge within my spirit to check my surroundings. I got up immediately amidst our conversation and headed for the door. My friend followed right behind. We both went outside my apartment building.

Once outside, we noticed it was tranquil. The quietness was unusual for the time of day. We did not have cell phones at the time, I didn't have any landline in the house either, so there was no way of receiving information. We decided to head further out to see what the reason for the silence could mean. Only to realize there was not a soul in sight.

All the stores were closed, which was odd as there were quite some stores on this usually busy street. It was surprising we could not hear a single sound within a quartile mile. All we saw were deserted cars lined up the road. It was undeniable by their random positions that people abandoned these cars in haste. It was the most heart-wrenching feeling to find oneself in such a deserted and completely silent, even lifeless, neighborhood.

With absolutely nothing in hand, we decided to walk to the campus, which was miles away. It seemed the safest place to go and where we hoped to find some clarity. Only a couple of miles walk, we were shocked when we finally saw a guy across the street from us with no one else in sight. He headed in the opposite direction. As he got closer, we could tell he didn't look okay.

A shirtless tall man, about 6'3", running unsteady like he was inebriated and would fall at any time. Instinctively, we began walking as fast as possible, keeping away from him. Once past, we looked back at this guy as he continued to stagger on helplessly.

What caught both our eyes sent a chill down our spines. We could see blood dripping down from the man's head. It seemed like the back of his head was cut deeply or partly chopped by something sharp like a machete or an axe. We were too scared to try to figure it out.

Seeing that, we were mortified and began running from thereon. The fear of the unknown scared us immensely.

The sequence of events, deserted cars, dead silence within the neighborhood, and a bleeding young man created fear beyond any we ever faced. Rosie and I were now unsure of what our fate was as we hurried towards the university campus.

At this point, we had lost the ability to talk while drowning in uncertainty in a seemingly endless walk. Caught up with these events' unveiling within this short span, I did not realize what was now in front of me.

Just then, I found myself staring in the face of a group of thugs carrying machetes. These guys were part of a larger violent Islamic radical group, which we can now identify as Boko haram, who planned to kill Christians on this day. This move, fueled by extremist groups, was seeking to Islamize the state.

People were brutally killed on the spot if these killer squads thought they were Christians, and sometimes the litmus test was just by the way a person dressed. I was the prime target for elimination due to my western-looking outfit.

While they used dress codes to decide Christian females, Christian men must recite some Islamic phrases in Arabic. Failing to do so led to their deaths. In several reported instances, pregnant women had their stomachs cut open or sliced through with fetal parts exposed. On some streets of Jos were dismembered human bodies of victims butchered by these religious assailants.

A few of my schoolmates and some of their family members who escaped death by these extremists did so with many scars and missing body parts, such as limbs, ears, etc., amidst bodily wounds so deep, it's a miracle that they survived.

These extremists looked cruel and unkept. They were screaming and shouting out hateful words with intense anger. As they continued their angry march, they would drag their machetes on the floor, making clunking sounds amidst loud and frantic cursing.

Of all places to be, I was walking right into their midst. It was terrifying. I looked around me and discovered I was all by myself.

My friend's survival instincts had kicked in. Being petite, about 5 feet, she had swiftly sneaked between some cars. She kept whispering my name and earnestly signaling to me from the other end of a lineup of deserted vehicles, but it was too late for me even to attempt to take a detour.

I was either too afraid to move another muscle or had no way of sneaking through any cars. None of that mattered now. They were already right there, within a few more feet in front of me.

At this point, I had given up, convinced that my end had come. I murmured in surrender, "Lord Jesus, if I perish, I perish."

I do not know how, but it seemed these people walked through me. Or shall I say I walked through them? All I know is that I walked through a group of violent killers, staring into their faces, and none of them appeared to have seen me.

None stared back into my face or even seemed to acknowledge a person walk past them. They just went on cursing, chanting, jumping, and moving past. I walked through a supernatural path. One they certainly didn't create.

I had no idea what or how it happened, but I continue to be in awe at what this calling in Christ Jesus has brought us into. A life-altering experience like this will change your life forever. When men speak of things they have no experience with and deny the possibility of the supernatural, you will beg to differ when you have had experiences like this.

It was such a relief when we finally made it to the campus. Upon arrival, we met students setting some extremists they had apprehended on fire. These brutality and demonic killing sprees in Jos City left unpleasant memories of a once peaceful and bustling city, starting on that unforgettable September day.

Once physically safe within the university's confines, we realized how worn out and emotionally drained we both were. We found some abandoned beds and spent the night in the hostel.

That night, I had a revelatory dream that appeared to be a replay of that moment I walked through the violent mob in the above narrative. It felt as though I was taken back in time. Only this time, I saw myself taken into a different realm when we came face-to-face with the mob. I could now see that Rosie and I were brought into the Heavenly Kingdom in that dream reality.

I could see we were both peaceful, happy, and actively having the best time of our lives. As I looked, I saw we were in an atmosphere of glory and splendor. We were in absolute bliss, having real conversations with different people and angelic beings.

I woke up to realize I had just been in a dream. Then it began to all make sense to me why the mob was oblivious of someone walking through their midst.

At the time, it was something I kept pondering. Years later, as I grew in my experiential relationship with the Lord Jesus, things became more apparent. I began to understand that, As a spirit being, I can step into Heaven by faith in Jesus Christ. That was my first experience stepping into the kingdom realm of Abba Father, howbeit unconsciously.

It is even more interesting that Jesus walked through an aggressive mob who were bent on killing him. Apostle Luke's account reports that; "**28** When everyone present heard those words, they erupted with furious rage. **29** They mobbed Jesus and threw him out of the city, dragging him to the edge of the cliff on the hill on which the city had been built, ready to hurl him off. **30** But he walked right through the crowd, leaving them all stunned." (Luke 4:28-30 TPT)

Imagine the shock on their faces when they attempted to push Jesus over to hurl him off the cliff, only to no longer see Him. He walked right through their midst because He had stepped into a realm to which they had no access. A realm where they were no longer able to see Him or lay hold of Him. A classic case of "now you see me, now you don't."

As a spirit being, Jesus stepped into Heaven and was no longer subject to His body's limitations. I am here today, writing these lines because Jesus did; and "...because as He is, so are we in this world."

"So now, with us awakening to our full inclusion in this love union, everything is perfect! Its completeness is not compromised in contradiction. Our confident conversation echoes this fellowship even in the face of crisis; **because as he is, so are we in this world** - our lives are mirrored in Him." (John 4:17 The Mirror)

PONDER POINT:

Can you imagine how this scenario must have taken place?

The same people who were about to hurl Him over the cliff became incapacitated as He walked through them. Jesus sets precedence for us on how to operate in the spirit-man. If our makeup can enable us to walk through a mob untouched, we can go through barriers unhindered - a limitless life indeed. Hallelujah!

I love this Irish hymn, *"Be thou my vision,"* which is a beautiful picture of Yahweh's protection in raising me heavenward:

"Be Thou my battle Shield, Sword for the fight.
Be Thou my Dignity, Thou my Delight
Thou my soul's Shelter, Thou my high Tower
Raise Thou me heavenward, O Pow'r of my pow'r".

The Rebirth

A famous lingo among Christians is the word **born-again.** I find it so interesting that Jesus explained the process so profoundly in John 3:1-13. It is pretty different from how we have portrayed it.

"That which is born of the flesh is flesh, and that which is born of the Spirit is spirit. 7 Do not marvel that I said to you, 'You must be born again.' **8** The wind blows where it wishes, and you hear the sound of it but cannot tell where it comes from and where it goes. So is everyone who is born of the Spirit." (John 3:6-8)

Jesus describes being born of the spirit as different from natural birth. You become like the wind.

It means that as the flesh and natural senses cannot discern the wind's direction, the natural man who is not born of the spirit cannot understand the Spirit's workings. Your supernatural movements, ways, and understanding are entirely undetectable and incomprehensible by the natural. However, the world can hear the sound of your actions. You can move in a way that does not make sense to biological (human) understanding. It's a remarkable thing that only takes one born of the spirit to understand fully.

It also means that there is a conflict when a natural-born interacts with a spirit-born. It was evident from Jesus's interaction with Nicodemus. Nicodemus, even though a learned man of the law (a Pharisee – a religious scholar) who could recite the entire Torah, yet was reasoning out this process in natural terms. He literally asked Jesus how a grown man could go into his mother's womb because to him, a natural-born, that was the limit of his comprehension on the matter.

We often encounter this conflict even among Christians. I pray that many resolutions come as we step into revelation from the *Son of man* in Heaven – One who explains the process of rebirth and speaks these words while present in both Heaven and Earth simultaneously.

Note that, while Jesus was speaking to Nicodemus on the earth, He also referred to Himself as being present in Heaven at the same time, when he said:

"And no man hath ascended up to Heaven, but he that came down from Heaven, even the Son of man which is in Heaven." (John 3:13)

Understanding that Jesus was essentially taking us into a rebirth mindset along with saving us becomes even more apparent when we see how He lived while on earth. Emphases like why He would not do something without first seeing his Father do it and the whole concept of this dual existence shows us a pattern of moving like the wind, the way of a spirit-born. (see John 3:8)

"But Jesus said [answered them], "I tell you the truth [Truly, truly I say to you], the Son can do nothing alone [on his own initiative; by himself]. The Son does only what he sees the Father doing because the Son does whatever the Father does [for whatever the Father does, the Son does likewise]. 20 [For] The Father loves the Son and shows the Son all the things he himself does. But the Father will show the Son even greater things than this so that you can all be amazed [marvel; be astonished]." (John 5:19-20 EXB)

He, thereby, was portraying the rebirth and essentially what this born-again phenomenon is actually all about. The challenge is how to get our minds away from being stuck on natural operations. How to receive the truth Jesus offers and move into rebirth by the spirit. Along with saving us from sin, redeeming us from death and the grave, He offers us such a life that religion has no grid for; it is a life that we can come into only by the love of God. It is a life:

- To be present in human flesh and yet be present in His Kingdom as a spirit beings.

- To be aware of on-goings within the Kingdom of God.

- To see what the Father is doing and flesh them out on the earth.

To be reborn means, you are like the wind; the kingdom in darkness cannot see you go in and out of Heaven. Therefore, the domain in darkness cannot see what you are seeing in the Father. However, you can see and begin to pray for it to manifest on the earth as it is in Heaven.

The purpose of your calling on earth is to flesh out the things God reveals to you in the spirit realm of His Kingdom. Through His love revealed in Jesus, God has given you the power and ability to be present in His kingdom and to see what He is doing so that you can make this kingdom like His.

You have a privileged stance to pray for His will as you see it in Heaven, concerning your healing, displayed as an overcomer, your children's deliverance, the restoration of your city, nation, and the earth at large!

The Rebirth Quickens our Spiritual Sight

It is interesting to see in Matthew, it was hard for even Jesus to perform a miracle where there was unbelief:

"And He did not do many miracles there [in Nazareth] because of their unbelief."

— MATTHEW 13:58 AMP

Since they could not see in the Spirit, therefore, it could not be!

However, in instances like Luke 5:17-39, where a man had friends who could see God's heart; they broke through the roof to reach Jesus. And it was as they saw – the lame man whose friends lowered down through the roof got up and walked, healed by Jesus.

I find that the path to spiritual rebirth requires breaking through many ceilings to reach Jesus, where He is today. I believe that it has been for us as we have seen. That, too, can change as we begin to seek to see Him through the revelation of His Word.

It is an onward desire to explore every spirit life encounter with Jesus through the revelation of His Word. It is for everyone who will break through the ceiling of culture, religion & belief systems and reach into His full provision.

I believe that Jesus is right here in the form of His Word, washing us clean with the revelation of His Word. You must understand that Jesus Christ, who is God the Son, also personifies the Godhead. He is the One who makes God reachable, touchable, seeable on the earth.

Jesus reveals everything written. He wants to use His Word to cleanse and display each of us, too, as a spirit-born and glorious, holy, spotless person. We will also find that we are living epistles, words in the spirit waiting for our revealing as we become reborn through Jesus.

> "25 Husbands, love your wives, even as Christ also loved the church, and gave himself for it;
>
> 26 That he might sanctify and cleanse it with the washing of water by the Word,
>
> 27 That he might present it to himself a glorious church, not having spot, or wrinkle, or any such thing; but that it should be holy and without blemish."

> — EPHESIANS 5:25-27

How can the natural mind comprehend these things?

Jesus is on the earth today through His Word. For as many who will enter into His Word to allow Him to cleanse them within will find that they become the Word. It will no longer be just reciting them from memory or to win an argument. His Word transforms us into the living epistles that Paul speaks about in 2 Corinthians 3:2.

My earnest desire on this shared journey is that we see ourselves revealed through the Word. Allow the revelation of the Word to cleanse you as He so desires. That way, He can present you spotless without the grime of man's interpretations. You can live free from the blemishes of religious indoctrinations and belief systems that do not attest to this rebirth.

"Jesus said to him, "I am the way, and the truth, and the life. No one comes to the Father except through me."

— JOHN 14:6 ESV

Jesus was not speaking as one who was not present with the Father in Spirit. He would have said no one goes. That way, it's like, okay, after I die and return to the Father, I will be able to carry you there.

No! Rather, He said *"no one comes"* because He was present in the Kingdom with God the Father that very moment He was speaking. And referring to them coming to the Kingdom, He said they could only *come in* through Him into this living Kingdom.

Jesus did not mean after His death or after they died. He would not factor in the death of any of them, which helps our understanding of those who died before Jesus did. It is significant to clarify that He remains *the Way* regardless of which time period people lived or died.

Jesus, through His words, debunks the ideology of having access to the Father in the Spirit only after death. He was particularly intentional with His speech, leaving no doubt to suggest death as access to the Father.

We can see that Jesus was invariably saying that I am here as a flesh being and relating to you in the flesh so that even now, I can carry your spirit man to where my Spirit man is right this moment. Jesus emphasizes Himself as the Way into the Kingdom of God.

Jesus is saying to you today; I am here to carry you here. I am presently in Heaven to give you access to Heaven. Our time is different now because He went through death and resurrection two thousand years ago, but He is still our access into Heaven.

Death is not a requirement for us to access God's Kingdom realm. The power of operating as a spirit being lies in the fact that we have access through Jesus in the Spirit today. The power of this rebirth signifies the duality of our existence within Him. When we come to Jesus and offer Him our lives in repentance, we are washed in His blood by His water, and the Holy Spirit quickens us to live by the Spirit.

When we set out on this journey to rebirth and moving like the wind, we must understand that its very foundations did not make natural sense to any flesh. Even Satan had no clue, for if he did, he wouldn't have crucified Jesus.

> "But we speak the wisdom of God in a mystery, the hidden wisdom which God ordained before the ages for our glory, 8 which none of the rulers of this age knew; for had they known, they would not have crucified the Lord of glory."

— I CORINTHIANS 2:7-8

We are part and parcel of a mystery. One that was by design not meant to make sense in the natural. However, this mystery is our glory. Hallelujah!

For Jesus, this mystery and our glory was the great joy set before Him. So even in the face of horrendous suffering and crucifixion, He chose to see joy. Through it all, His sights saw beyond the immediate. He was present in a different reality with every step as He got closer to physical death.

With each strike, every inch of the nail that pierced, and as the thorns pushed deeper into Him; He kept seeing you and me in that heavenly seated place with Him—the pain of a thorny crown drawing Him into seeing us crowned with Him in glory.

When all our physical eyes see is the gory sight He became and the pains He endured, what He saw in the Spirit was the glory and authority we would operate in. What He saw was giving His Daddy many sons and Himself gaining many brothers. Every insult, every act of hate, each one written for many generations to be revealed, drawing Him closer to the joy that had everything to do with who you will become - incredible!

> "Looking unto Jesus, the author, and finisher of our faith, who for the joy that was set before Him endured the cross, despising the shame, and has sat down at the right hand of the throne of God."

— HEBREWS 12:2

My earnest prayer has always been to see the joy He saw. I consider what our Savior - Jesus - passed through to death, all the horrors of the scorching, piercing, torture, and humiliation that no soul has ever experienced. And I think, "What in the world did you see me become that would make you even go through all that, Lord Jesus?"

For me, the ceiling break has been to become what He kept seeing through all of that. I desire to break through every human-made structure of the mind and soul and reach in to become a full expression of that joy that Jesus saw even through every inhumane drag towards death. To think you and I are the reason for His relentless pursuit must attest to who we are.

Go through Jesus into the necessary heavenly training, grooming, discipline, and teaching. Do not hold back as you grow your divine image to heavenly degrees, awards, and achievements.

~ Easy is not what we are made for; we were made to press in till we do all things through Christ Jesus. ~

"But whenever someone turns to the Lord, the veil is taken away. 17 For the Lord is Spirit, and wherever the Spirit of the Lord is, there is freedom. 18 So, all of us who have had that veil removed can see and reflect the Glory of the Lord. And the Lord-Who is the Spirit-makes us more and more like Him as we are changed into His Glorious Image." (2 Corinthians 3:16-18 NLT)

3

THE BLUEPRINT OF YOUR DESIGN

~ When you come to God & Unite with Him through Jesus Christ, you are the Image as He ~

~

CALLED TO FUNCTION

The Holy Scriptures establish that "God is a Spirit: and they that worship him must worship him in Spirit and in truth." (John 4:24). Our God is a Spirit. He calls us to a life of worshipping Him in that Spirit form and out of the Spirit realm of His Kingdom. In the above verse, Jesus was speaking to a person who had questions about a physical place of worship.

How many of you had a hard time during the Covid-19 pandemic lock-down days because you could not go into buildings as usual? Those were tough times indeed. God's word tells us not to forsake the gathering of His people (see Hebrews 10:25).

The Church or Christian gatherings are necessary. However, those times called for deep reflection. Many began to reflect on how to be in the Spirit with a God who is Spirit and not in a physical place they had gotten used to receiving a *spiritual fix*. Without which, many got discouraged quite quickly. It makes you wonder, who are we worshipping?

I want you to pause for a minute there because if it is the God who is Spirit you are worshipping, you must pay attention to how Jesus the Son of God said you should worship Him. He said it because He knew the ineffectiveness of doing otherwise. Jesus was emphatic in saying how we must worship God; we MUST do so in Spirit and Truth. Yet have we sought Him in all the physical ways and places.

As a Spirit, God made man in the image He is, which is a spirit as well. Our pattern of living in our natural spirit-habitat was after the blueprint within Adam and Eve, who engaged God in Eden's garden. Take note that Adam was on Earth and had a physical body. However, as a spirit being, he fellowshipped and interacted with God, Who is fully Spirit (not a physical body). God would come and walk in the garden, and man would have fellowship with God.

Adam and Eve knew God's sound; they knew how He walked and moved. They had great times together – God and man. They could see Him. And, hence, they were able to hide away from God's path on the day they sinned: "And they heard the sound of the Lord God walking in the garden in the cool of the day, and Adam and his wife hid from the presence of the Lord God among the trees of the garden." (Genesis 3:8)

We are still spirit beings with a soul and a body to operate on the Earth. You see, for us to function on Earth, God had to create man from the substance of the Earth. To rule over the Earth, we must possess the qualities that make us have legal rights to the Earth.

To be the president of America, you must be born in America. Thus God would use the dust of the Earth to mold the physical form that gave man the right to function and operate on the Earth he would rule over.

God did not create man before the physical form because He first had to make Earth. He separated from beneath the waters the stuff (see Genesis 1:9) from which He would make man's physical form before breathing life into that form. Man's spirit was entirely within God. Man as a spirit was within the *Breath* of God.

"And the Lord God formed man of the dust of the ground, and breathed into his nostrils the breath of life, and man became a living being."

— GENESIS 2:7

The God who is a Spirit is also known as the *Breath*; In Hebrew, He is "Ruach." Out of His inferno of Breath, He creates spirit beings. All spirits are born from this *Breath* that never dies or ends. As a spirit being, His *Breath* is our sustenance.

When you now come to God and unite with Him through Jesus Christ, you are the image as He. You become a spirit being living from and by the sustenance of the God-Spirit. The Father of all Spirits created all spirits. After a lifetime of bearing this earthly *bodysuit* all over the place, all spirits return to God - their Father.

"Furthermore, we have had human fathers who corrected us, and we paid them respect. Shall we not much more readily be in subjection to the Father of spirits and live?"

— HEBREWS 12:9

All the animals and birds had to be made from the Earth to have legal existence on the Earth.

"Now the Lord God had formed out of the ground all the wild animals and all the birds in the sky. He brought them to the man to see what he would name them, and whatever the man called each living creature, that was its name." (Genesis 2:19). Satan and his demons are not creations from the soil, dust, or grounds of the Earth, so they do not have legal grounds to operate until they can take on a body.

Even though God also made animal bodies from the ground (Earth), God began to establish who was/is boss by taking man through the tenets of his authority. God made man the ruler, giving him dominion over all the elements in the Earth. (see Genesis 1:26-28)

Our body is not who we are. Our Spirit is who we are. Jeff & Mark Bezos and two others recently went into space and back. They wore space gears to keep alive while out in space for eleven minutes. When humans go even further into space, to the moon, they wear special body gear to help live and adapt to that environment.

Astronauts know that without the proper equipment, they will not survive on the moon. However, just because they depend on that space body gear to function on the moon does not mean they are the body gear. They only wore the body gear to breathe and carry out their operations on the moon.

You are a spirit-being with a soul in your body so you can live, breathe, and function on the Earth. Does it mean then that you are just that body? No, you are within that body. You are given a body for the time you are here. Jeff Bezos and the three were given their space body gears for the 11 minutes they spent in space. You've got your *body gear* for an allotted time on Earth.

> "Since *his days are determined, the number of his months is with You;*
> *You have appointed his limits, so that he cannot pass."*
>
> — JOB 14:5

Every time we lose a loved one, we see that their spirit leaves the earthly suit in which they lived. At that moment, a once bubbly, active, impactful, and fully present being leaves behind a lifeless, no longer relevant, or usable body. That body is no longer functional on the Earth because the wearer is gone; who they are is gone.

Without hesitation on the value that lifeless body has on the Earth, we proceed to bury or cremate the earthly suit back to its original composite. And we recite, "dust to dust..." The main person who is a spirit has left to a place in the Spirit realm so, while we may say "dust to dust..." on the Earth, those at the Spirit realm may repeat, "spirit to Spirit."

This spirit-being God made in His image was to rule on the Earth. He is to physically take care of the Earth but not neglect his spiritual position in the Spirit realm of our God either. He is also to uproot principalities and powers that oppose his operations from the Spirit realm and into the physical realm of the Earth. Indeed, "For though we walk in the flesh, we do not war according to the flesh. 4 For the weapons of our warfare are not carnal but mighty in God for pulling down strongholds" (2 Corinthians 10:3-4)

The responsibility allocated in Psalm 115:16: "The highest heavens belong to the Lord, but the Earth he has given to mankind." may sound overwhelmingly huge. However, it is not impossible because as beings in the image of God, God placed man in that position to rule the Earth as He (God) rules the Heavens, even the highest heavens.

Apart from having access to worship the Lord in Spirit, God also gives you the unique capacity to become united with His Spirit. So you - man can come to a place where there is no separation between your spirit and the Spirit of God.

"But he who is joined to the Lord is one spirit with Him."

— 1 CORINTHIANS 6:17

How can that be? It almost sounds like blasphemy. Yep, however, it is as God says. The voices of familiar spirits are turning us away from what God's word says. We hear God's word just like it is, and then we feel uncomfortable instead of embracing it and rejoicing over it. We shut ourselves out of the very thing that keeps us far above principalities and powers. How ironic.

Can you see that that precisely is what the devil wants to achieve? Now here are we, thousands of years later, still trying to figure out who we are.

"19 and what is the exceeding greatness of His power toward us who believe, according to the working of His mighty power 20 which He worked in Christ when He raised Him from the dead and seated Him at His right hand in the heavenly places, 21 far above all principality and power and might and dominion, and every name that is named, not only in this age but also in that which is to come.

22 And He put all things under His feet, and gave Him to be head over all things to the church, 23 which is His body, the fullness of Him who fills all in all."

— EPHESIANS 1:19-23

Jesus has placed us in these Heavenly places to sit with Him. We are sitting right there. As one who has chosen Jesus, our spirit can now sit there and operate in the manner that Adam and Eve would sit in Eden and talk with God. We can become accustomed to the sound of our God, His movements, and His love in a tangible way like they did.

So if we will rather believe the voices of familiar spirits that want to hinder us from our original God-design and privilege (thereby agreeing with demonic beings that are less than us), what can God do?

"2 For look! The wicked bend their bow, they make ready their arrow on the string, that they may shoot secretly at the upright in heart.

3 If the foundations are destroyed, what can the righteous do?"

— PSALM 11:2-3

If the devil and his cohorts have secretly staged their arrows and lies to get to us (God's children), they can only succeed when we refuse to stay within the parameters of our foundations – in Jesus Christ.

God, in His righteousness, is unable to stop His people from destroying the foundation of their design. God has not placed His will to override our preferences. Man has free will with his life choices. See Joshua 24:15.

THE PROGRAMMING

"Do not allow current religious tradition to mold you into its pattern of reasoning. Like an inspired artist, give attention to the details of God's desire to find expression in you. Become acquainted with perfection. To accommodate yourself to the delight and good pleasure of him will transform your thoughts afresh from within."

— ROMANS 12:2 THE MIRROR

As living, breathing beings, we have developed a pre-dated mindset of how the world operates and how it should be. Most of us have learned to think a certain way, so much so that even when we read the Scriptures, we naturally gravitate towards that belief system.

Many have developed thought patterns that are precisely the way our forefathers thought. Some examples include:

- the perception of God as One who is unapproachable, unseeable;
- a belief system that we can only see the devil or demons but not God;
- fear of the demonic kingdom creating a fear to interact with God in His Heavenly Kingdom.

Perception That God is Unapproachable, Unseeable

For several years, doctrinal teachings alluding to God being unapproachable or even biblical references to death if anyone sees God has framed many Christians to turn away from such aspirations. Others have even taught that they would have to go through a human intermediary or spokesperson with that unique ability to approach God.

However, Satan has been more than willing to throw himself at people and bring them into a focus on spiritual practices that lead them straight to him. As spirit-beings, we will always crave spiritual encounters with God, the supreme Spirit-being. Satan, a deceptive, false god, will present himself as the substitution to an unapproachable God.

This erroneous perception has caused many to look into the wrong realm. The constant exposure to the counterfeit has also increased influence on how most believers go about spiritual matters.

The focus of our engagement determines which kingdom we empower around our lives.

When we place value or focus on certain things, whether within our minds or even in our sights, they multiply, so we have grown accustomed to our programs and ideologies. What would happen if we broke away from these ideologies and sought God through prayer, worship, and meditating on His word?

A Belief System That Only Sees the Devil but Not God

The erroneous practice of only seeing the devil or demons but not God has left the body of Christ looking deeper into the realm in darkness rather than to God's Kingdom realm. Christians are becoming much more comfortable identifying and seeing demons than seeing God and His ministering angels assigned to help us.

That pseudo comfort is what tethers many to the demonic realm. It's no surprise we have more books on the demonic than the Heavenly Kingdom. Sadly, it is becoming a more popular and acceptable approach for the *easy-way-seeking* Christian. It excites the demonic realm to give Christians more information to write about them as though unbelievers haven't written enough (and made movies) about them. Consequently, this increases fear in their readers.

With a lot more exposure to the activities of the demonic realm (through hearing or seeing), a belief system of its power begins to stick firmly in people's minds. With great fear, anxiety also increases. Faith in God's love and His willingness to interact with each one on this spiritual level diminishes.

When we address Satan's kingdom in the right way, we take away the power it has to govern people's lives. As spirit beings, we engage in ongoing warfare against the kingdom in darkness. The demonic realm insists on taking over our territory, and we must rise against it wherever we see it show up. We must stand in God's armor and establish God's rule on our territory. (see Ephesians 6:12-13)

We must not be afraid of the demonic realm. But teach and give people an understanding of how to overcome Satan and stop his kingdom from taking over our rule and reign by the Spirit of God. This way, we expose Satan's plan to go unnoticed and gain footholds. There has to be a balance and pursuit of Jesus with understanding that both kingdoms are real and that God's Kingdom holds ultimate authority.

Many Christians still go to psychics or engage in horoscopes and spells to seek answers to their challenging situations. And many are ignorant or unaware that such activities they partake in open them up to demonic oppression.

If the Holy Spirit reveals a "trespasser" on our property, we have the legal authority to tell such to leave! When talking about the demonic realm, we should only show believers how to walk in our authority over it. Jesus said to his disciples: "Behold, I give you the authority to trample on serpents and scorpions, and over all the power of the enemy, and nothing shall by any means hurt you." (Luke 10:19)

Jesus did not magnify the demonic; however, demons were shrieking off from the people whose bodies they possessed at the sight of Jesus. A legion of them asked Jesus not to come close to them, pleading with Him to send them into a sounder of pigs instead. (see Mark 5:1-20, Luke 8:26-39).

Once a guy came to my house. Soon we all noticed that he would jump out of his seat every time I walked past him to my kitchen. Even I did not know what was happening. We would later discover this guy was previously involved in the occult and did dark ritualistic things in his past. The demons within him were scared at the proximity of God's Spirit and His tangible authority, working in my life to chase them out and render them homeless.

You see, these demons know who you are; they know who you are even when you don't fully comprehend. As you walk with God, you keep discovering how much authority He has given you to trample on all the works of the devil.

Jesus has given you that same authority He walked in. You have the Holy Spirit within you that causes demons to tremble from God's presence in you because you can cast them out to where they don't want to be.

> "And these signs will follow those who believe: In My name, they will cast out demons; they will speak with new tongues; 18 they will take up serpents; and if they drink anything deadly, it will by no means hurt them; they will lay hands on the sick, and they will recover."
>
> — MARK 16:17-18

Fear of The Demonic Kingdom Creating A Fear to Interact with God

The fear of the demonic kingdom has left many afraid to seek interaction with God in His Heavenly Kingdom. We have become very interested in knowing more about what we have feared even though we never liked them. Our focus on them empowers their relevance within us.

We do not often realize that we allow our spirit beings to engage with many things we dislike. It's simple things like what we watch, hate, or even spiritual things like what demons did to people or us.

You always come across those precious people who always jokingly say irrelevant things centering on Satan. Even though most of these are said or done in ignorance, it reveals what our minds quickly settle on. We are well into the wrong kingdom by engaging with them long enough in our minds. You can also tell you are inching more towards this kingdom when you find that you can quickly identify demons but cannot discern angelic activities around you.

The book of Hebrews 1:5 says that we have angels ministering to us. When we draw towards the Father, we will embrace more of everything given to us by Him. Sadly, many can not tell they have been helped by an angel, let alone the unique moments a specific angel has been in their lives.

God created all the kingdoms of this world. However, there is a kingdom that does not have the light and glory of God in it. It is Satan's dark kingdom. It is a realm where Satan's rule and dominion are supreme. A domain where evil and wickedness are the norm. By frequently dwelling on what the devil is doing, we are focusing on the dark kingdom. We engage with Satan's kingdom without knowing it when we give excessive thought, reference, and action towards the demonic.

In Jesus, we are of God's Kingdom of light; we are to bring His light to every place darkness reigns. "This is the message which we have heard from Him and declare to you, that God is light and in Him is no darkness at all." (1 John 1:5)

When we understand that the more we engage God and His Kingdom, the more authority we have against Satan and his cohorts, it changes how we operate. We gain higher ground and get rid of demons. When you constantly submit to God, the devil is in constant flight at your very submission to the Lord. (See James 4:7)

God is so faithful, and if we draw near to Him, His great light will always expose what is hidden in the darkness so that we can have victory.

"But the Lord is faithful, who will establish you and guard you from the evil one."

— 2 THESSALONIANS 3:3

THE DANGERS OF PROGRAMMING

All around us, we see the dangers of taking on "*cultured*" belief systems on varying issues. Let's consider one typical programming of something as spiritual as prayer warfare as one quick example. Sometimes even as vibrant prayer warriors, many believers have suffered attacks from speaking to demons. Your call is to take authority over and not have some nice chit-chat with them until they trigger you to unbelief.

A Christian should recognize that they are seated high above principalities and powers. They should not be comfortable with activities that engage the demonic kingdom around them, even when they intend to cast them out. A believer must stay clear of all appearances of the evil kingdom (see 1 Thessalonians 5:22). Do not entertain them as spirit entities living in your house. Do not entertain them as the voice of your mother's familiar spirit or your dead girlfriend who is jealous of your female friends.

Peter warns, saying, "Be sober, be vigilant; because your adversary the devil walks about like a roaring lion, seeking whom he may devour. 9 Resist him, steadfast in the faith, knowing that the same sufferings are experienced by your brotherhood in the world." (Peter 5:8-9)

Jesus was not afraid of the devil, but He desires that His disciples know their authority and not doubt it. A genuine prayer warrior is led by the Holy Spirit and knows they are under God's covering protection. He has faith that God backs him up wherever he goes. You can be confident in God's word and assurance that:

"No weapon formed against you shall prosper,
And every tongue which rises against you in judgment
You shall condemn.
This is the heritage of the servants of the Lord,
And their righteousness is from Me,"
Says the Lord."

— ISAIAH 54:17

If demons come at you for dismantling their authority in, let's say, your child's life, you must not back down for any reason. Your stance is to recognize your spiritual armor (Ephesians 6:10-18), rise, and boldly take authority over them. If they try to follow you, show up in your dreams or gain a foothold, you bet God will expose it and give you the insight to cast it out of your abode! He is always so faithful in that!

That said, our shield of faith still has to be up. Meaning, we have to believe what God's word says about the authority and power He has given us and not provide a foothold for fear of critters well beneath us. Remember, we are seated in Heavenly places (see Ephesians 2:6).

Only a person living in sin would suffer from a lack of authority like the sons of Sceva in Acts 19:14-16. My good friend shared a story of an evangelist administering deliverance on a lady (and he had seen people possessed flying around the sanctuary and all sorts of crazy things before). Anyway, this man was there and asked, "Can I stay to help and watch?" As he said that, the demon in the lady said to the man, "How can you deliver her from me when you have drugs in your pocket!" The man was terrified and ran out of the church as fast as he could.

OUR REALM OF FOCUS

As you may notice, it is a matter of the effects of focusing on the wrong thing; in this case, the wrong kingdom. I have seen too many believers casting out demons yet, victims themselves. Many are oblivious to why it is so, some while trading into the ways of the world. Many are focusing on religious acts rather than knowing God intimately.

It's why Jesus said to those who cast out demons in His name in Mathew 7:21-23, "I never knew you; depart from Me, you who practice lawlessness!." These are all mighty works but no intimate relationship, and really, this means such did not fulfill their purpose either.

Many believers and even prayer warriors constantly focus on the demonic. Such approaches as going to Hollywood mountain to cast out territorial demons, etc., and yet, they were just victims of demonic oppression themselves. You don't force demons out of a place where people are willingly engaging them. However, when people are willing to turn to God and forsake their agreements with the demonic kingdom, you are operating in victory.

God's word reveals that they instead should spend that time engaging His face & His Kingdom; everything else will bow. Daniel, in Daniel 10, wasn't looking into demons; he was seeking to understand

God. In Chapter 7:9, he saw God, engaged angels, spiritual battles ensued in the Spirit realm, and dominions came tumbling down. An entire nation worshipped and revered the God of Daniel because of his commitment to God and His Kingdom.

Our authority is past dealing with demons, but it's about us "being." It is about us being who God designed us to be. It is about us being in a place where all spirit-beings and even demons recognize our positioning in God's Kingdom. And like Jesus, they know we have entered a city; they beg and seek to get out.

The Lord has given you His authority to pull down demonic strongholds. But along with that is so much more for you. Dealing with demons is not the pinnacle of our walk.

When Jesus' disciples rejoiced at the victory they exercised over demons (which is absolutely fantastic), Jesus pointed them to their greater positioning in God's Kingdom:

> "Nevertheless do not rejoice in this, that the spirits are subject to you, but rather rejoice because your names are written in heaven."

> — LUKE 10:20

One is not without the other; it's just that one should be of a greater focus.

Here, I emphasize the greater, which is often neglected and of which we have failed to reap its benefits without diminishing the relevance of the other.

So much will be taken care of here on Earth if we turn our face into God and the Kingdom He presents us now. There's so much beyond the veil we can be talking about and revealing here on Earth.

Avon

> "21 "Not everyone who says to Me, 'Lord, Lord,' shall enter the kingdom of Heaven, but he who does the will of My Father in Heaven. 22 Many will say

to Me in that day, 'Lord, Lord, have we not prophesied in Your name, cast out demons in Your name, and done many wonders in Your name?' 23 And then I will declare to them, 'I never knew you; depart from Me, you who practice lawlessness!'"

— MATTHEW 7:21-23

It is a sin when we become drawn away by any religious act rather than God. When you get hooked on the demonic, you need to understand it becomes your fascination, and this is one reason we have so much news on the demonic.

Hence, there are probably more books written on the demonic than there are of God's Kingdom. How many people are looking intently into God and His Kingdom?

We know many names of demons that aren't even in Scripture, yet we can not identify angels or what they are doing presently. Because we are fascinated with the demonic realm, iniquity prevails within the body of Christ. We are not to ignore the demonic realm, either. But there must be a higher value on God's Kingdom to see God's power and authority restored to the body of Christ.

Look into the kingdom you want to see multiply on the Earth. I once heard Shane Willard speak so wonderfully on Avon. The Hebrew word for iniquity is "Avon," it is three letters, namely a, v (vav), n (nun) = avn, the o is added for easy pronunciation, so it does not apply.

Every Hebrew letter has a picture; therefore, a, v, and n represent three pictures.

The picture of the letter 'a' is an eye, the picture of "vav" is a hook or a nail, and the picture of the "nun" is fish multiplying. The Hebrew word picture for iniquity is an eye, a hook, and a fish multiplying. What that means is that whatever your eye hooks to, multiples.

When a Hebrew person reads the word "iniquity," they read: whatever your eye hooks to multiplies. Whatever dominates your focus becomes increasingly prominent.

Based on the above, I will itemize these soul-searching questions to help you move into a heavenly place right now.

- Could it be that we have bought into a deception that has only multiplied the works of the devil among proclaiming Christians?

-Could we be missing the point of our call to set our affections in God's Kingdom (see Colossians 3:2)?

"A time will come, however, indeed it is already here when the true (genuine) worshipers will worship the Father in spirit and in truth (reality); for the Father is seeking just such people as these as His worshipers."

— JOHN 4:23 AMPC

When is the time to be which Jesus envisaged His true worshippers worshipping God in Spirit and Truth (see John 4:24)? How and when was it to be?

Here's an invitation, who will be a true worshipper?

- Was it to be a feeling, or was Jesus speaking about a place of worship in the Spirit realm of our God where we would ascend and worship God after the Holy Spirit had come into us?
- Would we receive such mighty power to be greater witnesses of a Kingdom we know by the Spirit of God? (see Acts 1:8)
- Could it be that by turning fully into God's Kingdom, we would see and put to effect the prayer that God's will be on Earth, as it is in Heaven? (see Matthew 6:10)
- Is this how we flip the authority sin and iniquity (Avon) has over us? (see 1 John 3:9)
- Is this how we turn the tables against the accuser who stands to accuse us of sin, day and night? (see Revelation 12:10)
- Will we begin to say no to our present evil ways, demonic inclinations, fascinations, and focus?

The focus on Satan's kingdom increases sin and all its demonic activities (hate, fear, sicknesses, etc., you name it) in people. We have embraced illness as God's will when indeed, it is Satan's. In many circles, we reject the supernatural access given to us in the gift of speaking in tongues.

The devil knows ways he can empower himself against the believers. He knows if he can get a group of powerful beings willingly looking towards his kingdom alone all of the time, he could sustain his hold on them.

But God gave us His word and has painted so many beautiful pictures of His Kingdom realm that is very endearing.

UNABLE TO WITHSTAND THE GLORY

What I find in engaging the personhood of God is I see more people set free by taking them before God into the Courts of Heaven. Other times, deliverance would happen by exalting God in worship or even in conversations. When I pray for people, I am consciously taking them into the presence of God. A common trend I see is:

First, as the person begins to repent before God, the demonic entities would manifest violently to shut the person up and keep their place. Do not let all that deter you from your focus. Follow through with repenting and renouncing.

There is nothing a demon can do to you when you stand before God. They cannot withstand the glory.

Next, in failure to withstand, they leave or, in some cases, begin to plead or ask through the voice of their host. Sometimes you hear a man speaking in a woman's voice or vice versa, asking you where they would go from there. Be warned; it is never time for conversations or negotiations with them.

Do not fear or feel pity for them. Cast them out. Keep the focus on the Lord, exalt the Lord, and establish His Kingdom within yourself or the person undergoing this deliverance. May the Lord open your spiritual eyes to see what is going on. Even if you don't see it, you engage in an actual deliverance session and get victory in a real Court.

Sometimes, I take authority and command the demon spirits to leave. Other times they just run out with a squirm, unable to withstand the glory, and I can see the person's countenance change as the demons leave. In all situations, still take authority and command them to leave.

In some cases, the person is badly hit, thrown around the floor, may feel pains in some body parts. Depending on the degree of oppression or the demon's hierarchical order making its way out, the victim may experience torment as the demons leave. Some may throw up, spit a lot, yawn, cough, fart, purge, itch, cry, etc. Don't worry; God is expelling them out of the subject. Other times a person may fall (also known as being slain by the Spirit). The person may be unable to move for a while but gradually become strengthened to get up after the oppressive spirit(s) leave(s) them.

In other instances, there may be no physical activity, but you feel light. You can sense weight lift from your shoulders, a release from tension, and you feel peaceful, joyous, etc. In all, know that you are not alone. If you don't see, only rely on the Holy Spirit's direct prompting.

A lovely brother had done a spell for peace. When he came to me, the Holy Spirit began to prompt me to call on Shalom - the Peace of God. I did not know about the peace spell until later. As we prayed and called on Shalom, his oppression intensified so I had to cast it out. The Devil gave him a pseudo-peace demon along with the spell; but it had to come out when the Peace of God was invited in. Be careful, my beloved, what you receive.

Finally, in exalting God, recognizing the brilliance in the purchasing power of the blood of Jesus to redeem every lost territory, I have seen it consistently prove its potency against Satan's kingdom. And God's people get set free.

Even though there are more aspects to deliverance and prayer warfare than these, it is vital to point out that even a wrong belief system on spiritual matters can increase damaging operations around us.

YOUR JOB

After an incredible victory, you have to work to maintain it, just like you maintain your car, house, looks, etc. Without maintenance, you might end up in a worse state. Hey, don't give up on your deliverance because of maintenance or fear of being in a worse state. Maintenance is growing in God, growing your spirit man, and walking in authority. You'll have supernatural fun while you are at it.

Prevent Re-Entry

Question: What if they attempt to return as Jesus said they could in Mathew 12:43-45?

> 43 *"When an evil [defiling; unclean] spirit comes out of a person, it travels through dry [waterless; arid] places, looking for a place to rest, but it doesn't find it. 44 So the spirit says, 'I will go back to the house [the person] I left.' When the spirit comes back, it finds the house still empty, swept clean, and made neat [put in order; fixed up]. 45 Then the evil spirit goes out and brings seven other spirits even more evil [wicked] than it is, and they go in and live there. So the person has even more trouble than before [the last state of that person is worse than the first]. It is the same way [So it will be] with the evil people who live today [this evil generation]."*
>
> — MATHEW 12:43-45 EXB

Make no mistake; God is greater than Satan and so is the power of God more than Satan's power. It does not even compare.

So if a Greater and Higher Power (the Power of God) has so radically delivered you beyond compare, how in the world can that evil spirit that ran out from you by God's power keep coming back to check if you are clean – unoccupied (not filled with the Holy Spirit and walking in holiness)? How is it possible that it can get seven more unclean spirits that are more powerful, powerful enough to put you in a worse state than before?

Can there be seven more powerful spirits than the Spirit of God that sent that evil spirit out?

When you ask these questions, you keep yourself from deceit and ignorance. You arm yourself with knowledge of how the Spirit Realm operates. The Bible says: "My people are destroyed for lack of knowledge." (Hosea 4:6a). Once you know how the Spirit Realm operates, you understand what to do to keep winning.

Indisputably, there are **no** more powerful spirits (demons) than the Spirit of God; that is a foundational truth. Praise the Lord Jesus! However, demons will keep checking back after being evicted from their host.

Demons will go around to seek legal grounds to return because their depraved minds believe your body is their territory, especially if they have lived long in the bloodline and have brought lesser demons underneath their rulership. They will find stronger ones who are willing to get the trophy - you.

These demonic entities will network or connect with stronger ones who have a stake in your bloodline and have legal grounds to operate. This multiplicity is why one person can have many demons in them (see Mark 5:1-20). They will attempt to fortify themselves so as not to leave quickly when their host person undergoes deliverance.

Jesus saved and delivered you, but you will have to effect your freedom and prevent re-entry into your territory - that's your job.

All Your Armor Is In the Spirit: Put Them On

As a Spirit-being standing against the demonic realm, God has given you spiritual armor to disperse all the wiles and arrows of the devil. All your armor is in the Spirit; use them to fortify your spirit man and prevent re-entry attempts of a former demon and seven stronger demons - that's your job! And to execute this, you will do well to take seriously what the Word of God instructs you to do.

- Put on the whole armor of God.

"10 Finally, my brethren, be strong in the Lord and in the power of His might. 11 Put on the whole armor of God, that you may be able to stand against the wiles of the devil. 12 For we do not wrestle against flesh and blood, but against principalities, against powers, against the rulers of the darkness of this age, against spiritual hosts of wickedness in the heavenly places. 13 Therefore take up the whole armor of God, that you may be able to withstand in the evil day, and having done all, to stand.

14 Stand therefore, having girded your waist with truth, having put on the breastplate of righteousness, 15 and having shod your feet with the preparation of the gospel of peace; 16 above all, taking the shield of faith with which you will be able to quench all the fiery darts of the wicked one. 17 And take the helmet of salvation, and the sword of the Spirit, which is the word of God; 18 praying always with all prayer and supplication in the Spirit, being watchful to this end with all perseverance and supplication for all the saints—

— EPHESIANS 6:10-18

The Word of God is your effective sword of the Spirit (Ephesians 6:17). Speaking of the place of God's word in the believer's life, King David wrote, "But his delight is in the law of the Lord, And in His law he meditates day and night." (Psalm 1:2)

To overcome;

- Pray in the Spirit with all prayer and supplications (Ephesians 6:17). Also, while at it, do not stop;
- "Pray without ceasing." (1 Thessalonians 5:17)
- Worship God in Spirit and Truth. (John 4:24)

God is a Spirit: and they that worship him must worship him in Spirit and in truth. (John 4:24)

To shut your doors from unclean spirits returning with even stronger ones, you must not harbor unforgiveness or unrepented sin.

You must pay close attention to repenting and shutting off, especially the sin of witchcraft/rebellion.

"For rebellion is as the sin of witchcraft, and stubbornness is as iniquity and idolatry."

— I SAMUEL 15:23A

Rebellion is as the sin of witchcraft. Therefore, you may claim not to practice witchcraft, but you are rebellious over every godly influence in your life. Some people will rebel so hard without knowing why they are that way. It may not be evident to them that they are operating from a seed of witchcraft. They do not recognize that the effects of the witchcraft their parents and ancestors practiced are active in them.

For instance, if you notice that you are rebelling against every godly influence in your life, if you want to be the prevailing voice-over everyone else regardless, then check yourself. You are deceived; you need to be free from engaging in witchcraft activities. The spirits of witchcraft operating in lives make it hard for them to receive and apply godly counsel.

If there is witchcraft in your bloodline, repent as though you were a part of it because it is in the genealogy. You have blood in you that is in covenant with witchcraft, just like you have blood in you which has already been in covenant with diabetes, high blood pressure, cancer, autoimmune diseases, etc.

How come it's easy to see the latter but not the former? And how come it's acceptable when doctors tell you? Yet Jesus Christ paid for your freedom from all curses and healed you by His stripes. Let His Word speak in your life for your good.

If you are rebellious, repent for both witchcraft and rebellion. Daniel did not just stop at repenting for his ignorance and sins, but he also repented for the sins of his ancestors and nation. (See Daniel 9).

Brother Ian tells a story of a man who stood before God in Court, and when demons began to call him a *goat rapist*, he was agitated. He said they were lying. However, his Mediator, Jesus Christ, told him that his uncle raped goats and that if it is 0.0001% in the bloodline, it is legal grounds; so, he should repent so that the Judge will judge the effects he is suffering from that sin. He did, and God placed a fierce verdict against the evil/unclean spirits.

When the Lord exposes the devil's plans to you while in your days of ignorance, do not feel like you need to defend yourself for your failings, the Lord will overlook your times of ignorance but now calls you to repent.

> *"Truly, these times of ignorance God overlooked, but now commands all men everywhere to repent."*
>
> — ACTS 17:30

Do not entertain pride, shame, guilt, or condemnation; repent to remove yourself from that contract of years ago. Accept responsibility for not being in your position of authority at the time you were passive or violated.

The point is that you want your violators judged. What you need and should want is to be free. But understand you have to establish victory in that very place of your violation, passivity, or ignorance—this is vital.

Do not give excuses for why you did what you did. It may be the sneaky unclean spirit giving you reasons to be defensive so that it can remain inside you. Act opposite to what the voice opposing repentance is saying to you. Remember, the devil cannot repent, and neither does he want you to.

When you repent, you are partaking in the action that dispels him from you. There are some key winning spiritual activities we overlook that are hurting us.

As a spirit-being fashioned in God's image, get on board with your spiritual life; get tools that empower your spirit man to thrive. Partner with God and repent to give the Righteous Judge legal grounds to judge in your favor.

Many people struggle when told to repent for things they feel they didn't do. Spiritual matters work differently than things in the natural; This is why the natural man cannot understand the things of the Spirit.

> "*14 But the natural man does not receive the things of the Spirit of God, for they are foolishness to him; nor can he know them, because they are spiritually discerned.*"

— 1 CORINTHIANS 2:14

When Jesus said that looking at a woman lustfully meant one has committed adultery with her (see Matthew 5:28), it was hard for people to receive it. It was hard for them because they only saw through natural lenses.

Through the natural lenses, one may argue even speaking to the lady they lusted over, let alone having sex with them bodily. On the other hand, being the Son of God operating in His Spirit capacity, Jesus was teaching them what really takes place in the Spirit realm, when we engage demons without paying attention (like lusting after a person).

Jesus taught them the real things and spiritual transactions taking place that they couldn't see with their natural eyes. All they needed to do, and all we need to do today, is to pay attention. The only person benefiting from your neglect is the devil. How long will you let it continue?

What have you got to lose by repenting? Honestly, the only thing you will lose is a major demonic influence over your life and children.

Jesus saved you so that you can now get up and begin to effect His finished work on the cross in your life. If you do not effect what Jesus has already done, you may (God's mercy prevails) continue to suffer from that affliction. Of course, God will always show you mercy and break you free from that stronghold, too, because Jesus mediates for you in Heaven's Courts.

I ask people, do you want to be free or not? Repentance means you are breaking free from that agreement you or your bloodline made (knowingly or unknowingly) that caused those harmful situations in your life. You want to get rid of the effect of that agreement upon your life.

Repentance means you are now getting into an agreement with God on that matter. It now means your agreement with God will take effect, and all the demons that held you bound in that area are receiving God's judgment. You can now be free from years of torment, sickness, failure, and shame.

This means you can also be more open to the ways and relationships God brings to you than when you formally only attracted the wrong people. You did not recognize that you lived by the dictates and biddings of a contract you do not remember making. However, once you do know, you must understand that Jesus has empowered you to destroy all the works of the devil.

"He who sins is of the devil, for the devil has sinned from the beginning. For this purpose the Son of God was manifested, that He might destroy the works of the devil."

— 1 JOHN 3:8

Total repentance, separation from even the likeness of your former ways, and a life of devotion to God will close any doors of re-entry.

Also, remember to step into Heaven's Courts immediately you sense demons come back; so they are all dealt with at that moment. When you are under attack, do not be afraid. Take authority and know that you are not alone in the Courts of Heaven – It is where you should be running. (Chapter 8, 9, and 10 discuss this in detail). Don't walk blindly and allow the devil to mess with your life and calling.

Many do not deliver God's way, but if God's Kingdom is the focus, everything engaging us will bow to this Higher Kingdom. Personally, administering deliverance to people became quicker as I began taking people to the Courts of Heaven with their cases. People I work with also find themselves empowered to get rid of demons when they attempt to return.

Refocus and Repurpose

God is multi-dimensional. We are made diverse for a reason and a purpose. Let us take a detour and see an example of a direct result of programming in the physical sense.

One of the many reasons we have conflicts in the physical world around us is that each group of people, tribe, ethnicity, race, community, etc., has acquired some incomplete or false knowledge of the other, which informs their perception. Reading or orally receiving information about others, generation after generation encourages stereotypical beliefs. In the same way, people have these ways of thinking about God.

Many genuine seekers have rejected or shied away from the truth that God is both approachable and reachable. Just as it would take a willingness to relate with and be open to knowing people who are different from us, it would take a conscious effort to break away from perceptions and belief systems to now engage with God from an entirely different perspective.

To this end, some claim their ways are absolute. Consequently, this has given rise to many disagreements and undue hatred for one another. There have been generations of dissentious beliefs festering enmity within us against one another through programming in a physical existence.

On spiritual matters, we have engaged with this falsity even concerning our perception of who God is. As a result, many hold a one-dimensional view of God that even causes an enmity towards God. I have met many followers of God who feel hatred towards the Lord even though they appear content in their spiritual journey. They perceive Him as loving others more based on the outcome of their own lives.

Imagine what difference it would make for you and me if we chose different programming. One of looking into the throne of God, seeing what He is doing. How about believing to see the angels around His throne in glorious worship?

For a brief moment, allow your imagination the thrill of chariots with wheels within a wheel as the spirit in Ezekiel-1 empowered it. And that is to name a few. Imagine the authority believers would walk in today if they began to set their gaze and affections towards God and His Kingdom realm?

When we come to the knowledge of God as Spirit and that we are spirit beings, it becomes a stepping stone to explore the more excellent plans God had when He designed us so. In engaging God in spirit and truth as we ought, we begin to find the truth of His nature.

We become accustomed to this all-magnificent Being, different from everything we have perceived Him to be. We also begin to approach Scripture and life within the reality (as spirit beings) in the Spirit which the Godhead framed us.

THREE BENEFITS OF AVOIDING THE PITFALLS OF PROGRAMMING THROUGH RELATIONSHIP

Just as it would take relationship, interaction, and a willingness to learn and understand people, in the natural sense (not just reading about them) to fully know them, it would take stepping into a conscious relationship with God to learn of Him in Spirit and Truth.

In a powerful and revelatory conversation with the Samaritan woman at the well, Jesus enlightens, saying: "God is Spirit, and those who worship Him must worship in spirit and truth." (John 4:24).

Like this woman, many see worship at a physical place on a mountain or church building where you sing and feel good with yourself. However, worship is what gives you access to God in the Spirit. And the place is the God's Heavenly realm.

The most effective ways of interacting with God come from taking time to worship Him in a quiet place alone with Him. When you seek out time with God in this way, you are taking time to engage your spirit with God's Spirit.

When this becomes the norm in your life, you will soon break through the veil that separates Heaven and Earth. You will come in direct encounter with God. It is the way God designed for you to meet with Him in His Kingdom.

Let us go beyond just reading about Him but engaging with and desiring a deep connection with Him. I urge us all to look into the face and nature of our God, Who is Spirit, and calls us into a life with Him that is achievable and reachable "in Spirit and Truth." There can be no greater truth!

From this place of worshiping Him in "Spirit and Truth," we see ourselves operating in our seated position with Jesus Christ. The results of this act of intimate worship of God are incredible. We shall consider 3 of such benefits.

- **Divine Guidance**

If we are open to knowing God-the-Father in the Spirit personally, we will get clear instructions on our calling within His Kingdom. The Lord speaking to Joshua in Zachariah 3, said: "Thus says the Lord of hosts: 'If you will walk in My ways, And if you will keep My command. Then you shall also judge My house. And likewise, have charge of My courts; I will give you places to walk among these who stand here." (verse 7)

Learning of Him in this way will ensure a functional spirit existence; One through which you can come to walk in heavenly places among those that stand in His presence and have charge of His courts in Heaven.

- **Know His Ways**

It is also in this place and state of being; we will allow the Holy Spirit to expound each Scripture into our hearts. God will increase the measure of revelation to the one who seeks Him. We no longer see through someone else's belief or the lens of some programming but learn His ways and His Kingdom's laws. God is Righteous and a God of Justice.

He is Love and the God who punishes iniquity. He is Patient and Kind. God's ways are Holy, and there is no shadow of turning with Him (see James 1:17). When you know how He moves, you become a fountain where others can receive nourishment in God's ways.

- **Clears out Enmity / Doubts Towards God**

We also come to experience the depths of God's love for us when we get personal with Him. We understand better the reasons for the challenges we face on Earth. When we suffer challenges, our perception of His heart is no longer in question, thereby clearing out doubts and hatred from our hearts.

His love grows within us so vigorously, assuring us that nothing ever separates us from it (see Romans 8:31-39).

THE PROGRAMMING FEARS YOU WILL DISCOVER YOUR IDENTITY

When we accept the Lord Jesus into our lives as our Lord and Savior from a life of sin and torture from the devil, He introduces us to ABBA Father and the Person of the Holy Spirit. It is truly a transformational journey when we embrace them with all our hearts. Allow the Lord to teach you; that way, you will never mistake your identity.

There is a promise in Isaiah 54:13 that God Himself will teach us. In reality, once we have embraced Him as His sons and daughters, we get the privilege of calling Him Abba Father. When we know who He is, we understand who we are as His children.

Romans 8:14-16 expressly suggests that "The mature children of God are those who are moved by the impulses of the Holy Spirit. 15 And you did not receive the "spirit of religious duty," leading you back into the fear of *never being good enough*. But you have received the "Spirit of full acceptance," enfolding you into the family of God. And you will never feel orphaned, for as he rises up within us, our spirits join him in saying the words of tender affection, "Beloved Father!" 16 For the Holy Spirit makes God's fatherhood real to us as he whispers into our innermost being, "You are God's beloved child!" (TPT).

With that, it means we have also stepped into a new inheritance that far outweighs our earthly bloodlines. We are not going about our business the way people do or how our parents did. Instead, you are quickly moving by the impulses of the Holy Spirit. You are moving in boldness, authority, and love, such as are of them within the family of God. You exhibit the family traits not of an earthly genealogy to impress an earthly lineage but a Heavenly genealogy to bring pleasure to the King of kings and the Lord of lords yet, also fondly Daddy.

It's never too late to begin to trust the Lord this way. I promise you that He will guide us through His Word to know His nature. Sooner or later, you too will begin to get accustomed to His face and voice as a child with his very present Dad. He is yours. Be His.

Systems, thrones, and perceptions all crumble before Him. These all crumble at our manifestation in Him. When you know Him this way, the entire Spirit realm sees His image in you, and Satan's kingdom crumbles at its attempts against you.

One more beauty of embracing being present with God is, you discover this was God's intent all along. One which began in Eden and never changed.

Knowing Abba Father on such a level becomes a two-way streak where we also know who we are as sons of God, making us a terror to the devil. It all makes sense that Satan is behind the programming that limits our reach into God. It's no wonder he is terrified of you finding out who you are as inspired all through Scriptures;

"But we all, with unveiled face, beholding as in a mirror the glory of the Lord, are being transformed into the same image from glory to glory, just as by the Spirit of the Lord."

— 2 CORINTHIANS 3:18

When you step into Heaven by faith to know God in Spirit, you do not carry that program into the realm of Heaven. On the contrary, you become and fully see who you are when you go into the Kingdom of Heaven.

When a child of God chooses to engage faith by going before the

Throne of God to know Him intimately, something happens. You do not go into the realm of Heaven and out as one feeble being. Even if you set out with that mindset, the act of faith qualifies you to receive what the Father has in store for you.

The more you step in, the more you engage who God designed you to be when you go into the realm of Heaven. When we look into the Face and Nature of our Three-in-One multifaceted God, we keep getting transformed into the very exact nature (2 Corinthians 3:18).

Today, take a trip in your spirit, get on a journey with Him, and you will not be disappointed.

What Happens when you step into Heaven?

My beloved, this is a truth I have walked in, with not enough vocabulary or earthly references to express how magnificent our lives can be in the Spirit even though we look very ordinary on Earth. I must not fail in my assignment to **let** you know that you can see your real Daddy in Spirit. Start today by only believing that God made you for a deeper walk with Him.

I pray you embrace love and relationship like never before. What you think love and relationship are pales in comparison to being with Abba Father. You were made for much more than your human brain can handle. Allow your Spirit to engage God in Spirit, for it was designed with the capacity to grasp what your human brain is unable to.

"My *heart* says of you, "Seek His face!" Your face, LORD, I will seek."

— PSALM 28:7

Knowing God this way reveals you as well. You begin a journey into sonship. For in knowing Him, are we fully known; In beholding Him, we see us.

In looking into the face and nature of our three-in-one multifaceted God, we continually get transformed into the very exact nature. Imagine why an opposing kingdom will create programming that keeps you away from this reality.

4

LIVING THE SUPERNATURAL

~He Loves you Boundlessly, Ordinary and All~

∾

On May 10th, 2008, about 1 a.m., my husband, Ime, had just returned from his usual Friday night evangelism. Ime was part of a group of amazing friends, Jim and Janet Colville, Tony and Mary (of blessed memory) Johnson, from Eternity Church in Guildford, Surrey, England.

Each Friday night, they set up a hot beverage stand outside on the side of the busy intersection, near the theatre and clubhouses (pubs) down Guildford High Street. On those nights, these amazing Jesus-loving couples we were honored to call friends made sure of a table or two of hot coffee and tea for strangers going about their fun evening out. Once they came out in those cold late nights, they had something hot to drink before proceeding to their next destination. Many came by the table.

This hot-drink setup they created provided the opportunity to love and share Jesus with all who stopped by. Many got to hear about the love of Jesus, and some accepted Him into their lives. They openly prayed over them and witnessed so many miracles on those cold nights for hours on end.

I remember I had joined them one night and got to pray over this guy who had been suffering from endless hiccups. He got healed and kept asking how that could be. I tried to explain it was the power of God, but he ended up running off screaming, "*this is weird, this is weird!*"

Ime eagerly looked forward to those Friday nights and would head there straight on from work to set up tables and prepare for their night of great ministry.

On this particular night, Ime had just returned, and I was slipping back to sleep after I had said my usual Friday night/Saturday morning, "'Sweeto', welcome!" as he came through the room door. However, he came over and woke me up to pray with him. His words were, "I have a burden on my heart." On hearing that, I got up, and together we began to pray.

At this time, worship was second nature to me, so we worshiped, and we started praying in tongues (our spiritual language), considering we didn't understand the nature of his burden. Neither could he say precisely.

So we leaned into the Spirit for help, as scripture says:

"*Likewise, the Spirit also helps in our weaknesses. For we do not know what we should pray for as we ought, but the Spirit Himself makes intercession for us with groanings which cannot be uttered. 27 Now He who searches the hearts knows what the mind of the Spirit is because He makes intercession for the saints according to the will of God.*"

— ROMANS 8:26-27

People of God, when in doubt, pray in the Holy Spirit. He helps take care of human limitations. Praying in your understanding can only take you as far as your knowledge goes. Anything beyond that would require the assistance of a higher understanding.

Suddenly, I found my spirit taken into the heavens. I could sense I quickly got rushed into very thick, deep darkness. In there, I felt much pain, sorrow, and despair that I could not handle. I started weeping, screaming, groaning, and making bizarre noises.

My heart pleaded for God to take away the darkness and this horror I found myself in. There was no fighting off these feelings. I had this feeling that this place was hell. There, I felt like there was no sense of Jesus around me.

Over the years, I cultivated a tangible relationship with Jesus that I knew how His presence felt when He showed up. However, even though in prayer, there was a total absence of Him in this place. I started searching for Him there to no avail. I was helpless.

Strangely, in my body, I was sweating and struggling to take the duvet off me. I was going through a spiritual experience that was simultaneously reflecting on my physical existence. Hot and helpless, I couldn't control what or how I felt. All I had was the voice within my heart I recognized to be my Lord's. After quite a while, I finally reached in, desperately pleading, "Lord, please take away this darkness."

Relief came as I began to move into another realm. It was fast, and it was Heaven. I was in Heaven. I was in an encounter I never imagined myself partaking in.

Heaven, on the other hand, was bustling with love and beauty. I was finally with the ONE I have loved ever since my childhood; Jesus, the lover of my soul, my very first. Both transitions were quiet yet swirly, like a wild ride.

The contrast between both realms was simply unbelievable. Now in Heaven, I could feel an intense passion engulf me. Unmistakable! I was professing my love for Jesus as He did the same to me. It went on for a while. I was having the time of my life.

It fails me to find a grid or frame of reference to put into words such an encounter. I didn't know such an experience existed. I saw men and women, bought by the blood of Jesus, seated in the same place as Jesus. They all had seats beside the Father. They were beautifully clad in gorgeous robes and making high-level decisions meant to impact the earth.

I saw me, but I was totally and utterly different from who I thought I was. I was in a body way better than what I was used to having on the earth. I wore bright and radiant colors, just like the rest there. The authority we had was off the charts. We spoke and interacted by knowing, and we all just knew what was, what is, and what should be. Unexplainable!

In the physical, I had taken Ime's arm in mine. I was kissing and cuddling it. Ime knew I was engaging in a spiritual activity with my Jesus. He could see that it was directly reflecting on him or his arm rather. I was in and out of this experience, such that I would step out and speak with Ime.

At a point, the power of God was so heavy on me that I began to ask Ime to pray for me. However, what was going on within my spirit was more tangible than I could hear him pray for me.

And so whenever Ime would mention God's attributes, like love, righteousness, holiness, etc., it gave me so much joy, and I would laugh uncontrollably.

When we are in God's presence, many of us experience His Spirit, bringing joy and laughter.

"Our mouths were filled with laughter, our tongues with songs of joy. Then it was said among the nations, "The LORD has done great things for them."

— PSALM 126:2

"He will yet fill your mouth with laughter and your lips with shouts of joy."

— JOB 8:21

"You make known to me the path of life; you will fill me with joy in your presence, with eternal pleasures at your right hand."

— PSALM 16:11

"Blessed are you who hunger now, for you will be satisfied. Blessed are you who weep now, for you will laugh."

— LUKE 6:21

While standing before the throne of God, I was more struck at how different I thought Heaven would be. The more the Lord kept answering my questions, the more our earthly existence paled in comparison with our heavenly one.

Just seeing all of us in our spiritual state knocked my socks off. Who we are was evident there. The confidence and importance we had, the authority we wielded. When you know who you are, you no longer struggle for man's affirmation. It's how Jesus operated by washing His disciples' feet because He already knew who He was (see John 13:3-6). In the coming years, I see a people who will seek to serve others because they know who they are.

It was also interesting that we had responsibilities and were active in many affairs. What bothered me was how we have not attained (on the earth) what seemed readily available unto us.

Even though I see it, I am yet to grasp all the abilities we have in Him or understand how to unlock them. Some things have gotten clearer over time. But all I felt at that moment was deep gratitude to be with my Jesus. Like, this can be a reality.

How does that even happen? Not many speak about it as though it is available to me, ordinary me. And, to you. Yes, ordinary you too.

It was many hours, with me laughing and having a heavenly rapture all at the same time. It was glorious. Ime was singing in the background as I remained lost in a world I never knew existed. I am not sure if it is the right word to use, but I was so 'weird' in my actions. I even had to call the name 'Jesus' several times. It was "the Jesus" right here to love, hold, and know like never before.

Finally, and what did it for me was, I needed to pee. When I told Jesus I had to go, He teased me and said I should go before I peed on myself. I laughed hysterically, pulling myself away into the bathroom.

Yes, physically. But I felt invincible. I had so much fire around me that was unmistakably God's glory and anointing.

I remained in that glory and began prophesying, declaring His word, singing a new song I had no prior knowledge of. I never remembered that same song again until my second visitation.

I continued to worship the ALL HOLY, ALL AWESOME, ALL BEAUTIFUL GOD. How privileged we are to be His.

Next Day

Finally, at about 5 a.m., I had to force myself to sleep since I had to be at work by 9 a.m. It was a short rest, but I woke up refreshed. All-day, I sensed God's presence all around me. I felt His Kingdom with me as I went to work.

It turned out to be an unusual Saturday. I found people willingly came up to me to talk. Some even shared their lives' concerns with me. I got to share God's love so freely with as many as would listen. I spent a significant part of that day encouraging people.

At some point, I began to feel people's pain before they shared them with me. I could relate to their burdens, and it was such a joy to take them to Jesus, who carried all their burdens; "Come to Me, all *you* who labor and are heavy laden, and I will give you rest." (Matthew 11:28).

Ministering to people became easier as I spoke in authority, from a solid place of knowing and being. How much easier life becomes for us and the people God places in our lives when we begin to step into Heaven.

MY UNUSUAL PRAYER GATHERING

A similar experience occurred on May 25th, 2008. This time around, it was at a prayer school session with Liz Wright. It was a highly impactful gathering of God's people. We all came together to learn to engage and grow in spiritual intimacy with Jesus.

It came time for taking the holy communion - the elements

symbolic of the body and blood of Jesus (see 1 Corinthians 11:23-26). I took the communion bread - representing Jesus' body - to my mouth. As soon as I began to chew the bread, I was spiritually translocated (see Acts 8:26-40) into another place on the earth.

In the physical, I was on the floor, vibrating, shaking, and pouring out revelation. However, at that same time, I saw myself in another setting where I witnessed a blind man's eyes pop open. I saw several other healings that sent me into an excited state for a considerable amount of time in the Spirit.

When this was all over, like a couple of hours later, I realized I never got to drink my cup of communion - representing Jesus' blood.

Since that encounter, I have met people who have also translocated into the Spirit realm of God. I also heard of a preacher caught on tape ministering at two places simultaneously. He even recounted the identical timestamps on the cameras at these different events.

I remember listening to a preacher speak of this encounter, saying it started with him having communion at one of the meetings only to show up at the same time at the other. Like with my experience, he began shaking when he took the communion. In one of his podcasts, he kept saying, "it's in the shaking, it's in vibrating..."

I have few references for many of my experiences with God. Many of which I never fully understand. However, I continue to receive clarity for many of my encounters as I walk through this life's journey with the Lord.

God's Kingdom is for Regular Folks Like Us

Over the years, I have met and seen many ordinary amazing people of God. I am so excited to see what the Lord is doing among everyday people who press into an intimate walk with Abba Father and discover Him in supernatural ways.

To think that God has made this degree of intimacy accessible for us, yet we question His love. It saddens my heart to think situations get us into ever doubting God's love for us. And I pray you who hold this book will know He loves you boundlessly, ordinary and all.

My joy is seeing that we passionately take hold of what is already ours in Christ Jesus, knowing God shows no favoritism (see Romans 2:11).

I would encourage those who have had these personal encounters with God to continue cultivating their relationship with Him. Let us lead a lifestyle of continual worship and intimacy in our quiet place. Please do not feel like it's a one-off encounter for the books. Hold onto Him tightly and pursue an ongoing relationship with Him.

God designed that spiritual encounters come out of a relationship with Him. They are to enhance our walk with the Lord and enable us to function beyond the limitation of the flesh. This function is to see His glory revealed on the earth. In Acts 8:26-40, we see that Philip could preach the gospel with greater ease and speed in Azotus as the Lord supernaturally transported him there.

The eunuch that Philip preached to before his translocation is said to have been used by God to bring the good news of Jesus into all of Nubia in Northern Sudan. God wants to do many of these in our day. When you walk closely with Him, there is no limit to what He will do through you for His mighty purposes.

God wants to see His passion expressed on the earth. Therefore, He brings us into a place where we can have a bird's eye view of things which then informs our choices and decisions on earth. When we can see and be a part of the glorious activities going on in the Spirit realm of our God, we can bring that way of life to the world.

If I promised you lots of diamonds to give your friends, you'd have to see them, embrace the possibility of having them, then receive them and set off to give them to your friends. All of these are simple when we get used to operating as spirit beings.

Relationship Over Experience

We must understand that wherever there is a counterfeit or fake, there must be a genuine copy. Although the counterfeit is usually more aggressive and widespread, it does not negate the existence or relevance of the real.

The devil's activities and his kingdom are all for oppression. He quickly drives people into spiritual experiences that oppress, create fear, or fulfills desires that eventually work against them. It is a good reason why it is not profitable to desire God just for the spiritual experiences but that you love Him. Love does cover a multitude of sins. Where the motive isn't pure, we easily fall victims to the devil's manipulation.

Merely seeking supernatural encounters comes from a wrong motive and makes people vulnerable to ungodly spiritual encounters. We can't force an encounter in our own strength or flesh, either. It is on the Holy Spirit's time and say so.

Naturally, many people gravitate to the demonic realm due to covenants made in their genealogies. People who come from a bloodline that dabbled into witchcraft and other ungodly supernatural ways, pass them on to their children. So many have grown up with tales of encounters with demonic entities like marine spirit connections and ghosts living in their homes.

Many more have received stories of encounters with other spirits. They have built more critical mindsets on demonic realities. So, it is common for many to become victims of demonic operations, nightmares, etc. In deliverance, there are no ingrained mindsets and bloodline ties that the name of Jesus cannot break.

All through Scripture, our God is referred to as the God of Abraham, Isaac & Jacob, and on it goes. Typically, you see their sons toe the line of wanting the Lord to be their God. Covenants like Hannah devoting Samuel to the Lord led to Samuel encountering God supernaturally at a very young age (see 1 Samuel 1:21-28). A child being spoken to by God – it's just priceless.

There are generational covenants that empower God's purposes in our lives. In like manner, people make demonic covenants, such as those who come from bloodlines of free-masonry or religious cults that empower demonic tendencies in their children's lives through cutting, animal sacrifices, to name a few. Those demonic alters are serviced generation after generation. As a result, they grow up listening to the voices of demons.

We see many covenants that result in the demonic upholding their bargain. In many cases leaving generations dealing with suicidal thoughts and untimely deaths until someone steps into the lineage to break those demonic agreements and start a new covenant in Jesus.

For people who have found themselves in the demonic spirit realm, the outcome often leads to torment. Therefore, many prefer to shut the door to supernatural experiences altogether. A rule of thumb is, if Jesus Christ is not the one leading you into a spiritual encounter, then a demon is. And you don't need to say this, but we know that even in "Christian" church settings, there are encounters that are not of Jesus but done in His name. This is why relationship with God is also key to discernment.

The spiritual realm as a whole is broad. As earlier mentioned, there is God's Kingdom realm - Heaven. There is also Satan's kingdom realm - the demonic realm/world (in darkness). Both domains are within the spirit/spiritual realm, referred to as the unseen realm or unknown universe.

I want you to understand that the devil parades his counterfeit before the unsuspecting soul. Satan has created false heaven where he takes many people to. I have heard people express their experiences and how real they were to them. But in reality, they do not line up with Scripture. Many of them even see a false Jesus on a cross along with other idols and demonic beings. Some have seen what they described as a female god they title mother or mother earth.

So, you must beware of encounters that do not line up with the Word of God, the Bible. If you do have these encounters, you need to head into the Courts of Heaven for deliverance.

Even some churches are involved in these charades. They give the appearance of love, helping the poor and many other outward services that are easy to coax people into deception. So, beware of how you go in search of the Lord.

If you have been a member of these religious organizations, I urge you to seek deliverance in the Courts of Heaven. Some people feel they are strong enough to withstand influences towards the new age wave going on right now, for instance.

"This does not surprise us [And no wonder, since...]. Even Satan changes himself to look like [disguises himself as; masquerades as] an angel [messenger] of light [trying to fool people into thinking he is from God, who is pure light]."

— 2 CORINTHIANS 11:14 EXB

Many proclaiming Christians have opened their souls to "chakras" – an ancient Hindu religious practice. Some have "mantras" they live by, which only open them up to pseudo-spiritual encounters. It is a sad deception. (the *mantra* is a sacred utterance, a numinous sound, syllables, or group of words in Sanskrit and other Indo-European languages that its practitioners believed to have religious, magical, or spiritual powers).

If you are reading this and feel you are benefitting from these activities, beware it starts innocently. Gradually, you begin centering your entire lifestyle, choices of what to eat, where to go, live, what to buy & even what to wear, around these beliefs. That is the point where you have given demonic spirits the go-ahead to dictate what happens to you.

Then you begin to have series of spiritual encounters that are impressionable on your soul. You might come to find out that you are knee-deep into the demonic realm. Sooner or later, you begin to suffer the rebuffs of spiritual attacks, but at this point, you may have enjoyed some other *benefits* that it becomes difficult or scary to pull out for fear of losing those. Sadly, many have lost their lives trying to pull out on their own.

I promise you, Jesus can pull you out if you give up everything you took from the dark kingdom and start afresh in God. If you do, only then will you remain in His covenant of protection. But if you do not, even though Jesus wants to protect you, by your action, you are rejecting His covering and opening the door for the demonic; Satan now has access to mess with your mind and make you feel unworthy at all times.

You can be in the way by holding on to the little pleasures you enjoyed from the connections. You cannot hold onto anything that belongs to the devil when you decide to give your entire life to Jesus, or else Satan has legal grounds to come after you. Whatever you are holding on to; be it in a job, a gift you got, a connection, etc., you name it, that could be the hook the demonic realm has to get to you. The devil seeks to meddle in your entire existence so he can always have legal grounds of continual access to you.

I tell Christians who want to experiment with the devil that the devil is a master player and knows how to give you enough interest as bait. Chasing after encounters you feel are educational or enlightening is the chief of all tricks. The devil will give you enough appeal based on your desire to explore supernatural encounters rather than a deep love for God.

If you have been moving with spiritual guides, even to have them boost your career or lead you to your future spouse, this is a good time to separate yourselves and call on Jesus Christ to be your only Lord and Savior.

Make the Holy Spirit your only guide. Every other spiritual guide is an imposter. Allow the Holy Spirit to lead you into that victorious future you seek.

"However, when He, the Spirit of truth, has come, He will guide you into all truth; for He will not speak on His own *authority,* but whatever He hears He will speak; and He will tell you things to come."

— JOHN 16:13

Question: *Will you commit today?*

From your heart, pray out loud with me:

Lord Jesus, I forsake all other loves and make You my Lord and Saviour. Come inside of me and pull out everything of the demonic from my life.

Prayer

Continue by praying thus:

In Jesus' name, I repent for housing (these, any) spirit guides. I repent for observing chakras. I repent for living by these mantras.

I repent and renounce every covenant I have made with them.

I repent and commit to throwing out the material benefits I have received from these covenants. I cut ties and all associations with people and items within these cults. I break away from elitist functions that take me deeper into their lifestyles.

I repent for seeking their help. I repent for believing in spirit guides.

I break every agreement I have made with them to (be very specific on the ways you have partnered with them. for example, *seeking them out before you leave the house, obey them, etc.*)

Lord, break every soul ties that give them access to my body and soul.

I repent for engaging in blood covenants. I repent for the soulish covenants I made. Forgive me for the oaths I have taken and the potions I have drunk. Forgive me, Lord. Deliver me from the life and effects of the orgies I have had.

I repent for the use of occult or witchcraft items such as crystals used to channel the demons into my life, causing depression and sadness. I repent for indulging in horoscopes, tarot cards, boards, casting of spells, etc.

I ask the blood of Jesus to cleanse me. I ask the blood of Jesus to wash me clean from all the patterns I have observed from them. Wash me clean from all their habits of operation in my mind. I ask the blood of Jesus to heal me from the desire to return to them.

I ask the Holy Spirit to come and be my only Guide.

Lord, I ask that You strengthen my resolve with the challenges I am about to face.

I know You are even more real than all I have experienced. I ask that You fight my battles as they come.

I will not succumb to the pressure and threats on my life because I know you will keep me safe. I will not hold on to some of their stuff while I walk with You. I am all in with You, Lord.

Jesus, be my only Lord and Savior. Show me Your ways that I may walk with you alone. In Jesus' mighty name, I pray.
Thank You, Lord Jesus, for setting me free.
I am free indeed.
Amen!

Pray these prayers for as long as three months till there are no traces of occultic or demonic function in how you process things. Send me an email when you do, and you can be sure I will be praying for you.

Only Be True

I have also met people who think their experiences with the demonic gives them a better knowledge of God. If you have this mindset, you must know that no institution studies the counterfeit to discern the real stuff. You must understand that cashiers who handle money are well-trained to know the qualities of the original dollar.

Other experienced tutors take time to expose an upcoming cashier to the actual dollar for a time. It is by knowing the original that they can recognize the fake. Their exposure to the original currency is the primary determinant that makes it easier to identify the fake than a layperson (without that training).

So, do not assume you can *wing* spiritual encounters. The more you desire and cultivate a deep *relationship* with the Lord than just *experiences*, you will soon realize the latter comes with the former. To try and force it (experiences) leaves you more vulnerable to the devil's deception instead of enjoying the blessings of God's divine presence in your life.

It takes being genuine in your desire for God and a willingness to submit to have a strong relationship with Him. It's humbling to have the privilege of sharing the beautiful encounters with Him. These encounters do not exclude you, my beloved. I have seen a bit of what He has for you; therefore, I must be honest that God's Word centers around genuine supernatural encounters.

The more we spend time in His Word, we receive the needed exposure to His ways. It is no longer something we read for reading sake; instead, it becomes our reality and way of life. His attributes come alive within us. The more time we spend worshiping Him, we are setting our affection on Him. We attract everything from God's Kingdom. We also begin to change, becoming His holiness and desiring to please Him only. We make choices to be holy, and He trusts us with His face.

In a world where the essential characteristics of being a Christian are tainted, and grey areas are encouraged, the Holy Scriptures urges us to "Pursue peace with all *people,* and holiness, without which no one will see the Lord:" (Hebrews 12:14).

I owe you this caution in love. Our generation has blurred many lines with lots of opinions and less of God's Word. God's standards will never change, no matter how sophisticated we get. He is a Holy God and (putting it simply) will not take us to His Kingdom for us to make a smear campaign on His image.

"but as He who called you is holy, you also be holy in all your conduct, 16 because it is written, "Be holy, for I am holy."

— I PETER 1:15-16

Throwing in The Grace Card

With a lot of godly living and character lost in the body of Christ, I cannot over-emphasize the need for an authentic and holy walk with God. Let no one with a compromised walk jump up from a sinful and wicked lifestyle to claiming true intimacy with God along with supernatural encounters. Not even with an attempt at claiming grace. It does not happen that way, and a person will know this because neither is it being authentic in your walk with God.

The grace God gives you is for you to be empowered to come to Him with every sin imaginable, every failure heard/unheard of, and He will receive you that way and wash you clean. The grace He gives you is that those ways you walked in do not scare Him or make Him turn away from you. On the contrary, the deeper you have walked in darkness, the more extraordinary grace attracts Him to love you; This is His grace for you! (Romans 5:20)

Regardless of individuality or opinion, "Nevertheless, the firm foundation of God [which He has laid] stands [sure and unshaken despite attacks], bearing this seal: "The Lord knows those who are His," and, "Let everyone who names the name of the Lord stand apart from wickedness *and* withdraw from wrongdoing" (2 Timothy 2:19 AMP).

The closer you draw to Him, the more He strips you of your ungodly ways. If you invest daily in a lifestyle of seeking the Lord through worship, prayer, and in the study of His Word, He daily transforms you into His nature.

When you are in love with God, doing things He says to do is no longer a chore because all you want to do is make Him happy. The truth is that you will find you have a more successful walk when your desire is as simple as "I want to make Daddy happy!"

~ We make choices to be holy, and He trusts us with His face ~

Prompted by a question from Judas' Iscariot, "Jesus answered, "If anyone [really] loves Me, he will keep My word (teaching); and My Father will love him, and We will come to him and make Our dwelling place with him. 24 One who does not [really] love Me does not keep My words. And the word (teaching) which you hear is not Mine, but is the Father's who sent Me." (John 14:23-24 AMP)

When you love God, you obey Him. And the evidence is seen in the life you live, whether in public or behind closed doors. That's how this goes. Also, this reminds me of Romans 7, where Paul talks about the battle with flesh vs. spirit. How we have this battle raging within us, but when we rely on Christ's power, He helps us to overcome things of the flesh and be free from the power of sin.

The key is that when a righteous man falls, he gets back up. The key is knowing that we long to obey God, but even if we fail, we genuinely repent and ask God to forgive us, and we get back up (not allowing shame or guilt to hold us down).

I think some people do love God but sometimes obedience is a challenge. Like King David, they repent and ask God to help them. So, when you love God, you long (strive) to obey Him.

We know God and His Kingdom by constant exposure and effective times of walking in God's ways, growing to know His character, His holiness, righteousness, and justice. Only by these can we tell when something is not of God or from God's kingdom.

Please make no mistake; the fake by design is to look as close enough as the original so that you think it is the original. If it does not mimic the original, then it does not qualify as a counterfeit.

A life devoid of a relationship with Jesus is vulnerable in the spirit realm. Therefore, seek a relationship with the Lord. Worship Him in the beauty of His Holiness, and love being with Him every moment you get.

I tell people it feels like a lifetime of being in love for the first time. His love for you is new every morning (See Lamentations 3:22-23 ESV).

The Father's extravagant love consumes a true seeker, and all you want is just to be with Him. Don't stand on the sidelines. Come on in!

5

WAYS THE HOLY SPIRIT WILL DRAW YOU IN

~ Never Underestimate the Impact of a Yes to God's Invitation - Magic does not even Cut it ~

∾

Before we go further, I want to acknowledge many believers still struggle with building a healthy relationship with the Holy Spirit. You might be in this type of situation because of how the relationship took off in the first place.

It might be that you are unsure if you can even be in a relationship with the Holy Spirit or how to get started. If you do not have one altogether but always desired, that is okay still. Just follow along as we dive into this chapter to unlock truths every believer must fully understand.

Recognizing the Early Stages of Life in the Spirit

I want to take out the mystery aspect of building a relationship with God by stating how you can recognize when the Lord (who is Spirit) is reaching into your spirit (you are also a spirit being) for a relationship.

If you have never willingly asked the Lord Jesus into your life, this is an excellent point to do so.

There is no problem if you do not know what to say. Ask Jesus to come into your life and take over. Tell Him you want Him to be your Lord and Savior; also, ask Him to cleanse you from your sins. Below is a prayer of faith to guide you through.

Prayer of Faith
Say this prayer with me:

> "Lord Jesus, today, I come to you by faith. I choose to believe that you are the son of God who died to set me free from sin and death. Thank you for loving me regardless of what I have done or where I have been. I ask that you forgive me for rejecting your call. Forgive me for walking away from you.
>
> I repent of all my ungodly ways. I ask that you take over my life. I ask that You would sit on the throne of my heart. Be my Lord and Savior starting now! I join myself to You, Jesus. I unite myself to You, Holy Spirit. I join myself to God the Father. In Jesus' name, I pray. Amen!"

Ok, if you just said that prayer and meant it, then I can assure you that you have that which you have asked. I greatly rejoice with you; the entire Kingdom of God is rejoicing with you right now. I would love to hear from you and keep you in prayer, so send me an email.

You have now received Jesus Christ into your life. Rivers of living water symbolizing the unlimited power and presence of the Holy Spirit courses through you (see John 7:38-39).

Jesus also promises that if you love & obey His command to you, as revealed in the Bible, He and His Father will come and live within you (see John 14:23). Now, what this means is that you will begin to notice some changes in your life. Many begin to experience the peace of God come upon them. Others start to lose the desire to sin, do drugs, smoke, drink, lie, steal, manipulate, live a false lifestyle, etc.

The list is endless but what this means is, you have allowed the Lord to arrest the demons that held you in bondage. The desires you had from being under the control of Satan are heading out, along with the unclean thoughts and spirits you once entertained. Although they will check in from time to time to see if you will have them back because they must live in a place they claim is theirs. Do not let them, or you will regret it. Keep guard by staying in prayer and running away from enticing situations.

What that also means is, God is empowering you to have new desires so that He can bless you incredibly. You chose Him to be Lord over your life; now that decision has positioned you for God's protection & favor always.

After such a prayer is consciously made and one is determined to walk with God, it is good to note the many changes that will begin to occur.

It is of great benefit to read your Bible and learn the ways of God daily; this is how you build your spirit. Talk to the Lord about connecting you with people who love Him genuinely. I am sorry, but there are so many counterfeits out there. You'll soon find that Jesus warned us about that too. I am stating this so that you are aware. You will not change your mind on God based on anything you experience with fellow Christians when you know this. Stay focused on Daddy, not people.

Now let's go into practical ways the Holy Spirit will draw you to Himself. I chose to include this because many people feel that it takes a special person to have an intimate relationship with God, which is not true. We are all called by the same Spirit. The Lord is crazy about you in the same way He is about me and anyone else.

AN IMPRESSION, A NUDGE

You will begin to sense these nudges to pray or read your Bible when you least expect it or are not in the mood for it. Sometimes, the Holy Spirit will awaken you out of your sleep to do so. You might even see a picture of yourself kneeling to pray or worshipping in tears. I find that when I retreat in those moments to step into that picture that flashed before my face, it ends up being the most rewarding moment.

As you begin to make these simple moments a priority, you will be amazed where your investment into getting intimate with the Holy Spirit may lead you. An easy one is driving to work; the thought of those moments of worship before a hectic workday may be something you look forward to.

When times have been challenging or in those moments where you would instead do something else like drowning yourself in binge-watching a television series, I have found the most outstanding results by choosing to spend time with God. I find investing time in Bible passages that I have always sought to understand more builds further interest for my quest. I talk to God about them as I read. You will find me making conversation and even exclamations with Him as one aware of His presence. I find great success in this practice as I write down the impressions He places in my heart.

Your response to the nudge of the Holy Spirit in those unlikely moments plays a big part in your spiritual growth. I have found it to be a Kingdom of sacrifice. The more your positive response in those situations, the more your desire for Him grows, and that ultimately leads to a deeper relationship with Him. It is just like spending time with your favorite person.

For those married or continuously in the company of family and friends, you will find that constant urge to step away from everything else. It may feel as though the Holy Spirit were pulling on your heart-strings. The desire to run off to Him every little chance you get as though you are in a secret affair. Over time, you will discover that you can be amongst people and still have your spirit fully engaged with Him in your heavenly reality as well.

All of this sounds fun, but there will be challenges. There are forces from the other kingdom that hate this budding relationship you are having. You are growing into a spirit being who is aware of the power he has with God. That is huge because your growth is detrimental to Satan's operations. Have no fear, though; we were built for this too. We are here to pull down the devil's operations against our lives, so we expect to have victories.

Challenges will come to throw you off, but you have to keep

pressing in. In the past, I was not great at immediately turning into God's Presence in those moments. And in those times, after my victory, I would look back and wonder why I didn't come to Him sooner. Don't wait to have lost so much before you remember to run straight into God's presence. He is always faithful and ready to draw you in.

WHERE SECRECY IS KING

One of the most challenging things in this age of technology and social media is being still or alone with God. We tend to want to be with people, whether they add value to us or not. As an extrovert who loves people and enjoys entertaining, I understand that it may sometimes be challenging to take time away from these soothing pleasures.

I must also emphasize the need for creating a particular time to engage with the Lord, where it's just you and Him. And when you do create that, make each moment as special as can be. Place value on it like you don't let people look into your loaded account. Blowing your trumpet about how much time you are spending with God does ruin things for you, though, so make it private and personal.

You may ask why it should be confidential. In the spiritual realm, when you boast about your achievements, you have men praise you. However, when you are focused on God's approval, you get rewards beyond what any man can give you. You get greater access to eternal, more than life – exceeding, abundant – rewards.

There is a reward that comes with making an effort to keep your prayer times secret. This caution will not come to you as a surprise if you recall the Lord Jesus Christ's words in Matthew 6:

"When you pray, you should go into your [private; inner] room and close the door and pray to your Father ·who cannot be seen [or who is in that secret place; or secretly; in private]. Your Father can see what is done in ·secret [private], and he will reward you."

— MATTHEW 6:6 EXB

When Jesus Christ was on earth, He made it a habit to go to a quiet place with God. "[Very] Early the next morning, while it was still dark, Jesus woke [got up] and left the house. He went to a lonely [isolated; deserted] place, where he prayed." (Mark 1:35-36 EXB)

I find a practical advantage with spending a good chunk of time alone with God is the uninterrupted freedom of expression I have. Especially when my kids were little, I had to plan my prayer routine when their dad was home, and they were all asleep, so I could wander off to a nice quiet spot around 5 am. There I would be alone with the Lord in the fields, by the lake, in deep yearning for Him to draw me into His Kingdom.

Once I sense His heart, I go into Him; and you'll find me alone, screaming my lungs out and crying my heart out till someone comes walking their dog around 7 am; then that would be my queue to leave.

I remember one such occasion, I opened my eyes to see two big dogs next to me and their owner staring at me—so much for privacy.

I also found a 3-hour window when my older daughter was away in pre-K for 3 hours. I just made sure my little one was napping after I must have fed her. Sometimes she woke up and found me praying or worshipping; she would sit and stare. Other times she would come to wipe my tears with her cute little hands or baby blanket and ask me, "Mommy, why are you crying?" I would tell her, "God is so good, and... those were happy tears."

As she grew, I saw her cry uncontrollably during worship services. And I would ask her, "why are you crying?" She would say, "Mommy, it's the Holy Spirit."

Regardless of age, we have had our special moments with God's supernatural realm as a family. We consciously take time to plan out the things that are important to us. All of this nurtures our spirit man into God's desire for us.

These uninterrupted moments of prayer and worship are the moments where we step into Heaven without knowing it. Sometimes we go to sleep after some of those extensive times of prayer and dream we are in Heaven or in someplace healing a sick child, etc.

Every spiritual experience must come out of a relationship with

Jesus Christ. He then becomes the door into God's Kingdom realm, where all our spiritual experiences train and mature us into sonship.

I have since then found a way of losing myself in deep heavenly, and desperate worship that translates me into where Papa – our Abba Father - is.

Uncountable rewards for moments before the audience of One that grows you await. Rewards that make you confident of God's presence even in very trying times. Rewards that fill you up so much to filling many others with love, joy, hope, and deliverance from demonic strongholds.

I have also seen the power in the body and blood of Jesus. I have experienced the power of gathering with a group of people who desire God intensely. I have found Him to be enough and faithful to satisfy every longing heart.

I can speak to God's desire to release miracles, signs, and wonders in many lives due to being in God's secret place. Also, remember that grace? I can also speak to the grace for self-control, faith, and more grace to live a godly life. (John 1:16)

As we release ourselves to God's flow and Spirit presence, we also grow in authority. We begin to understand our function as His sons. Before long, you must have found a new way of living.

AN INVITATION TO GOD'S THRONE

~ In Knowing Him, Are We Fully Known; In Beholding Him, We See Us ~

When you go into Heaven's realm, you transform into who you are there, entirely different from who you or humans perceive you to be. God calls you to come boldly before His throne because He has provided you with access to Him through Jesus.

Jesus, our Great High Priest, went before us and passed through the Heavens; we can follow Him right through the Heavens to stand before the Majestic Throne of God.

"Seeing then that we have a Great High Priest who has passed through the heavens, Jesus the son of god, let us hold fast our confession.

15 for we do not have a high priest who cannot sympathize with our weaknesses but was in all points tempted as we are, yet without sin.

16 let us, therefore, come boldly to the throne of grace, that we may obtain mercy and find grace to help in time of need."

— HEBREWS 4:14-16

His glory in you will transform you into His Son's image, enabling you to present yourself before Him.

There are inadequacies and areas of need within our earthly experiences that limit our full expression as sons of God. Therefore, the Lord is urging us to come boldly before His throne because it is within His glory and presence that His grace can transform us, raising us above those limitations.

He made this provision for us through His Son, Jesus Christ, who walked through our experiences and passed through death into life. God is passionate about you. He desire for you is to live and walk in the image of His Son.

The Veil

"But whenever someone turns to the Lord, the veil is taken away. 17 For the Lord is Spirit, and wherever the Spirit of the Lord is, there is freedom. 18 So, all of us who have had that veil removed can see and reflect the Glory of the Lord. And the Lord-Who is the Spirit-makes us more and more like Him as we are changed into His Glorious Image."

— 2 CORINTHIANS 3:16-18 NLT

Why Walk as Though Veiled?

The purpose of removing the veil is to open you to a Spirit-to-Spirit engagement with God. That veil is the barrier. Without the veil, you can see God now, Spirit-to-Spirit!

Suppose you are questioning if this is real or of God; it is what the veil has done to God's people for many generations. Think, why is the devil able to take people into spiritual experiences with Him, and it's easy for you to believe it? Why will your mind think of ways to resist knowing you can have a tangible relationship with God now in His Kingdom Realm?

I wouldn't have known it were possible because no one told me about it till I bumped into it through lots of desperation for God in worship. A new world opened up for me that I have continued to experience and have since spent my life teaching others and they too have come to experience.

Daddy wants His children! Now you are aware. I hope you desire Him deeply enough and choose to know Him this way.

Maybe if there were more movies made of this real Kingdom relationship and the powerful beings we become in the Spirit realm due to it, you would be more used to it. Maybe if we had more viewings of super Spirit-led sons of God with authority to destroy the works of the devil than those of people gaining power from drinking dark potions, bitten by creepy aliens, and looking hideously scary, that would do it for some. Doubtfully so.

Do you notice how we are naturally programmed to enjoy that sort of thing? At this point, if we came up with what happens in the Spirit Kingdom realm of our God, will we even be interested? We already have an inkling towards a counterfeit. Needless to say that we can give an opening or gateway to the enemy by watching these creepy demonic movies.

If only most movies, books, and people who do the devil's job weren't portraying sons of God as weak religious people who run at the sight of an attack. If we have as many movies, books, etc., show the victories we have had over the devil and of our encounters with God; as there are of those of the dark realm cultured to saturate our minds as it is, then maybe, just maybe, we would aim for a more remarkable life in God. We can only wish that for now.

As adults, we know that we get nowhere with wishing. We rise and do the work, which brings me to a surer way.

Another way we can reveal this truth is that you, my beloved, can run with it when you read this. Consciously pray and go for it. When many of us begin to live this way and teach it, God's glory will begin to fill the earth and its people. We will have many Heaven bringers — People who can take what they experience in Heaven and bring it to Earth. God's will, will then be done on Earth as it is in Heaven. How about that?

You know it can't be that easy when a devil fully functional on Earth ensures all these aren't revealed. However, it doesn't mean it is impossible. Easy is not what we are made for; we were made to press in till we do *all things through Christ Jesus*. (see Philippians 4:13) Make no mistake, only until this true gospel of Jesus and our positioning in God through His sacrifice is preached, then will the end come.

I got tired of expecting everyone else to do the work when I found out God was waiting on me.

Beware of the Counterfeit

God designed us as spirit beings that have a soul and live in a body. He engages with us in the Spirit. The devil delights in twisting this truth to blacklist what is real and empower his kingdom. Always know that the counterfeit cannot exist without the existence of the original. Satan also offers counterfeit love, joy, peace, and the fruits of the Spirit. He also counterfeits spiritual gifts (like slaying people under the kundalini spirits), thereby hindering the church from operating in the gifts of the Spirit.

Truth is so powerful. The devil, the wannabe god, is always known to take God's truth and corrupt it with many lies. Every lie will need a little bit of truth to bait the receiver. Every form of corruption and darkness has an element of truth to guarantee that people will believe it.

The truth is that there is a dark kingdom realm with some measure of power; the lie is that they don't win; we do.

All religious systems have some degree of truth to them. The occults and high-level demonic organizations thrive with a little bit of truth to mask up the darkness. Even though it is also primarily based on the perversion of truth, just a little bit of truth is a hook that draws people into believing a lie. With the deception and many theatrics that appeal to the human senses, these systems fool people and continue to operate significantly.

A bank official once said that the only way to tell a counterfeit currency is by examining and handling more of the original. Hence, studying fake money does much less good overall. Many Christians cannot discern the counterfeit the devil parades, mainly due to not having an ongoing quality relationship with God - The Original Supreme Spirit.

But when we come to the Lord who is the Truth Himself, He removes the veil which separates us from entirely knowing Him in Spirit (2 Corinthians 3:14). We experience total liberty from deception and all earthly programming as we live within the Person who is the Truth. By Way of Truth and Life - Jesus (John 14:6), our spirit-man, is escorted into Heaven to commune with God, who is the Spirit.

Turning towards God in repentance and faith allows for the removal of the veil. Otherwise, we could live many years without knowing a great relationship beyond the veil, beyond the flesh barrier. The Apostle Paul discloses in Hebrew 10:

"Therefore, *brethren, having boldness to enter the Holiest by the blood of Jesus, 20 by a new and living way which he consecrated for us, through the veil, that is, his flesh, 21 and having a High Priest over the house of God, 22 let us draw near with a true heart in full assurance of faith, having our hearts sprinkled from an evil conscience and our bodies washed with pure water."*

— HEBREW 10:19-22

In all sincerity and with an open heart, come to the Lord consistently and then watch that veil lift.

How You Move in The Spirit

Freedom is living in the Spirit—freedom to live in a relationship with your Father in His Kingdom realm in Heaven and yet walk the Earth.

The way of the natural mind cannot comprehend how you reason or operate. The physical realm cannot determine your whereabouts.

> "*The wind blows where it wishes, and you hear the sound of it, but cannot tell where it comes from and where it goes. So is everyone who is born of the Spirit.*"

> — JOHN 3:8

Like the wind, when you move, you are undetected by the elements of the flesh but your sound! Yes, your sound can be heard in the Spirit Realm when you move. You sound like the movement of your Father, the Supreme Spirit, in Eden's garden (see Genesis 3:8). Will you go to Him or hide away because you have eaten from the wrong tree and are now naked?

You have the above scriptures to remind you of the facts. Now there is no need to convince you further.

Are you born of the Spirit? Here, let us pray.

Prayer

Say;

Lord Jesus, I come to You. I repent for all my sinful ways and sinful mindsets. I ask You to save me. Deliver me from the lies of the devil. I give my spirit, soul, and body to You. I ask You, Jesus, for a supernatural rebirth. Spirit of God, fill me, lead me, guide me. I ask You to change me, Lord.

I break every tie to remain on this side of the veil. I ask You to take me into Your Holy Place by the blood of Jesus. Sprinkle me from an evil conscience and evil desires. Thank You for accepting me as I come. Hold me close to You. Keep me desiring after You for all my days. Please help me out of my weakness. I make You Lord over every aspect of my life.

Thank You for seating me in Heavenly places, dear Jesus. You are my Savior. I believe You have saved me from death, shame, and fleshly ways. I make You mine. I give myself to be Yours. Do in me what You will.

I hear Your Sound in Eden's Garden, and I run towards You.

In Jesus' name, I pray.

Hallelujah! Welcome on board. I join with all of Heaven to rejoice with you. You are born of God's Spirit through Christ Jesus. It would help if you chose Him daily, in His word, in worship, and prayer.

A great prayer to pray daily is to ask the Lord to deliver you from deception. Jesus paid a great price to get us to the Father right now, but we still allow the effects of the veil to hold us back. Go through, my beloved. Go through.

6

TRADE AGREEMENTS

~ God Presents you as His Kingdom to Serve Him here on Earth; do not be of service to Another ~

We know there are kingdoms, which stand out uniquely in lifestyle, economics, politics, etc. As with any established kingdom, its citizens get to exhibit certain traits because of their inclinations. We display the nature and heart of the kingdom we belong to through speech, tendencies towards the simplest things like spices, lifestyle choices, etc.

"For the kingdom of God is not a matter of rules about food and drink, but is in the realm of the Holy Spirit, filled with righteousness, peace, and joy."

— ROMANS 14:17 TPT

HE PRESENTS ME A KINGDOM

Time and again, Abba has told me that He has come to present to us a kingdom. He wants us to know what great kingdom we are a part of due to Jesus making the ultimate choice to die for us. Thus, we become a kingdom drenched - bought and paid for - with His blood.

Every kingdom has its unique ways of operation, which we usually refer to as culture. God's Kingdom is not exempt from having its unique culture as well. The Holy Spirit empowers God's Kingdom culture; therefore, we can seek to exhibit the nature of the Holy Spirit when we accept Jesus. It's not a chore; it's supposed to be our way of life. I have often heard repeatedly in Christian circles that we need to follow God's rules when we come to Christ. Unfortunately, when people fall short of these rules, it appears as though God were a boss with a bunch of regulations to set traps for them to fail so He could, in turn, afflict them. There could not be anything farther from the truth.

On the contrary, God makes provision to restore us to His nature and the culture of His Kingdom. As a son of God, you have every support from the Holy Spirit interceding for you. He intercedes for you in a supernatural language of groans, a language so cultured in the Holy Spirit to take you out of your weaknesses. The Holy Spirit helps you with groanings that cannot, I repeat, cannot be uttered. The process of upholding you as God's kingdom is by a means beyond the formation of earthly words - a language so profound that no human language can express. Know who you are.

> "Likewise, the Spirit also helps in our weaknesses. For we do not know what we should pray for as we ought, but the Spirit Himself makes intercession for us with groanings which cannot be uttered."

> — ROMANS 8:26

Your support system is so tight, from God the Father, Son, and Holy Spirit. The Trinity is all about restoring the image they made in the beginning. Invest your time in knowing God's ways and the nature of His kingdom.

We find that we have different opinions of people when we invest in knowing them. As with all lasting relationships, time is of the essence.

We will know more of Him and the Kingdom He offers us as we diligently study about Him and nurture our relationship with His Spirit. The same applies to His kingdom.

*"and has made us to be a kingdom and priests to serve his God and Father—
to him be glory and power forever and ever! Amen."*

— REVELATIONS 1:6 NIV

God is presenting you as His Kingdom here on earth. You are God's Kingdom - a Kingdom He has positioned to reveal Him - to allow His reign over your spirit, soul, and body.

EVERY KINGDOM TRADES

We must know that every kingdom engages in trade with others. The earthly realm is just a picture of the Spirit realm. We see special trade agreements among different nations or countries, such as the North Atlantic Treaty Organization (NATO) or the European Union (EU). These regional trade entities are supposed to be for the benefit of the member nations involved.

The stronger the agreement, the greater access to the support these countries have between them. The more countries that ally within that agreement, the harder it is to break, as we have seen in recent times with "Brexit*."

I love to see how the Spirit realm is screaming through every earthly channel to get our attention. Simply incredible how often we miss the signs all around us.

We have to understand that it takes at least two parties to have a contract. Both come into an understanding or covenant which each party becomes bound to uphold. It is as though pledged in blood. If one party decides to pull out after very many rewarding years of doing business, should the other feel threatened, it may elect that the trade should not dissolve. It is difficult to end such a contract where the other party stands (and hence is unwilling) to lose the partnership benefits.

It is the same in pretty much all partnerships, be it in marriage or business. You are stuck with and tied into whatever the other party's motives are.

Once you have sealed that partnership, you become one with your partner's motives, whether they expressed them on paper or not. Whether the unexpressed motives would be detrimental to you or not, you are at the mercy of your agreement.

At first, some trades may appear to be very rewarding, and all parties involved may benefit. However, the implications of trade become more evident with time. Sometimes it is so hard to pull out of these agreements when we want to.

The covenants can weigh in heavily, like a soul tie. You may no longer want to remain in it but find yourself going through the same ugly cycle over and over. It's as though you lost your power of choice by going into such a partnership, and in a sense, you do, more so if it is a transaction where you already made an exchange or merged your resources.

As a kingdom, we also choose which kingdom(s) to trade with on different platforms. God gave us the power to choose freely. And that is one of the most potent things because we get to choose the kingdom with which to trade – God's Kingdom or Satan's.

You are God's Temple

Consider the earthly temple as a picture of us being God's temples. Jesus shows us that God has openly revealed the pattern of our spiritual existence throughout Scripture. As a result, we will see a pattern of who we are as spirit beings – God's temple.

> "Do you not know that you are the temple of God and that the Spirit of God dwells in you?"

— 1 CORINTHIANS 3:16

There are godly trades as there are also ungodly trades that many engage within the spiritual realm. So fascinating was Jesus' response when He saw the various trading activities going on within the temple. He did not take it lightly because it was all about you. "And He said to them, "It is written, 'My house shall be called a house of prayer,' but you have made it a 'den of thieves.' " (Matthew 21:13)

Here, Jesus was zealously rescuing us (His temple) from an ungodly trade with Satan - the thief. It was all about saving us from wrongly motivated people taking advantage and involving you and me - His temple, His kingdom, and carriers of His Spirit - in ungodly trades. It was all about Him stopping the influx of demonic operations within your spiritual life. We shall get into much detail on this in the next chapter.

The Location of this Temple - In God's Kingdom Realm

Jesus made it very clear to the Samaritan woman that the temple is in "Spirit and Truth." He said to her, "But the hour is coming, and now is, when the true worshipers will worship the Father in spirit and truth; for the Father is seeking such to worship Him." (John 4:23)

In the pattern, the physical temple had its location in Jerusalem, but the original temple (you and me) are spirit beings with a place and position in the Spirit, in God's Kingdom realm. It is about time we realize the duality of our existence. We are not physical bodies seeking earthly recognition. We are spirit beings, temples located in the Kingdom realm of God that should offer up spiritual sacrifices to Him.

God yearns for you to come into an experiential relationship with Him in the Kingdom realm. It is the highest and most authentic worship, not limited to anything external or subject to physical limitations. It is worship, not within temporal structures. It is, however, the union of the spirit of man with the nature of God.

The Design of this Temple - To Offer Holy Sacrifice to God

The Lord has called us to offer spiritual sacrifices to God in our temples. Jesus came and revealed that the temple where holy sacrifices and offerings took place was indeed our lives. The pattern God gave demonstrated how to keep our temples victorious by staying active in our spiritual connection with Him.

We are not to be dormant in our interaction with God because that will allow for active trading with the devil. Thus, we are either trading with the Kingdom realm of God or are in trades with the devil's kingdom. You may have heard the saying, "An idle mind is the devil's workshop." Scripture in Proverbs 16:27-29 (TLB) renders: "Idle hands are the devil's workshop; idle lips are his mouthpiece. An evil man sows strife; gossip separates the best of friends."

> "As living *stones, you are being built up a spiritual house, a holy priesthood,*
> *to offer up spiritual sacrifices acceptable to God through Jesus Christ."*
>
> — 1PETER 2:5

Let us take a moment to consider some offerings you can render in holy sacrifice to God within your temple:

1. **Holiness.** Our temples are to offer the spiritual sacrifice of holiness. We can interpret that through the lens of this Scripture in 1 Peter;

> "As God's *obedient children, never again shape your lives by the desires that*
> *you followed when you didn't know better. 15 Instead, shape your lives to*
> *become like the Holy One who called you. 16 For Scripture says: "You are to*
> *be holy because I am holy."*
>
> — 1 PETER 1:14-16 TPT

The Lord would not tell us to be holy if He did not know we were capable of holiness. He made way for us to be through Jesus Christ. Through the blood of Jesus, we can shape our lives as God intends. We can hear His voice and respond to Him in a loving relationship. Obeying God is easier when you are in love with Him.

2. Obedience. We are to engage in the spiritual sacrifices of obedience. Obedience to God is not a chore when you realize that He is not a power-thirsty God, but that is what empowers you to overcome the devil and his works. The devil disobeyed and lost his place in Heaven as the anointed cherub. As the serpent, the devil deceived Adam and Eve to sin, and they lost their dominion.

As the biggest loser of all time, the devil will dig into any measure of dominion he can take from anyone who will hand it over to him by disobeying God. But, unfortunately, the devil knows the power of obedience. So he continues to drive people to disobey God so that he can take their place.

All of humanity come through a fallen seed. Jesus Christ paid the price of Adam's disobedience and restored us to our place of dominion. Those who accept Jesus as their Lord and savior go through a process of the old nature's death. They also resurrect as new creations through the resurrection of Jesus Christ from the dead. To the torture of the devil, believers in Christ can even now sit with Him, reigning with Him in Heaven while they are alive on the earth.

How empowering to know that "He raised us up with Christ the exalted One, and we ascended with him into the glorious perfection and authority of the heavenly realm, for we are now co-seated as one with Christ!" (Ephesians 2:6 TPT).

Talk about an insurmountable temple; You are now in a place in Christ and with God, where Satan can never get to; therefore, you always win.

3. Prayers. Our temple sacrifices include day and night prayers, just as the priests offered before God. Part of our active interaction with God is a life of worship and prayer. Our temples are to remain soaked in prayer, continually (see also 1Thessalonians 5:16-18).

A prayer-less Christian is a powerless Christian; he is not a terror to the demonic realm while not offering this spiritual sacrifice – prayer.

As we progress, you will see, in John 2:13-17, that this was not the case when Jesus walked into the temple and saw the active offerings for trades within the physical temple. That was not the sacrifice required for the temple that carried God. Praise God, Jesus came to save and redeem us from the tyrant and the merchant he found invading our spiritual temple. Jesus reinstated God's temple as a house of prayer (ref Matthew 21:13).

No matter how far your ungodly trades have been, Jesus will cast out the evil merchants that have you bound in pornography, drug abuse, suicidal propensities, and all the activities that happen within your temple as a result of trades within your bloodline.

Jesus demonstrated it physically and even went ahead to prophesy that He would rebuild the temple in Jerusalem after three days if they destroyed it. He spoke about Himself. Jesus destroyed the works of darkness. He went through death for three days to restore His temple into a place of glory that we can all come through the blood of His sacrifice.

PONDER POINT:

Today, if you look within yourself, you would see that your temples' offerings are not what God intended them to be. However, just as Jesus physically restored His temple, He can restore yours. He will also re-establish your purpose to offer spiritual sacrifices of holiness, obedience, and prayers. Only abide within Him. It is a conscious practice of abiding *in* Jesus and His word.

"I am the Vine; you are the branches. The one who remains in Me and I in him bears much fruit, for [otherwise] apart from Me [that is, cut off from vital union with Me] you can do nothing."

— JOHN 15:5 AMP

Now begin to speak to God from your heart, say, "Lord, I will remain in You, all my days. I commit to stay in vital union with You all my days."

OUR HOLY SACRIFICE HAS A DOUBLE IMPACT

There were important activities designed to take place in the temple that God instructed Moses to build. It was not a lifeless structure. There were all kinds of sacrifices, incenses, and sweet-smelling spices burning up within the physical temple.

In Exodus 30:8, we see some of the sweet-smelling aromas that came out of the physical temple. Talk about the engagement of all our senses of smell, sight, hearing, touch, and taste like God's temple.

Through Jesus Christ, we offer up a sweet smell of holy lives to God. We offer up our passions by setting our affections on Him, touch, and feel Him with our hearts. We pour out our affections on Him in the spirit like Mary Magdalene poured out her alabaster box upon Jesus.

"Then Mary took about a pint of pure nard, an expensive perfume; she poured it on Jesus' feet and wiped his feet with her hair. And the house was filled with the fragrance of the perfume."

— JOHN 12:3 NIV

We choose to set our gaze in heavenly places where God is seated (Colossians 3:2-17). We consciously make choices to taste His ways and see that He is good (Psalm 34:8). When my kids were little, they would reject a fruit or a meal without even tasting it. Their dad would always tell them not to form an opinion about the foods we offered them until they had tasted it. That worked most times because they would taste a little and end up finishing the lot.

I hope you can see what God shows you today; go on further and taste it. You'll find He is so good. You'll discover everyone who told you otherwise did not really taste Him themselves, and you may have built your ideologies on another man's opinion of God.

Here's the cool part of all these, whereas you are building up your spirit-man with the spiritual sacrifices you offer to God with your life, you are also pulling down demonic strongholds over your life and generations after you. The saying "one man's food is another man's poison comes to mind.

Many of us do not realize that offering our lives to God in faith, holiness, and worship is very repulsive to the devil and his cohorts. Talk about a twist on killing two birds with one stone.

How exciting to read in Scripture of the double impact when we offer up these sacrifices?

> "We have become the unmistakable aroma of the victory of the Anointed One to God—A perfume of life to those being saved and the odor of death to those who are perishing. 16 the unbelievers smell a deadly stench that leads to death, but believers smell the life-giving aroma that leads to abundant life. And who of us can rise to this challenge?"

— 2 CORINTHIANS 2:15-16 TPT

The body of Christ must understand that when the Lord shows us how to live, it is not because He is a killjoy or because He wants us to suffer. Instead, the body of Christ must realize that the very things that bring glory to God are the same things that empower us against the devil and his demons.

I must also emphasize that it is an enjoyable life to have. It may not be the fun that the flesh is accustomed to, but a higher level of joy and peace that those who have tasted can attest to. Those who only form opinions about what they have not partaken of will never know what lies beyond the natural sight.

Many people have walked in holiness and enjoyed a life of victory. But, unfortunately, some feel compelled to be accepted into individual circles and end up compromising along the line. Do all it takes to guard against the temptation of going with the latter.

So many are deeply hurt right now from going against their temples' glory. These people didn't understand the depth of their pain when they compromised because while they offered up holy sacrifices within their temple, they drew the presence and glory of God to themselves and so were repulsive to the devil; as a result, Satan could not touch them. The only way demons could easily access them was if they would change the focus and realm of their offerings and becoming a repulsion to God.

Today, we see many practices worldwide where people burn sage and hope that they would ward off evil spirits by so doing. But, unfortunately, demons are not scared of spices, herbs, or the likes. They are only afraid of the authority and power of God operating through the life of a child of God.

The burning of incense and spices offered in the earthly temple depicted a life burning for God in holiness and obedience. These sacrifices are repulsive and frightening to the devil and people who give themselves to him. A life like this offers up a sweet-smelling fragrance to God, but it is also a stick of walking dynamite to the demonic kingdom.

Many people wonder why they step into an ungodly work environment to reveal love, empathy, and grace but then find they are immediately let go. They try hard but can sense the resistance in the spirit. It is the repulsive smell. Please note that I specifically said you step in with love, empathy, holy living, and grace. Do not mistake this if you carry around a judgmental attitude. That will repulse any kingdom.

Finally, you must fully activate your sense of hearing within your temple. When the devil cannot get you to listen and do his biddings, you are a winner.

"And when he brings out his own sheep, he goes before them, and the sheep follow him, for they know his voice. 5 Yet they will by no means follow a stranger, but will flee from him, for they do not know the voice of strangers."

— JOHN 10:4-5

When people tell you it is okay to do what the Lord said you shouldn't do, resist that voice. It is the voice that wants to destroy you. It is the voice of a demon speaking through a human.

Demons can only talk and express their filthy nature through a human body because they are spirit beings with no physical body. So they will even use a human vessel who avails them his voice, someone you trust to make you do the things that displease God to infiltrate your life and destroy you.

Satan's kingdom is at risk when you are intimate with your Abba Father and can recognize His voice.

> "*My* sheep *hear My voice, and I know them, and they follow Me.*"

— JOHN 10:27

When your temple offerings involve hearing God's voice, you become one more life that threatens him. You are also one more life that will teach others to follow after God through your temple offerings.

I see God bringing you out of that place of loss and hurt from compromising your temple. I see Him redefining you as His right now in Jesus' name. He says to you, "I know you."

Hey, it's not a one-way streak; you too can speak to Him.

> "*The* Lord *is near to all who call upon Him, to all who call upon Him sincerely and in truth.*"

— PSALM 145:18

What will you say to Him right now? He is close to you.

Addressing the Trades

"13 But the time was close for the Jewish Passover to begin, so Jesus walked to Jerusalem. 14 as he went into the temple courtyard, he noticed it was filled with merchants selling oxen, lambs, and doves for exorbitant prices, while others were overcharging as they exchanged currency behind their counters. 15 So Jesus found some rope and made it into a whip. Then He drove out every one of them and their animals from the courtyard of the temple, and He kicked over their tables filled with money, scattering it everywhere! 16 And he shouted at the merchants, "get these things out of here! Don't you dare make My Father's House into a center for merchandise!" 17 that's when His disciples remembered the scripture: "I am consumed with a fiery passion to keep Your House pure!"

— JOHN 2:13-17 TPT

Suppose we keep in mind that the trade within this physical temple is a picture of how we are supposed to be trading in the Spirit. In that case, we will understand what made Jesus upset about some activities within a physical house/structure - within a physical temple. Well, it wasn't about a physical temple; it was about the passion for the ones for whom He came to die.

To understand His reasoning, we must look beyond the physical structure and activities conducted there. The reality is, Jesus operated out of the provisions of a higher reality. This higher reality is of the Kingdom realm of His Father, God. Therefore, it is the provisions of this realm that should govern the motivations within the temple.

We will find that Jesus came to teach us the ways of a higher existence. His parables were to take those who were willing to a level of comprehension that will enable them look at things from the spiritual perspective. Such that he would conceal that understanding from those who were not His followers. (see Mathew 13:10-17).

Jesus saw through to the spiritual reasons behind the trade activities taking place. The temple trading reeked of the demonic seeking to have a functional existence in the earth. Satan had corrupted the religious practice with the same desires that consumed him; greed and self-seeking gains.

Anything that only pleases the flesh and its senses while dishonoring God has its origins from the demonic kingdom. Jesus knew the eternal consequences of trading with our temples for mundane gains.

Now compare the below text with the rendition according to John's gospel we just read. You will catch a more in-depth glimpse of Jesus's reaction.

> *"Jesus* entered *the temple courts and drove out all who were buying and selling there. He overturned the tables of the money-changers and the benches of those selling doves. 13 "It is written," He said to them," 'My House will be called a House of prayer, but you are making it 'a den of robbers.'"*
>
> — MATTHEW 21:12-13 NIV

Before we pick back up on our story of Jesus overturning the money changers table, it is good we pause for a moment. Pause and weigh what decisions we make with this body, how they affect who we become, how they affect us—the successes (not ungodly gains) or failures (not how the world views it) of this life, the trial, and the pains.

We must consider these victories or losses in our spirit man through our trades' lenses and how our (trade) choices may have influenced or caused them.

Now, Jesus came in and saw so much trading going on within the temple. The very temple the people traveled for days and weeks on end to worship God. Rather than people worshipping God in the Spirit and Truth, it was a trading frenzy that had taken over.

Right there, on the temple grounds, men and women were defrauded by very greedy traders. Money changers made it a point to take advantage of people by forcing the exchange rate. Trade agents were at hand to make sure none came in with their animal for sacrifice. It had to be one bought within the grounds, thereby allowing them to fix *exorbitant* prices.

It was a sellers' market frenzy in the temple of God! No one could stop these trades but One - Jesus. He is the same One who stands to prevent the ungodly transactions from taking place in your life with His speaking blood. (see Hebrews 12:24)

Is it not surprising that the religious leaders who seemed to revere God and supposedly upheld the temple activities to high standards were okay with such conduct within the temple? What a sight it must have been - a sight that set Jesus off so much so that men stood in bewilderment at His reaction.

If you can take a minute and picture a passion-consumed Jesus as He overturned the tables and chased out even the doves, you will be able to see how zealous He has always been for you, even to the cross. It was not a passion for a physical building since God cannot dwell in temples made with hands (see Acts 7:48). It was a passion for a spiritual temple sovereignly designed with the capacity to house God. God, in His sovereignty, created a being with the capacity to accommodate Him.

Jesus answered, "If anyone [really] loves Me, he will keep My word (teaching); and My Father will love him, and We will come to him and make Our dwelling place with him. (John 14:23 AMP)

Oh, the gravity of passion that consumes Him for our revealing. When everyone else could care less, Jesus stepped in on our behalf. He defends us even today. When He announces that the zeal for His Father's house consumed Him, it was the zeal for you and me.

It is you and I Jesus saw going in to trade with the super greedy and heartless Satan (the merchants and his agents). He saw that his people, his body was being coerced into some trading exchange with the demonic.

The merchandise we thought we needed for offerings was but bait. Jesus did not only step into the temple to stop the trading then; He still steps in today when we are offered juicy trades on demonic platforms. So when we feel tempted to make excuses to engage with the corrupt system, remember that His death on the cross makes you always overcome. He stepped into this world so that we can be truly free from all sin and its consequences.

We can see Jesus staked His life on every platform on the earth to redeem humanity. When the religious and political leaders and the demonic kingdom hated Him for it, He persisted.

Even when the devil would manifest through the very creation Jesus died to redeem, Jesus did not give up on us. He remained relentless. We must realize that no one can have our back as He. No one could love us as He. None can—only the Lord Jesus.

SEE BEYOND THE HYPE

The Passover is when the Jews celebrated how God delivered them from slavery in Egypt by placing the lamb's blood on their doorposts to prevent the angel of death from killing their firstborn children. (see Exodus 12). It's the picture and a pattern of the original Lamb of God slain for our salvation through His blood.

It was Passover season, and everyone was busy caught up in fulfilling a religious service. Here they were swooning over counterfeits, led on by those who were trusted and expected to know better, oblivious to the majestic presence of the Passover Lamb in their midst.

The original design for Passover is about Jesus, but everyone was carried away with the trades that sounded like Him, the types and shadows of Him that they could not see or perceive. After many years of expecting Him, prophecies and sacrifices, He was now with them. He was theirs to love, worship, celebrate, yet here they were, blinded by the god of this world.

> "Satan, who is the god of this world, has blinded the minds of those who don't believe. They are unable to see the glorious light of the Good News. They don't understand this message about the glory of Christ, who is the exact likeness of God."

> — 2 CORINTHIANS 4:4 NLT

The Jews were busy stocking up on spotless lambs, doves, and whatever the merchants were offering them. But, while it all looked religious and exciting to the natural senses, it was trashing the very essence of the spiritual design of the temple of God.

To make it relevant to our understanding, it could be likened to the Christmas season in our time. I love Christmas and Christmas season. But, there are some activities that have become commonplace which rival the true essence of celebrating the birth of the messiah. We must not lose their true essence.

Jesus is here for you, Emmanuel is close to you, He is yours, to love, yours to worship and build an intimate relationship with. You can choose to make great trades with Him today.

The activities within the temple in Jerusalem were deplorable and offensive to God. The temple of God is to be a house of prayer, a place that offers up spiritual sacrifices of true worship and prayers to God. It is not to offer up spiritual sacrifices to demonic platforms. Jesus Christ, the original Passover Lamb, was not pleased with what He saw in His people - the temple. He had come to redeem them.

Leading to the celebration of this Passover, patterned after Jesus's crucifixion, His heart broke for what He saw. The original Passover sacrifice was there in real-time to redeem His people through His blood, and they could not recognize Him.

PONDER POINT:

Can you see the original? or are you simply turning a blind eye to the detriment of your soul?

Pray with me:

Lord, I repent for partaking in all the activities with the external looks and flavors of You. I now see that they are not You.

I take charge of my life, and I place it in Your loving hands, let nothing creep in with smoke screens snatching me away from You.

I see You now, and I run towards You. Thank you, I see!

7

THE MERCHANT

~ The Kingdom of Heaven is all Around Us and Releasing Treasures to Those who would Come in and Trade ~

❧

A t the temple in Jerusalem, merchants profited from the hallowed acts of sacrifice, concerning which Jesus was not happy. See Matthew 21:10-13.

But Jesus, having chased those who were trading out of the temple, declared: "saying to them, "Is it not written, 'My house shall be called a house of prayer for all nations? But you have made it a 'den of thieves.'" (Mark 11:17)

As we continue looking through the lens of Jesus, it is shocking to realize the spiritual ramification of the transactions within temple grounds. So, who were the merchants that brought in spiritual trades within God's temple? You may wonder. The identity of the merchant is not unknown. He was the *covering cherub* who walked *amid the fiery stones.*

14 "You *were* the anointed cherub who covers; I established you; you were on the holy mountain of God; you walked back and forth in the midst of fiery stones.

15 You *were* perfect in your ways from the day you were created, till iniquity was found in you.

16 "By the abundance of your trading, you became filled with violence within, And you sinned;

Therefore I cast you as a profane thing out of the mountain of God; And I destroyed you, O covering cherub, from the midst of the fiery stones.

— EZEKIEL 28:14-16

From the above opening Scripture reading, this cherub lost his privileged position through his trade but has never stopped trading with the hearts of men. There is an exchange that takes place when you trade. In the spiritual realm, you give over your dominion in certain areas of your life through your desires, and the merchant gives you his junk.

The being we know as Satan, the devil, was once in Heaven as a glorious cherub covering God's throne. But, the gravity of Satan's defilement was enormous. And so, when we look at scriptures like the one below, you cannot help but wonder how Satan's trading could have defiled the heavenly sanctuaries.

"21 And later Moses also sprinkled the tabernacle with blood and every utensil and item used in their service of worship. 22 Actually, nearly everything under the law was purified with blood, since forgiveness only comes through an outpouring of blood.

23 And so it was necessary for all the earthly symbols of the heavenly realities to be purified with these animal sacrifices, but the Heavenly things themselves required a superior sacrifice than these. 24 For the Messiah did not enter into the earthly tabernacle made by men, which was but an echo of the true sanctuary, but he entered into Heaven itself to appear before the face of God in our place."

Did you get that? All these protocols were meticulously observed and established for generations as types and shadows of the Original.

God the Son, and being the original sacrifice, comes to the earth scene to take on human flesh, ending that gruesome process with much greater and more profound work. In taking on human flesh, Jesus would go through the traditions of these Mosaic procedures and become the fulfillment of the spiritual requirements for our redemption. And for what?

It all culminates with Jesus standing before the Face of God in our place. All of that to provide room for us before the Face of God! Hallelujah. That is where we belong.

God instructed Moses to build an *Earthly Temple* that looked and had the same utensils that exist within the *Heavenly Temple*. The earthly sacrifices were only useful to cleanse the Israelites for a year. Then, they had to go through the process again the following year on Yom Kippur, also known as the day of atonement. See Leviticus 23:27-32.

The sacrifices within the earthly temple could only cleanse the people yearly. But, unfortunately, that only brought in a greater awareness of their sins. Their spirit man still suffered from the guilt of the evil they committed. It was more like a holder in place for proper redemption.

"For if animal sacrifices could once and for all eliminate sin, they would have ceased to be offered, and the worshipers would have clean consciences. Instead, once was not enough, so the repetitive sacrifices year after year made the worshipers continually reminded of their sins, with their hearts still impure. 4 For what power does the blood of bulls and goats have to remove sin's guilt?"

— HEBREWS *10: 2–4 TPT*

Just as the Israelites were cleansed yearly by sacrifices within the earthly temple on Yom Kippur, in a greater measure, the singular sacrifice of Himself, Jesus purified the Heavenly temple. His superior blood cleansed us of sin and its consequences (past, present, and future) for those who choose Him as Lord and Savior.

Jesus had to take His blood into the true sanctuary or the Heavenly temple and cleansed it of all defilement. Earthly sacrifices of bulls and animals were not even a requirement for cleansing the Heavenly temple - the original. Sacrifices within the temporal physical structure were only a picture of what Jesus will do with the original sanctuary positioned in Heaven.

However, Jesus took His blood into the Heavenly Temple and sanctified it. The gravity of Satan's constant pursuit to defile God's temple started in the heavens and the blood of Jesus, that original Passover Lamb has been cleansing all of Heaven and Earth of his filthy trails.

A PASSION FOR YOU

We must understand our value as temples of God and keep the merchant out of our sanctuaries. Whatever we allow in our temple will manifest in the spirit realm - light or darkness, freedom in Christ Jesus, or bondage. If you enable the one who defiled his sanctuaries within your sanctuary by going into trade with him, you will officially defile your temple.

The merchant had no regard for his holy placement and chose to become the darkest being in all creation, defacing defilement trails on whoever entertained him.

Do not be a castaway by willfully messing around with the profane; sooner than later, the merchant gets hold of you, and you become a castaway. I really cannot say this enough, the body of Christ must beware of messing with the stuff the merchant presents; be mindful of the grey areas.

Satan once was the anointed cherub, and he still disguises himself as an angel of light (see 2 Corinthians 11:14). Many who trade with him claim you should do whatever makes you happy because God wants you happy. Yet, I wonder if people knew what real happiness is. Who, or what, defines happiness for you? How would you know happiness if you never experience the "real"? Many embrace sin in its different shades and make a mockery of God's holiness.

You must understand that God the Father gave up His Son for this. It must not be all fun to be the one to defile God's temple. Your body is God's temple. (see 1 Corinthians 6:19-20)

THE MERCHANT WILL LEAVE YOU NAKED

"15 I know your works, that you are neither cold nor hot. I could wish you were cold or hot. 16 so then, because you are lukewarm, and neither cold nor hot, I will vomit you out of my mouth. 17 because you say, 'I am rich, have become wealthy, and have need of nothing'—and do not know that you are wretched, miserable, poor, blind, and naked— 18 I counsel you to buy from Me gold refined in the fire, that you may be rich; and white garments, that you may be clothed, that the shame of your nakedness may not be revealed; and anoint your eyes with eye salve, that you may see. 19 as many as I love, I rebuke and chasten. Therefore be zealous and repent."

— REVELATIONS 3:15-19

As temples of God, there is an endless trade that goes on within us. The church of Laodicea received a letter from Jesus through the Apostle John. It was pretty similar to the way Jesus reacted in the temple in Jerusalem.

The Laodiceans had made their temples a den of robbers by trading with the merchant. They prided themselves on the things they had. They had lots of gold and sold huge supplies of white clothing. They flourished in producing eye salves that cured eye diseases.

Jesus likened their confidence in their financial security and clothing business as wretched, poor, blind, and even naked. That is the fallen state of trading with the devil. You become naked and lose your spiritual covering. Adam and Eve realized they were naked after they traded with the serpent in the garden.

> *"10 The man answered, "I heard you walking in the garden [your voice/sound], and I was afraid because I was naked, so I hid." 11 God [He] asked, "Who told you that you were naked? Did you eat fruit from the tree from which I commanded you not to eat?"*

— GENESIS 3:10-11 EXB

This form of nakedness is the spiritual state of anyone who deals with the merchant. It is a state of falling out from under God's sovereign covering. You lose your identity and ability to see God's light. You even hide from God because you feel unworthy. You believe the merchant's lies that your evil trades are also hidden from God which only festers more evil trades.

By being neither hot nor cold, the church of Laodicea seemed religious. But unfortunately, the worse thing about religion is giving the appearance of godliness, thereby luring unsuspecting minds deep into the darkness.

Paul puts it beautifully in his second letter to Timothy, that: "*5 They will act religious, but they will reject the power that could make them godly. So stay away from people like that! 6 They are the kind who work their way into people's homes and win the confidence of vulnerable women who are burdened with the guilt of sin and controlled by various desires. 7 (Such women are forever following new teachings, but they are never able to understand the truth.)*" (2 Timothy 3:5-7 NLT)

If indeed we see the polar ends of God's Kingdom and that of Satan, we will find there is no such thing as being neither one nor the other. God does not like mixture, and He will spit such a lukewarm people out. See Revelation 3:16. "For what fellowship has righteousness with lawlessness? And what communion has light with darkness?" (2 Corinthians 6:14)

There is no such thing as fellowship between righteousness and lawlessness; neither is there communion between light and darkness.

Be warned; it is the nature of the devil to disguise himself as an angel of light. When people trade with the merchant in this manner, they cause others to fall. You cannot take from the Kingdom of God and the demonic at the same time.

"No servant can serve two masters; for either he will hate the one and love the other, or else he will be loyal to the one and despise the other. You cannot serve God and mammon."

— LUKE *16:13*

Your love for the goods the merchant presents will cause you to question God's love and God's Word. You will begin to question why you aren't allowed to do the things you like, e.g., have pre-marital sex when your organs are yearning for it. You may challenge the wisdom to wait for the appropriate time with what else did God create the organs for.

You will question them without considering that these laws are in the very fabric of the Spiritual realm. You will not understand that you open doorways for the devil to pull down your calling by disobeying God.

You will not understand that God is the Good One, protecting you from soul-ties that can haunt you and future generations. It is how this works, folks. The demonic realm will have junk in you if your temple does not offer only holy spiritual sacrifices to God.

Our Spiritual Trade Affects Generations

We enable the merchant access to our lives when we allow greed, envy, bitterness, and other evil desires to take hold of us. Jesus knows what strongholds we come under when we let Satan into our hearts and temples. Not only do we suffer, but future generations also will when we let the merchant succeed in selling us his goods.

Jesus knew the pain we would suffer having to live with the consequences of our wrong trading. As with trade agreements, those who made the deals may die. But generations after are born into a pre-existing covenant that they are bound to comply. So many live under curses placed upon the families that they know nothing about.

When diagnosing a condition, doctors check family history for traits. First, they do so to isolate the possibility of a medical condition being hereditary. Second, they need the information so they can administer the proper treatment.

The Cambridge dictionary* (online) meaning for the term hereditary is: "(Of characteristic or diseases) passed from the genes of a parent to a child, or (of titles and positions in society) passed from parent to a child as a right:"

When something is hereditary, it is the same as a possession of the family line; family lineage. Medical science has shown physiological conditions can get carried across through the bloodline. So also can spiritual needs get dragged across the genealogy. It, therefore, explains bloodline covenants and their legal bindings.

> "You stiff-necked and stubborn people, uncircumcised in heart and ears, you are always actively resisting the Holy Spirit. You are doing just as your fathers did."
>
> — ACTS 7:51 AMP

Being stiff-necked (or obstinate), stubborn, and even resisting the Holy Spirit is a trade an ancestor has made with the merchant. Through the bloodline, we inherit the covenants that our ancestors made with either God or the devil. In this case, Stephen stated that these people had inherited resistance to the Holy Spirit from their genealogy.

You may ask, "how can there be an inherited resistance to the Holy Spirit from one generation to another as though it were a contract written on paper?" My answer to that would be: "it is a contract signed in blood; it is the result of trade agreements enforced by demonic alters raised in the bloodline to ensure continuity."

One generation makes deals with the merchant, and generations after will uphold and keep paying for it. A magnificent change occurs when one person stands up within the bloodline to break that cycle and makes a different trade with the blood of Jesus. Only then do they become free from that demonic trade.

The above is so powerful when you understand that this person brings a new government into his family. It's a whole kingdom take over. When another kingdom, or a new government, takes over a domain, the previous government no longer exists. The new kingdom comes and establishes its laws, rules, and governance. It is what happens when someone steps into the bloodline with a new speaking voice in the lineage. The blood of Jesus will supersede all.

Unlike God, who gives man absolute free will, the devil does not give anyone the freedom to choose; therefore, many suffer for things they did not do. They see the actions of their parents within themselves. They even find themselves inheriting their parent's enemies like they do their diseases.

The good news is that Jesus came to break every curse off of us. He also lives to show us, by His Spirit, how to walk in true freedom. Jesus promised that they would make their home in us with God the Father and the Holy Spirit. See John 14:23.

With your freedom comes freedom for generations after you who will also choose Jesus and trade with His kingdom only. (see Exodus 20:5-6, Deuteronomy 7:9)

PONDER POINT:

Look internally and be ready to give a proper assessment of your life. Look at the habits and propensities you see in you that seem to be generational. Look at the things that may have been passed on to you through your lineage. Consider them all, whether they be;

1. Physical examples include a talisman, charms, idols, crystals for enchantments, freemasonry rings/rods, swords, protection beads, etc. You are holding on to some things that activate demonic strongholds in your life. These are leading

causes of lingering diseases and a spirit of death around a
person's life. People who possess these things struggle with
suicide and terminal illnesses.

2. Character-wise – if you find in you such shrewdness in
business that you must not take a loss, but your employees
or business partner should, it is the mind of the merchant,
and you must seek deliverance from it. Likewise, if you have
anger issues inherited from a parent, you must deal with
them in the Heavenly Courts.

3. Mental strongholds – such as a poverty mindset, inferiority,
and superior complexes. Also, consider mottos or words to
live by, such as, oh, you get them before they get you, and
your life ends up becoming one lived out of fear, betrayal,
and suspicion. I have seen many marriages broken due to
such mental trades within the bloodline. Many hold onto
words from their ancestors that are not words of God's
Kingdom of light.

4. Materialism – suppose it's wealth gotten from defrauding
others? Seek to uncover its history. Then, repent in the
Heavenly Courts and ask the Lord to show you how to make
restitution on it. there is a movement of restitution going on
now; it is God. Close the doors of strife and the family
tragedies that come from ill-gotten means.

5. Traditions of men – This list is endless, so you may want to
check with God's word if what you practice is based on
God's standard for your life. Many of these practices service
demonic alters. They include not eating certain things on
certain days, celebrating ghosts, and appeasing the dead.
Here's the perfect word of God on this;

"6 Jesus replied, "You are hypocrites! How accurately did Isaiah prophesy about you phonies when he said: 'These people honor me with their words while their hearts run far away from me!

7 Their worship is nothing more than a charade! For they continue to insist that their man-made traditions are equal to the instructions of God.'

8 "You abandon God's commandments just to keep men's rituals, such as ceremonially washing utensils, cups, and other things."

— MARK 7:6-8 TPT

Good job digging deep on this ponder point. Now, ask yourself, "is the Holy Spirit revealed in any of them? If not, why are you still resisting the Holy Spirit like your ancestors?

Prepare your case and get ready to present yourself before God's Court in repentance. Throw out all the inherited ungodly items and break free of all the trades in your bloodline. Be free! In Jesus name.

Agents of the Merchant in Religious Garb

"18 But the Jewish religious leaders challenged Jesus, "what authorization do you have to do this sort of thing? if God gave you this kind of authority, what supernatural sign will you show us to prove it?"

19 Jesus answered, "after you've destroyed this temple, I will raise it up again in three days."

20 Then the Jewish leaders sneered, "this temple took forty-six years to build, and you mean to tell us that you will raise it up in three days?" 21 But they didn't understand that Jesus was speaking of the "temple" of his body."

— JOHN 2:18-21 TPT

The religious leaders failed to relate to the spiritual insight of the above passage. The natural man cannot conceive the spiritual; therefore, they could not understand how he would rebuild a temple in three days that took forty-six years to build.

How cool that there are forty-six chromosomes in every cell of the human body (the temple)? I was so stoked when brother Ian said this. Oh! What is there not to love about revelation?

And so when Jesus comes to find some strange things taking space/place within us, that breaks His heart. These activities could not go on within the temple if the leaders reverenced the holiness of God.

Instead, the Jewish religious leaders had given free rein to the devil, the merchant. They allowed, received cuts from the merchants, and contributed to the exploitation of the people. They did not honor the temple instructions Moses upheld in his day; instead, they enabled these filthy activities to continue.

Many religious leaders are enablers of demonic trades. They compromise God's holy standards, and their hearers do the same. The merchant uses them as his sales agents to facilitate transactions within the individual temples of their hearers. As a result, many people will receive false teachings from a pulpit rather than from anywhere else.

These leaders teach God's grace as a message that gives many opportunities to sin while they pad their pockets. Without an emphasis on holiness, many temples become victims of ungodly trades. Unfortunately, many people fall into the trap of listening to them instead of God's voice.

Trading with the demonic is one reason many remain in bondage within the body of Christ; it is why the believer's authority is uncommon. True freedom and spiritual authority can only come from trading with God's Kingdom and offering spiritual sacrifices to Him within our temples.

At the beginning of this book, we looked at how the first man, Adam and Eve, fell in Eden. As a result of their sin, death entered the scene. What was once God's dwelling place became desecrated by disobedience, greed, and a self-centered quest.

Place value on your life by understanding the spiritual implications of what Jesus did, overturning the tables in the temple, and chasing out the merchants. The impact of living life without the awareness of our more meaningful existence as spirit beings are robbing us of passion for our true calling.

Begin to align with this powerful Kingdom realm of our all-loving God. Engage in the realities within God, and be the holy temple pleasing to Him.

Jesus would demonstrate the power of His redemption to us by cleaning out the demonic trades within our temples. Today Jesus is saying and seeking to do the same things within you. He wants to clean you out so that you can be the habitation of His Father once again. As is written, "*the true God is the Creator of all things. He is the Owner and Lord of the heavenly realm and the earthly realm, and He doesn't live in man-made temples.*" (See Acts 17:24-31 TPT)

PONDER POINT:

Now, let's relive these words as though Jesus were saying this to you and me right this moment. Read the following scriptures out loud and let every word sink in.

> "*Do you not know that you are the temple of God and that the Spirit of God dwells in you?*"
>
> — I CORINTHIANS 3:16

> "*Have you forgotten that your body is now the sacred temple of the Spirit of Holiness, Who lives in you? You don't belong to yourself any longer, for the gift of God; the Holy Spirit lives inside your sanctuary.*"
>
> — I CORINTHIANS 6:19 TPT

A NEW TRADE SEALED IN HIS BLOOD

You must understand that all marketers look at the demographics of their target market to get the most out of the marketing campaign. Satan, the merchant, researches his target market's genealogy in the same manner a business owner invests heavily in studying his target market's spending habits.

Typically, a smart and successful merchant considers his target market's age group, occupation, vacation habits, race, and earning potential, to mention a few. He even looks at the places they hang out and their family sizes. It is most important to get accurate details of his target market's lifestyle to enable him tailor his products to their delight and enticement.

High-tech companies and social media companies will not expect to be very successful in targeting baby boomers as they would the Gen Z. You cannot successfully target a low-income earning demographic with Bentley cars.

More extraordinary measures are in place with the spiritual realm because our lives and genealogy become very visible to this realm. The Bible records that Noah's lineage was perfect: "This is the genealogy of Noah. Noah was a just man, perfect in his generations. Noah walked with God." (See Genesis 6:9). Therefore God would work with him.

Noah's genealogy was free of the demonic trade; there was no Nephilim/giborim seed in his bloodline. Likewise, some of our genealogies are free of specific spiritual transactions, so there would be no point presenting us with baits to which we may not be quite easily susceptible.

Noah's genealogy walked with God and refused to trade their seed with fallen angels, unlike the other people in his day who lusted after the fallen angels and birthed giants from their union.

The people in Noah's day had mixed up their seed with heavenly beings and defiled their DNA: "*1 Now it came to pass, when men began to multiply on the face of the earth, and daughters were born to them, 2 that the sons of God saw the daughters of men, that they were beautiful; and they took wives for themselves of all whom they chose.*" *(Genesis 6:1-2).* The Hebrew words for the "sons of God" are B'nai Ha Elohim, which means these are heavenly beings, giving credence to them being offsprings of fallen angels.

Unfortunately, many have become contaminated with demonic genetic interference. So God had to preserve humanity with the DNA that had none of that contamination.

The good news is, our Lord Jesus is still in the DNA preservation work today. In Jesus Christ we are drawn into a new covenant through His Blood. Jesus paid for our salvation with His shed blood.

The merchant will provide product offerings that appeal to his target demographics. One common way is by presenting the things their ancestors enjoyed. People are likely to enjoy the things their ancestors did. So the questions here would go along the lines of;

- What has been the trade of previous generations?
- What triggers do they have towards Satan's range of spiritual offerings like anger, pain, unforgiveness, jealousy, wickedness in high places, witchcraft, hypocrisy, etc.?
- Have they had a history of drugs and drunkenness? Their offsprings will be more susceptible. Introduce that and many other mind-altering narcotics to them to seal that deal in this generation as well.
- Have they been a family of greed? Present them with opportunities where they can manipulate their way into positions to take advantage of people.
- Did their fathers make deals with idols for fame, money, and power?
- How about sexual perversion? Child trafficking would appeal to them.

Satan's strategy is gradual, making people's conscience seared and accustomed to a certain level of compromise, introducing pedophilia and the muddiest of them. The process is carefully mapped out like in a business plan to get you to a place of no return – much like a sound business model aims at making converts and even evangelists of its target market.

That place can be where you often hear people say they have sold their souls to the devil. It is a place many call the point of no return due to a severe constraint and an inability to step out of it. These could go as far as making oaths, blood covenants, rituals where they sacrifice people and animals.

Other cases could include compromising situations with the potential of a tarnished image or even death threats if they attempted to break away. So it's either they keep going downhill, or many become consumed with guilt and hatred for themselves that they seek an escape via suicide.

Like addiction cases, the devil has a grip on such a soul tied to him in a spiritual trade. Always remember that whenever you buy from the merchant, you give him a layer of your soul in exchange for the image of God that resides within you.

Like I pointed earlier, the merchant engages in a process to get you hooked on his product selection. We saw that this process dates back to our forefathers and their spiritual trades. Trades sealed in the bloodline for generations, which require the blood of Jesus for its cleansing.

Your desires are the spiritual currency that you use to engage with any of these trades. James admonishes us:

> *"Blessed is the man who endures temptation; for when he has been approved, he will receive the crown of life which the Lord has promised to those who love him. 13 Let no one say when he is tempted, "I am tempted by God"; for God cannot be tempted by evil, nor does He Himself tempt anyone. 14 But each one is tempted when he is drawn away by his own desires and enticed. 15 Then, when desire has conceived, it gives birth to sin; and sin, when it is full-grown, brings forth death."*

Therefore, go to the Courts of Heaven consistently till you receive total freedom from trades with the merchant. Jesus knows what it feels like to be us; consequently, He mediates for us and sympathizes with our weaknesses. See Hebrews 4:15.

The Kingdom of God is great and powerful. It is an honor to be a part of it in every sense of the word. We belong there in Christ Jesus. By His sacrificial offering on the cross, we have full access to God. But, sadly, many doubt how this can be. And so go about life as pitiful ordinary beings, bereft of purpose and vision.

By the Spirit of God, we become active citizens of the heavenly Kingdom through faith. We are alive through the Spirit of God. It is the promise of God. Let this realization sink in until your entire being aligns with it. Then, as you sow into this truth with your faith, you will reap the fulfillment of this powerful promise of God.

My prayer is that you would walk in the awareness of your spirit-life existence. I pray, as you keep your heart and desire locked into God's Kingdom realm, this Kingdom will open up to you in extraordinary measures. I pray that the realities in this Kingdom and the full provisions of it would become yours today. And that you become this new creation the Father meant for you to be, in Jesus' name.

I am so grateful that we can now make a new trade through Christ's gift of His life. One where we each house a glorious Kingdom, God's Kingdom, within us. A Kingdom where God the Father, Son, and Holy Spirit can sup with our spirits within our body, His temple. (See John 14:23)

A CONSCIOUS TRADE

Consider a realm operated by entities. Let us call this realm the spirit world. Within this spirit world is a vast collection of the heavenly and the demonic. The heavenly realm is the Kingdom realm of God. It is where God sits enthroned, and from this Kingdom, He reveals His glorious purpose.

Within the heavenly Kingdom realm, there are the angelic and myriads of unique spiritual beings. Some of them are for worship, war, peace, some carry destiny scrolls of nations, and some are assigned to facilitate us achieving our destiny, amidst other things.

> *"What role then, do the angels have? The angels are spirit-messengers sent by God to serve those who are going to be saved."*
>
> — HEBREWS 1:14 TPT

These have different assignments and functions. You and I are also among these beings, seated in heavenly places, in Christ. Yet, we are beings with earthly bodies.

There are other spirit beings that no longer have earthly bodies. These are also in Christ Jesus. They have passed on and no longer operate from an earthly body. Still, there are several other spirit beings utterly different from us.

But when we come to the Lord Jesus as our Savior, we receive the Spirit of God. Whether with a present earthly body or not, we are all alive within God today. United and one in Him, we are part of the whole. We become new creatures in Christ.

The book of Galatians sums it that we died and we're resurrected with Christ. And now, living within His resurrection, we have the mark of Jesus Christ on us.

> "*My old* identity *has been co-crucified with Messiah and no longer lives; for the nails of His cross crucified me with Him. And now the essence of this new life is no longer mine, for the Anointed One lives his life through me—we live in union as one! My new life is empowered by the faith of the Son of God, who loves me so much that he gave Himself for me and dispenses His life into mine.*"

> — GALATIANS 2:20 TPT

The spirit world watches the motives and activities of every living being. A person on fire for the Lord visibly walks with the Holy Spirit's flame. The spirit world recognizes the authority of a true believer in Christ Jesus.

However, many believers do not know who they are. It calls to mind what played out between the sons of Sceva and the demon-possessed man in Acts 19:11-17.

THE HEAVENLY TRADE

The Kingdom of Heaven is all around us and releasing treasure to those who would come in and trade. Jesus made the ultimate trade when He gave us His righteousness in exchange for our sins. Jesus gave us abundant life in exchange for death, sickness, and disease.

In Jerusalem, Jesus chased out the merchants from the earthly temple, and it is what He did for us in the Spirit realm. Jesus chased out the enticing entities that preyed on our weaknesses and lusts. He declared that His Father's house was not trading grounds for thieves.

My beloved, Jesus said that you and I are not temples for the thief to steal God's inheritance within us. See John 10:10. We have willingly traded with the enemy for so long, thereby handing him the authority to access our inheritance, to steal from us. Yes, to steal, kill and destroy us spiritually.

Then came the day when Jesus walked right into our temple and established us as the house of God! Even today, Jesus stands at the door to your temple and knocks so that you would open up to Him and have fellowship with Him.

He says to you, "*Look! I stand at the door and knock. If you hear my voice and open the door, I will come in, and we will share a meal together as friends.* (Revelation 3:20 NLT)

Therefore know then that you are the house of God. Know that Jesus has decreed you so. After His declaration, Jesus challenged the ungodly powers saying He will rebuild the temple within three days when they destroy it.

In saying this, Jesus spoke about His death and resurrection after three days. He took on all of our ungodly trades with the demonic kingdom and nailed it to the cross. He then rebuilt us within His new resurrected body. What a Heavenly transaction. Hallelujah!

Restored in His Trade

As temples and houses of the God of Heaven, we can come with boldness into Heaven. We can begin taking the treasures of Heaven and fruits of the Spirit into our temples. We will now glean into Jesus as He shows us how to be partakers of a new trade by our choices and desires.

"*44 heaven's kingdom realm can be illustrated like this:*

"*A person discovered that there was a hidden treasure in a field. Upon finding it, he hid it again. Because of uncovering such treasure, he was over-joyed and sold all that he possessed to buy the entire field just so he could have the treasure. 45 "heaven's kingdom realm is also like a jewel merchant in search of rare pearls. 46 when he discovered one very precious and exquisite pearl, he immediately gave up all he had in exchange for it."*

— MATTHEW 13:44-46 TPT

There are highlights from the above passage I need you to grasp; they are to help you recognize and identify similar situations around you:

- Nature of what we buy in God's Kingdom – treasure, pearls.
- In what form? – hidden, rare
- Worth – highly valuable/priceless
- Who goes after the treasure? – a person (you and I), a jewel merchant (a spirit being in an active trade),
- How did they come in contact with treasure and pearl? – diligently seeking, discovering, in search
- Method of acquisition – an exchange/transaction/trade.
- Location – field (spirit world, and in this case, Heaven)
- State of heart upon discovery – overjoyed, nothing else is more valuable to him than this treasure.
- Action/response - sells everything to acquire it.
- How to get it? – demands action in attaining the Kingdom of Heaven
- Degree of importance/Desperation - The man bought the entire field to gain the treasure.

The moral of this parable is that only those willing to stake their whole life to seek and have it are worthy to obtain it. Today so many of us go for parts and pieces of God's Kingdom. A seeking heart will go for all of God's eternal Kingdom. (see Matthew 6:33)

A seeking heart will not hold back when he finds Jesus but will sell everything and give up every previously owned possession, whether physical or spiritual, in exchange for being a part of God's Kingdom. Empty out every previous transaction for this eternal life-giving treasure.

"And you will seek Me and find Me, when you search for Me with all your heart."

— JEREMIAH 29:13

I pray for you that you begin to see that the trades made with the Spirit world (heavenly or demonic) determine the outcome we see within our earthly existence. Our lives do not just happen by chance.

Every decision we make in the natural world is a play out of decisions we (or our generations) have already made (consciously or unconsciously) in the Spirit realm.

Humanity will always trade. In the earthly realm, we see that the trade market is an ongoing activity that determines the fate of individuals, corporations, nations, and the world. The trade market essentially determines the quality of life. On 9/11 terrorists went after the World Trade Center. Even on the Earth, this is key.

Whether you are a stockbroker, buying stocks or not, we are all involved and affected by what goes on in the market. Sometimes one man's decision affects an entire stock market.

We see how the markets react after a US presidential election based on who wins. Recall Nike's controversial Colin Kaepernick ad campaign case. We saw Nike stocks fall in one day and go 100% back up again on the same day based on people's reactions to the market.

A marketplace reaction also sufficed with the case of infidelity involving big names like Amazon's Jeff Bezos, to name a few. Our emotions are engaged in our earthly trades even if our finances aren't.

Looking at the natural world, you find that we are all trading, whether actively or not. Knowing our daily living evolves around trades should empower us towards intentionality. We can choose the transactions our spirit engages in so that we don't walk blindly.

Take back your trading power and stop being a victim of circumstances. Do not let other people's choices affect you; the activities that people in your bloodline engaged in should not be your story. Instead, rise up and actively take charge of your life in the Spirit. Take the bold step and enforce God's Kingdom in your everyday life!

You must see that the former kingdom can no longer dictate what happens in your life anymore. Its leader falls every time you enforce God's call on your life. You have a Kingdom mandate, with authority, to trample upon all the power of the enemy that none can question. There is no higher power than the one you exude inn Christ.

Look into the ways of your kingdom and teach your children. Teach all those around you to see that they are now at the very top with Christ. All pre-existing legislations bow to His authority. The kingdom you bear is the greatest of all.

"18 And He said to them, "I saw Satan fall like lightning from Heaven. 19 Behold, I give you the authority to trample on serpents and scorpions, and over all the power of the enemy, and nothing shall by any means hurt you."

— LUKE 10:18-19

"I have found in engaging the personhood of God; I see more people set free by taking them before God into the Courts of Heaven. Other times, deliverance would happen by exalting God in worship or even in conversations. When I pray for people, I am consciously taking them into the presence of God."

8

THE COURT SYSTEM

~ Whereas the Earthly Courts Present Evidence of Physical Actions; the Heavenly Courts Receive Heart Actions as Evidence where Man makes Spiritual Covenants ~

A key thing for a bible student is the hunger and eagerness to study Scripture; Taking time to comprehend by comparing Scripture with Scripture, verifying truth verse by verse, and allowing revelation to come through by the Holy Spirit. The Berean Jews sought Scripture in this way.

"They found that the Jews of Berea were of more noble character and much more open-minded than those of Thessalonica. They were hungry to learn and eagerly received the word. Every day they opened the scrolls of Scripture to search and examine them, to verify that what Paul taught them was true."

— ACTS 17:11 TPT

Like the Bereans who sought to confirm and not to find faults, twist God's truths or unjustly criticize, let us go ahead and examine the Courts of Heaven, shall we?

Ok, we will begin our reading of the Book of Job in chapter 1 (NLT):

"1 There once was a man named Job who lived in the land of Uz. He was blameless—a man of complete integrity. He feared God and stayed away from evil. 2 He had seven sons and three daughters. 3 He owned 7,000 sheep, 3,000 camels, 500 teams of oxen, and 500 female donkeys. He also had many servants. He was, in fact, the richest person in that entire area.

4 Job's sons would take turns preparing feasts in their homes, and they would also invite their three sisters to celebrate with them. 5 When these celebrations ended—sometimes after several days—Job would purify his children. He would get up early in the morning and offer a burnt offering for each of them. For Job said to himself, "Perhaps my children have sinned and have cursed God in their hearts." This was Job's regular practice

6 One day, the members of the heavenly court came to present themselves before the Lord, and the Accuser, Satan, came with them. 7 "Where have you come from?" the Lord asked Satan.

Satan answered the Lord, "I have been patrolling the earth, watching everything that's going on."

8 Then the Lord asked Satan, "Have you noticed my servant Job? He is the finest man in all the earth. He is blameless—a man of complete integrity. He fears God and stays away from evil."

9 Satan replied to the Lord, "Yes, but Job has good reason to fear God. 10 You have always put a wall of protection around him and his home and his property. You have made him prosper in everything he does. Look how rich he is! 11 But reach out and take away everything he has, and he will surely curse you to your face!"

12 "All right, you may test him," the Lord said to Satan. "Do whatever you want with everything he possesses, but don't harm him physically." So Satan left the Lord's presence."

— JOB 1:1-12 NLT

In the early part of Job 1, we see a man who had everything going for him. *Is it not typical of us to assume that they must be doing everything right when one has everything going for them?*

Job had a practice that guaranteed his prosperity and the protection of his children. When we practice something long enough, it becomes an ingrained part of us, whether right or wrong.

We will move on to events of *the day*:

In a realm that is as active as the Earth, we see a day when members of the Heavenly Courts present themselves before the Lord. The accuser, Satan, also came with them. We see him (accuser) and the Lord having a meaningful conversation that would determine the course of Job's life. A scenario like this should make one wonder if their present circumstances result from a Court of Heaven type discussion Satan is having with God.

Even though we may have full and busy lives here on the Earth, we must not neglect a realm involved in our lives' eternal outcome. This (the Spirit) realm appears even more important than our daily existence on the earth. In a way, Job's righteous ways were no match to the actions taking place in the Heavenly Courts.

What if Job was privy to the info about his life? Would that have made life a little easier for him?

In verse 8, it appears the Lord was bragging on his son, Job. Excitingly, this verse causes me to know the Lord can have reason to boast on you and me in the Spirit world.

The verses we read from Job 1 have five spiritual truths that will ensure your success in navigating the Courts of Heaven and your spiritual life as a whole.

1. Satan - The Accuser of the Brethren

First, we see Satan, the accuser, agreeing to the facts the Lord presented about his son Job. Yet, at the same time, Satan is heard giving reason(s) why that was. They were not just reasons; Satan was making accusations. Do not doubt it. Satan is your accuser.

The accuser is determined to accuse the believer in the Court consistently. He shows up to the Courts of Heaven every time to charge a child of God.

"For the accuser of our brothers and sisters
has been thrown down to earth—
the one who accuses them
before our God day and night."

— REVELATION 12:10B NLT

The Scripture here is not referring to accusations against unbelievers. Still, the emphasis is on "brothers and sisters" or "brethren," as other translations put it, which references believers in Christ Jesus. The fact that he accuses day and night means he does it consistently.

To steal, kill, and destroy (see John 10:10), the devil must win a case in the position of "*Ha'satan*." Satan's name comes from the Hebrew root 'Ha'satan,' which is "the satan." In Hebrew, it translates as - prosecutor, also known as "the accuser in court."

A prosecutor is a principal member of every court. His (prosecutor's) top three tasks include;

i. Investigating Crimes.

Satan is great at making sure he documents every record of your weakness and failings.

The accuser is not custom to Job alone. His assignment is not peculiar to Job either. The Bible makes it clear that he accuses you day and night. He very well knows who you are, but he will walk to and from your generational bloodline to gain evidence that discredits you. When his job description searches for your destruction, he will eventually find something that legally gives him the right to afflict.

"Be sober *[well balanced and self-disciplined], be alert and cautious at all times. That enemy of yours, the devil, prowls around like a roaring lion [fiercely hungry], seeking someone to devour."*

— 1 PETER 5:8 AMP

'The Lord said to Satan, "From where have you come?" Then Satan answered the Lord, "From roaming around on the earth and from walking around on it."'

— JOB 1:7 AMP

ii. Make Decisions to Instigate Legal Proceedings Based on Evidence.

Since the Court is in Heaven, the evidence is in the Spirit realm. Ha'satan's case would primarily establish on;

- *Heart level*: Regarding spiritual matters, the life of a spirit being is visible through the heart's lens motivations. The Lord showed the prophet this principle. We must understand this truth because we are very visual beings. We always tend to look at things from face value. God warned Samuel that, His sight lasered into the heart of a man.

'But the Lord said to Samuel, "Do not look at his appearance or at his physical stature, because I have refused him. For the Lord does not see as man sees; for man looks at the outward appearance, but the Lord looks at the heart."'

— 1 SAMUEL 16:7

- Many years later, Jesus also taught us that the level to which the Spirit realm weighs a man is on the heart's ongoings – what goes on in the heart. The contracts you made within your heart are binding. You make them with your soul in the spirit, and the prosecutor will use them as evidence against you in Heavens' Court. Whereas the earthly courts present/receive physical actions as evidence, the Courts of

Heaven receive heart actions as evidence where man makes spiritual covenants.

"27 You have heard that it was said, 'You shall not commit adultery; 28 but I say to you that everyone who [so much as] looks at a woman with lust for her has already committed adultery with her in his heart."

— MATTHEW 5:27-28 AMP

- *Motive and Intent*: Why do we do the things we do? Why do I serve God? Is it for the benefits? These, and more such like, were the basis Satan used for instigating legal proceedings against Job.

"9 Then Satan answered the Lord, "Does Job fear God for nothing? 10 Have You not put a hedge [of protection] around him and his house and all that he has, on every side? You have blessed the work of his hands [and conferred prosperity and happiness upon him], and his possessions have increased in the land. 11 But put forth Your hand now and touch (destroy) all that he has, and he will surely curse You to Your face."

— JOB 1:9-11 AMP

iii. Being Present in Court.

Satan is there day and night (see Rev 12:10)

His role (as with any prosecutor) is to convince the Judge with hard evidence of the crime(s) committed by the defendant/accused. His persuasive abilities and the weight of evidence acquired on a person are vital to the Court's ruling.

It perfectly describes "Ha'satan," a function he has in the Courts of Heaven. He has a legal position in the Court, and he stays consistent with it. Therefore he will look to see that everything we ever did wrong is under a microscope.

Satan will see to it that every detail of our actions at the motive level where no physical eyes can see receives condemnation according to the law stating, "the wages of sin is death" (see Romans 6:23).

Consequently, when you see a person always accusing you of something, whether you did it or not, know that the person is displaying a nature of "*Ha'satan.*" It may be something you don't remember doing.

In most rampant cases, things you didn't do; But he traces someone in your genealogy who did and brings it to the forefront as an act committed in your bloodline. When you suddenly get wind of some strange news flying around about you, out of nowhere, this spells much demonic activity may be going on.

That is why I continue to urge Christians never to spread gossip or false stories of people because you help promote the activities of this evil being. In reality, you are displaying the nature of *Ha'satan.*

Every time we choose to walk like the devil, we allow ourselves to be displayed in a spirit that will, in turn, accuse us of claiming to be God's but demonstrating a nature that is Satan's. That also is grounds for Ha'satan to build a case against a person.

> "*The one who practices sin [separating himself from God, and offending Him by acts of disobedience, indifference, or rebellion] is of the devil [and takes his inner character and moral values from him, not God]; for the devil has sinned and violated God's law from the beginning. The Son of God appeared for this purpose to destroy the works of the devil. 9 No one who is born of God [deliberately, knowingly, and habitually] practices sin, because God's seed [His principle of life, the essence of His righteous character] remains [permanently] in him [who is born again—who is reborn from above—spiritually transformed, renewed, and set apart for His purpose]; and he [who is born again] cannot habitually [live a life characterized by] sin, because he is born of God and longs to please Him.*"

— 1 JOHN 3:8-9 (AMP

We are not to (with this knowledge) go about calling people devils whenever they exhibit these characteristics. Instead, it reveals the truth of the operations in the Spirit realm that we seem to be oblivious to. It shows that we are not wrestling against people but with "a nature" that hates us and always desires to pull us down (see Ephesians 6:12).

We wrestle against a being who is actively seeking to get us to break the hedge of God over our lives. He knows that he wouldn't have a winning case without our choice to break the hedge by indulging in his nature.

In the book of Ecclesiastes 10:8 (JUB) warns, "He that digs a pit shall fall into it, and whosoever breaks a hedge, a serpent shall bite him."

This truth is the secret to generations and generations of going through troubling and unsurmountable torments as God's creation.

The Lord is equipping His people to see the bigger picture of who we are in Jesus. God wants us to understand why an entire kingdom is in such a contest for our souls! We are the prize and the ones who get to choose. We are so worth it!

The guaranteed way to not be the same ones breaking God's hedge of protection around ourselves is, "2 We look away from the natural realm, and we fasten our gaze onto Jesus, who birthed faith within us and who leads us forward into faith's perfection. His example is this: Because his heart was focused on the joy of knowing that you would be his, he endured the agony of the cross and conquered its humiliation, and now sits exalted at the right hand of the throne of God!" (Hebrews 12:2 (TPT)

That said, we need to step in and answer every accusation as the Lord Jesus, our Mediator reveals to us.

We can stop giving Satan legal rights against us. We can also present our cases against him and even win at his ongoing claims against us.

2. You have a Hedge of Protection

The accuser complains about the hedge of protection the Lord placed around Job. He acknowledges it makes it impossible for him (Satan) to touch Job. Wow! this is an excellent insight into the enemy's frustrations concerning God's love for us.

There is a covering hedge around you that the entire Spirit world can see even if you don't. We all need to be aware of what divine covering we have. With that hedge of protection that the Lord has placed around you, the enemy is unable to touch you. So naturally, the enemy is very upset about this.

In one of his come back at God, Satan's questions in the following text reveals his strategy.

"Have You not made a hedge around him, around his household, and around all that he has on every side? You have blessed the work of his hands, and his possessions have increased in the land."

— JOB 1:10

The enemy is aware of the hedge that stands in the way of him afflicting us. When we get into the Word of God and no longer choose to remain a bystander enjoying a good story, we see nuggets of who we are. Our confidence hinges on the premise of what we learn about our spiritual coverage.

Look quickly at Psalm 23, you probably know this Psalm by heart. In the second half of verse 4, David declares of the Lord's protection over him. He says: "...for thou art with me; thy rod and thy staff they comfort me."

You probably do not realize that you have a hedge around you; even right now. That's right! As it is written; *"He that digs a pit shall fall into it, and whoso breaks an hedge, a serpent shall bite him."* (Ecclesiastes 10:8 KJV).

Now, take a moment, son/daughter of God, and look at that verse again and begin to notice the hedge about you for the first time.

Can you see it? When you stay in the Lord, making Him your shepherd like David did, all you see is the hedge of protection all around you. Check you out, all arrayed in a supernatural bulletproofing barrier. You are untouchable by the devil. Take that truth into your spirit and soul and thank the Lord.

"You have hedged me behind and before, And laid Your hand upon me."

— PSALM 139:5

3. You are Powerful to Break the Hedge

Understand that even though the enemy cannot break your hedge, you can. Like the serpent he is, the enemy will strike once he sees that barrier lifted (see Ecclesiastes 10:8). The enemy will go out of his way to make sure he presents you with opportunities to break that hedge yourself.

Recently, a church removed its pastor as a result of adultery. It was regrettable also due to the impact he had made on people's lives. Some people felt the punishment was too severe and public. The call to walk in a leadership position as a son of God places you under a public microscope; many may not realize that you are even under greater scrutiny in the Spirit realm.

When a leader's impact transforms his community for Jesus Christ, it frustrates the devil because he cannot stop what God is doing through him. People's mass repentance from a chained life into freedom in Christ Jesus does not make the devil happy. He seeks to go after the influencer by presenting opportunities for compromise. When a preacher (or son/daughter of God) falls for any of the devil's schemes, that means he broke his hedge.

In most cases, the serpent strikes. In this pastor's situation, people got upset about how the church handled the preacher's case. But know that this case is a clear example of how a broken hedge appears. The devil comes at a person who breaks his hedge to such a degree that not only wears him down entirely, but it causes the lives impacted to;

- acquire a spirit of offense,
- return to their old lifestyles,
- lose sight of their salvation and hope in a life with God,
- speak less about God's keeping power,
- further make light the holy life believers are to live.

A famous phrase for making excuses for sin goes like this, "He is only human." This excuse does nothing but fall in line with what the devil feeds off of because it causes others to break the hedge they didn't realize they had. It is a strategy that has worked for the accuser for generations.

No one can break that hedge about you but yourself.

Notice also that no one can break that hedge about us but you and me. However, we break that hedge when we choose to trade on the enemy's turf. Only then will the devil, who is the serpent, gain legal grounds to bite.

"He that digs a pit shall fall into it, and whosoever breaks a hedge, a serpent shall bite him."

— ECCLESIASTES 10:8 JUB

You may have heard of the famous way to boil snails. First, the cook places the snails in a pot of water to make sure they are comfortable for a while because when you pick them up, they naturally retreat into their shells. The snails will not step out till they no longer feel threatened by their environment.

Ok, the next step is, set the water to boil under low heat. Aha, it's all nice and cozy in here, the snails think. Before long, they begin to feel comfortable stepping out of their shell and glide into the pot of water.

The snails gradually start exploring this new environment and feel comfortable letting themselves out over time; as the snails are almost entirely out of their shell, the cook ramps up the fire. The snails are unsuspecting because it has become very comfortable with its territory.

By the time the snails sense danger, it would be too late. They are too far out of their protection and are unable to retreat. And, the cook has the snails exactly where he wanted. This end state makes the cook's job easier; it's way better for the cook than when the snails remained within the protection their shell provided.

Do not get comfortable with the ways of the world, gratifying your fleshy desires that you lose sensitivity to the Spirit of God as He draws you back into your hedge. When you begin to play around the *grey areas*, it never starts at the extremes; you will only gradually warm up into stronger addictions which means a massive demonic habitation and tougher demonic oppressions till you can no longer retreat.

Your spiritual death (insensitivity) is good for the devil but not for you. Always *REMEMBER* that *YOU CAN COME BACK* whenever you've failed. You have those warning signs and a few great people around you who will always speak to you when you start going off the rails. That is the Holy Spirit using every means to get to you; listen and return.

> *"Those who listen to instruction will prosper;*
> *those who trust the Lord will be joyful."*

— PROVERBS 16:20 NLT

4. The Attack on Motive

The "accuser" displays his nature. Not only accusing Job but blaming even God. Understand that there is no limit to how far he can go with his stench. It is ingrained in his character. Permit me to paint a little picture here. Satan went sort of like;

- *duh! Who wouldn't revere You (God) if You covered them the way You have protected Job?*

- *how are You bragging on someone who has good reason to fear/revere you?*

- *he (Job) isn't doing it from his heart, but for the benefits he receives.*

- *look how rich he is; who wouldn't serve you if you made them rich and untouchable? Why would anyone do something to lose those benefits? They do so to humans who provide for them as well,*

- *is this not like a job description where you pay him for serving you?*

- *how do You (as God) give a man covering and luxury then turn around to brag about him serving You as though they did it with the right motive? We both understand motives, so why boast about him?*

Pause a bit and see where this is going.

"But reach out your hand, and destroy his bones and flesh, and he will curse you to your face."

— JOB 2:5 EXB

The certainty in this statement pretty much sounds like the premise upon which the accuser has won many cases. The weighing upon our motive is key in the Spirit realm. Jesus even taught that looking at a woman lustfully was already an action of adultery through spiritual lenses (see Matthew 5:27-28). Therefore, motive is spiritual evidence, not necessary physical evidence as the case is in an earthly/human court system. Many people serve God for goods like protection from poverty, disease, hell. Things like, serve God and get rich. Wonder why the extreme prosperity gospel is a steal?

The accuser is an old dog in the game. He can speak confidently on this because the facts are there. When life takes a drastic turn, many turn away from God.

Ask yourself, "why do I serve God?"

5. An Attempt to Discredit

Another thing to note is that when Job lost everything, his wife advised him to do exactly what the accuser said Job would - curse God.

"Job's wife said to him, "Why are you ·trying to stay innocent [maintaining your innocence]? Curse God and die!"

— JOB 2:9-10 EXB

It almost sounds like the same voice that spoke to God had whispered to Job's wife to influence Job's reaction to his favor. Virtually, Satan orchestrated everything behind the scenes to prove that Job was not who God was making him out to be. The devil will use every avenue to win a case against you. He will even use the people closest to you.

When you are going through life's trials, instead of listening to the voices of human emotions, present yourself in the Court of Heaven and continue to seek God's face until it passes. Be wise and realize that God has provided a way for you to answer the accusations Satan is staging against you in the Heavenly Courts.

The devil knows your worth as paid by the blood of Jesus; he knows God's covering upon your life. He knows what value and great calling were given to you by God, so he will attempt to discredit you. Satan was doing this here.

A typical move made by attorneys is to find ways to discredit the witness. Instead of looking into what the witness is presenting, the focus becomes about disproving who the witness is, his character, and his motivations. Sometimes stuff is dug up on things that have no bearing to the case.

It is just like when one comes out to declare their intention to run for Presidency. Oh, boy, do they come under scrutiny! I feel we all can get it from there.

A common trend in human nature is that when they desire what you have or cannot control another, they give themselves over to demon control. It could show up as jealousy, envy, or backstabbing, to name a few. That is the devil seeking to discredit you.

When the Hand of God is upon your life, the same people you think know your character will propagate horrible things about you. Don't fret over them; it is all the accuser's way of discrediting who you are in the Courts of Heaven. The exact words expressed by the accuser to the Judge of Heaven are Job's wife's same words.

As you read the book of Job, you will see that the accusation pattern continues through his friends as well. For this reason, I encourage people who do not yet see the Heavenly Court proceedings to answer for and repent of every horrible thing they have heard concerning themselves.

PONDER POINT:

If your life takes a drastic turn, what would you do?

In typical Job fashion, below we see his response to the accuser's words, who, by the way, was in the voice of his wife.

> *"Job answered, "You are talking like a foolish woman. Should we take only good things from God and not ·trouble [or evil]?" In spite of all this, Job did not sin in what he said"*

— JOB 2:10 EXB

Repent of anything known or unknown, even if you feel it is false. How privy are you to Satan's constant accusations against you? Would you be able to identify a motive that he is using against you?

Allow your Advocate (Jesus) to reveal these allegations to you and humbly repent of them. The Lord, the Righteous Judge, will rule in your favor when you do.

SATAN IS MAKING A DEMAND FOR YOU

The sayings and teachings of Jesus are purposeful to open us up into the Spirit realm's reality. Scripture iterates that if all Jesus said and taught were written, the libraries of this world would not contain it (see John 21:25). To think we have just one book and only a few pages with the words of Jesus, let's hold onto these words as life.

We should acknowledge that even though little, what we have is by the blood and sacrifice of many. It should motivate us to seek and rightly divide the word of truth.

The enemy has taken a lot from the believers in Christ; however, we are responsible for what we do with what we have. A seeking heart must therefore grasp every word and run with it. Seek to understand what is going on in the Courts of Heaven concerning your life.

Simon Peter's case is an example and insight for all who walk with God.

In Luke 22:31, we see a fragment of a pattern whereby the accuser persistently makes a demand for a son of God, in this case, Simon Peter. Luke wrote: "31 And the Lord said, "Simon, Simon! Indeed, Satan has asked for you that he may sift you as wheat. 32 But I have prayed for you, that your faith should not fail; and when you have returned to Me, strengthen your brethren." (Luke 22:31)

There, Jesus was letting Peter in on the heavenly conversations over his life. These conversations would affect the course of Peters' life and existence on earth. What was going on would change the trajectory of Peter's life. He was under accusation. His loyalty was put to the test, quite similar to Satan's conversations with God concerning Job.

Jesus had to be in both places simultaneously to witness this constant demand for Simon Peter by Satan in the Heavenly Courts even though he was also with His disciples. Satan was asking to sift Simon Peter.

According to Merriam-Webster's dictionary, the word 's*ift*'* means *"to examine (something) very carefully to find something useful or valuable."*

The adversary was going through Simon Peter's life to take value out of his life. Simon Peter's value and impact are profound. Peter was one of the best human friends Jesus had in His earthly existence. Peter revealed Jesus as the Christ.

Peter was the leader of the disciples and one of the essential foundational leaders of Christianity. Peter even walked on water. Peter's life would end on the cross like Jesus, but Peter requested to be crucified upside down in typical Peter fashion. He felt unworthy to be crucified like Jesus and chose a lesser position even in death.

I do not know about you, but I marvel at this; who thinks this way at the point of death? The stakes seem so high when you look at the precedence set by these martyrs. What manner of men were these?

It is no wonder Satan wanted him to fail so badly. Satan was coming after the foundation of Christianity when he came after Peter. Like, Job, he had to find grounds to discredit Peter.

Now that we can see how Peter excelled, we can all say what a worthy leader he was. Satan saw this possibility, which was why he came after Peter to discredit him before God.

Jesus continued to exemplify His undeniable existence in Heaven and Earth, even in human flesh. Jesus was conscious of being present with them both on earth and in Heaven's Courts as an advocate mediating on Simon Peter's behalf. The presence of the Mediator – Jesus, in Court, would be a game-changer for Simon Peter.

Although Peter did go through a sift but, because Jesus prayed for him, He was restored to his glory state and divine calling big time. Sometimes you may go through a sifting situation in life, but through Jesus, it only re-enforces your calling. On the other hand, what would have been the story if Peter stood to answer to Satan's accusations all by himself?

In Zachariah 3, Satan's accusations didn't fall through as Joshua was present in Court. But we shall return to discuss this in detail later. Let's stay on Job's story for now.

When Job began to realize the issue with him was a Court issue, he desired a mediator. He recognized that God was his Judge in the Heavenly Courts and that his own righteousness would not grant him victory. Then Job went on to say, *"For though I were righteous, I could not answer Him; I would beg mercy of my Judge."* (Job 9:15)

After all, Scripture says, "our righteous acts are like filthy rags" (see Isaiah 64:6 NIV)

Job also needed a mediator. His mediator's description was someone who was both man and God, someone to bridge the gap. Job thought God was beating him. But he would later find out who the author of his affliction was.

"*32 God is not a mortal like me,*
　　so I cannot argue with him or take him to trial.
　33 If only there were a mediator between us,
　　someone who could bring us together.
　34 The Mediator could make God stop beating me,
　　and I would no longer live in terror of his punishment."

— JOB 9:32-34 NLT

In Job's case, Jesus had not yet come to earth as a man. Even so, Job could attest that his *Mediator* had to be one that was in Heaven. Job's next statement is profound as he declares, "Even now, my witness is in heaven. My advocate is there on high." (Job 16:19 NLT)

In the Messiah's dispensation, Simeon Peter had The Mediator in earthly existence, both man and God. Again, Jesus was equally present in the Courts of Heaven to stand in mediation for Simon Peter, and as a result, Simon would overcome. He would go on to experience God's love and justice in a personal way. Not only that, but Peter received a higher mandate to strengthen his brethren after he had risen from his fall.

Recall this is the same Peter who denied knowing Jesus three times for fear of death (see Matthew 26:69-75). Through Peter's restoration experience, we see that God gives second chances to all who would turn to Him. God also turns good, whatever evil the enemy intended for our harm (Genesis 50:20).

RESPONSIBILITY TOWARDS JUSTICE

Peter received a verdict that would change his life and empower others. Peter would pull down Satan's kingdom for many generations as one of the fathers of Christendom. Such is the comfort and certainty we have in being mediated by Jesus. His mediation strengthens our faith to fulfill our destiny.

The relevance of us winning in the Courts of Heaven transcends our needs and wants. It goes beyond the physical into taking spiritual grounds in the Kingdom of God, laying the building blocks for generations to further on the build. The devil is scared of God's sons ruining him for many generations.

As sons of God, we've got to look beyond the here and now. We've got to know the Godhead made us for more - God's excellent ways. We have a responsibility to establish God's justice system on earth. We are the seed that will crush Satan's head, and he knows it.

Prayer:

May we be awakened to know who we are and what kingdom legislation backs us up. May we know that our life on earth is an opportunity to bring forth God's kingdom into it. And gain territory so that the kingdom of this world becomes the Kingdom of our God (see Revelation 11:15), in Jesus's all mighty name. Amen!

9

MEDIATION

~ Upon the Weight of the House of Mediation, no Man or Spirit-being Stands a Chance ~

THE MEDIATOR

It is another day in Court. In Job chapter 2, Satan is present to accuse Job a second time. He is determined to prove Job wrong and secure a way to ruining his life. God sets a limit to how far the devil goes against Job's life - "spare his life." In the same vein, God has set a limit to how far the devil goes against your life.

Now let's get deeper into the events on *Day 2* at Court;

"One day the members of the Heavenly Court came again to present themselves before the Lord, and the Accuser, Satan, came with them.

2 "Where have you come from?" the Lord asked Satan.

Satan answered the Lord, "I have been patrolling the earth, watching everything that's going on."

3 Then the Lord asked Satan, "Have you noticed my servant Job? He is the finest man in all the earth. He is blameless—a man of complete integrity. He fears God and stays away from evil. And he has maintained his integrity, even though you urged me to harm him without cause."

4 Satan replied to the Lord, "Skin for skin! A man will give up everything he has to save his life. 5 But reach out and take away his health, and he will surely curse you to your face!"

6 "All right, do with him as you please," the Lord said to Satan. "But spare his life."

— JOB 2:1-6 NLT

You get a sense (or picture) of what Job was dealing with unknowingly. It is also a reflection of the things we go through without knowing their origins. While God continues to speak highly of His son, Job, Satan presses hard at it to get legal grounds for afflicting Job.

The devil dragged on to the point of getting permission to afflict Job. And that he did straight away, starting with all his possessions, children, and to afflicting Job with a skin disease.

If you are going through an endless cycle of affliction, it is most likely that Satan has found legal grounds to bring affliction. Amid most of life's challenges, that endless cycle of pain, suffering, sicknesses, I urge that you seize every opportunity to take any situation to Heaven's Court. A good reason to go to the Court of Heaven is getting a diagnosis from your doctor.

After so much suffering and hurtful interactions with his wife and friends, Job began to perceive he needed to take his situation to Court. Not just any court.

Job could sense he needed a mediator who could defend him against his accuser. He also felt something even more potent in his spirit – he would also need the Mediator when he gets to stand before God, The Righteous Judge.

"32 God is not a mortal like me,
    so I cannot argue with him or take him to trial.
    33 If only there were a mediator between us,

someone who could bring us together.
34 The Mediator could make God stop beating me,
and I would no longer live in terror of his punishment."

— JOB 9:32-34 NLT

Oh, someone needs to go to trial now! Indeed, it was not God that Job needed to take to trial. Job thought otherwise because somehow, he never knew he had an accuser. Through Job's lament, Job never mentioned or seemed aware of an accuser who was frustrated he could not harm Job's testimony before God.

Job believed in the power of this Mediator to end all his sufferings through His mediation. He saw the need for an intermediate between him and God in Court. Someone to bring them together. He said, "Nor is there any mediator between us, *Who* may lay his hand on us both." (Job 9:33)

For Job to come up with the thought of a mediator who had the power to place His hands on The Almighty God and on Job, a mortal, was incomprehensible to the ordinary mind. A Being who can lay His hand on God; a Redeemer Being who can place His other hand on Job and bring Job face-to-face with God into a union. One who could bring about an agreement between Job and God could only be possible through this Being. It is something we have not seen any mortal man could envisage as a possibility. But Job will think this. If not by the Spirit, how would Job even conceive of that possibility? Hold on a minute, did Job know in that day who he was seeking?

Somehow Job saw the need for a mediator who was both God and *Man* to stand between God and man. This person had to be fully God and fully man to rescue him from accusations that brought about his predicament. The mediation had to fulfill the requirement that would guarantee his freedom from all the calamity. We know who fits the description Job seeks—the only One who does.

Later in 1 Timothy 2:5, the Apostle Paul offers an exciting revelation clarifying how this Mediator that qualifies to stand between man and

God is both God and Man at the same time; This is Jesus, the Son of God, born of a woman. Wholly God and yet fully man.

> "[For] There is one God and one Mediator [intermediary] so that human beings can reach God [between God and human beings], Christ Jesus, who is himself human."

> — 1 TIMOTHY 2:5 EXB.

We all had a debt to sin through Adam, but Jesus Christ, the son of God, came to earth as a man and fulfilled all the requirements necessary for our redemption. He became the overpayment for our sin and delivered us from the death penalty. He is our one Mediator. He is the same mediator Job perceived would deliver him from his present predicament even before Jesus had come to Earth to die.

Job figured that his Mediator and Witness was in Heaven too, all pointing us to the ONE – Jesus.

> "Even now, my witness is in Heaven. My advocate is there on high."

> — JOB 16:19 NLT.

Marvel with me for a moment. Did Job in his day know about Jesus, His witness, and His advocacy? Perhaps Job encountered Him in the Spirit.

We can see from Scripture accounts that Job was doing everything you and I would try to do to get Heaven to intervene on our behalf. Job's predicament notwithstanding, we may not fault him for lack of effort.

Job understood the 'Triune' nature of the God-head. Somehow during his grueling search for a mediator to stand between him and God, Job appears certain of the nature of this Mediator – one who is not just man. One who would have the authority as God (see Job 9: 32-33 NIV) and represent him before the Almighty God – The Judge. Haven established that his Mediator was in Heaven; he still did not know how to get to this Mediator. (see Job 23:1-9 NIV).

As we continue the journey with Job, we will begin to see that Job was no longer an earthbound man. We will see that Job had transcended into a man who could step into the Heavenly Court. Job realized he needed someone to witness for him and one who would advocate for him. Job knew that he needed both (witness & advocate) to establish a valid case once in Court. Job finally saw that he had a witness in Heaven who could testify on his behalf.

The Apostle Paul enlightens us how that "The Spirit Himself bears witness with our spirit that we are children of God." (Romans 8:16). Then John writes in His first epistle: "My dear children, I am writing this to you so that you will not sin. But if anyone does sin, we have an advocate who pleads our case before the Father. He is Jesus Christ, the one who is truly righteous." (1 John 2:1 NLT). Both Scriptures are complementing Job's standpoint.

So, indeed Job became aware that his advocate had complete jurisdiction in the courts of Heaven where he had to go. He realized he had the Son of God who could mediate for him, and it was not by any acts of his righteousness or endless sacrifices that made him a blessed man.

Can you picture Job's relief and joy at the encounter with the one who redeems him? What a beautiful thing that Job was able and willing to reach out to the pre-incarnate Jesus in his day. Jesus' atoning work for humanity is for all time – past, present, and future. (see Romans 6:10)

The Lord would do this for Job when many would have thought that since Jesus hadn't come to die for us, then he couldn't possibly advocate on Job's behalf. Let's throw out the belief systems that have only but hindered us and take a journey into the great love of God that transcends time, space, distance, and dimensions.

Job's search was for that One who would be both God and Man; One *"who may lay His hand on us both."* (see Job 9:33) None but Jesus qualifies. Only Jesus fits this bill. Upon the weight of the House of Mediation, no man or spirit-being stands a chance. Job's voice through recognizing the need to prepare a case and go before God was weightier than seeing that person who would mediate for him be just anyone (see Job 13:18). No being, no man can lay his hand on God. On Job, sure. But not on God, for no ordinary man could, nor ever will. Only God-the-Son can.

Amazing how Job caught on quite well on things, one may say. He knew his case was no match for a mere man like himself; hence he laments, "For *He* is not a man, as I *am*, *That* I may answer Him, *And that* we should go to court together. Nor is there any mediator between us, *Who* may lay his hand on us both." (Job 9:32, 33). Such a timeless revelation!

Also, this is where we go back to the existence of the Trinity and the reality of their operations. In the center of their unity was, and still is, Jesus; His presence and role did not start after coming to earth, dying on the cross, and resurrecting. Not at all. Jesus existed in the Godhead as Mediator before and after His resurrection. He offered Peter that mediation even while on earth as a man. Jesus said to Peter;

> "*31 Simon, Simon (Peter), listen! Satan has demanded permission to sift [all of] you like grain; 32 but I have prayed [especially] for you [Peter], that your faith [and confidence in Me] may not fail; and you, once you have turned back again [to Me], strengthen and support your brothers [in the faith].*"

> — LUKE 22:31-32 AMP.

He has always been the Mediator and the Savior-Lamb, slain from the foundation of the world (see Revelation 13:8, 1 Peter 1:19-20)

Just as David would ask for the Holy Spirit not to be taken from him (see Psalm 51:11) long before Pentecost in Acts 2, so was Job seeking for his Mediator. The Triune Being played their roles before they manifested on the earth in the ways they did. We record Christ as crucified in human time about 2000 years ago, but here He was before time began, as revealed in Revelations 13:8.

"All who dwell on the earth will worship him, whose names have not been written inn the Book of Life of the Lamb slain from the foundation of the world."

Some believe Job was relating to God, but you have to sit in with the Spirit of Revelation to understand revelation. The mediation was between Job and God; God as the Judge cannot turn and be the defense counsel. Consider this. Suppose I am searching and relating to the Trinity on a specific issue; then the One who qualifies or sits enthroned in the seat of my search is the One I am connecting to within the Godhead. He is the One directing me towards what He alone provides. I am, therefore, receiving what I need from that Person of the Godhead regarding my unique need.

Again, when it comes to mediation, through all of eternity, Jesus stands alone. "For there is only one Mediator between God and men, the man Christ Jesus" (1 Timothy 2:5)

Through Job's affliction, the Lord never left Job's side as He never leaves any of us when we are afflicted. The Lord walked him through it. Similarly, He is walking with you through these pages and preparing you to head into His Courts.

Now personalize this when you think about going to the Heavenly Courts. Personalize the joy of knowing God-the-Son, who has imputed His righteousness to you, and therefore He answers for you when you call out to Him in your day of trial. Isn't that the greatest treasure imaginable? Such powerful justification.

God will go to every length to bring us freedom. And today, His Word is proven right in the way God preserves us. We see the confirmation of this timeless truth in both the Old and New Testaments. He is the same God, yesterday, today, and forever. (see Hebrews 13:8)

Beloved, we will find that Jesus and the Holy Spirit were available and active in the lives of all who called out to them in a relationship. Over the years, I have seen many beautiful people shut off from engaging the Old Testament's beauty while embracing only the New Testament. It almost seems like they think it makes Jesus happier that they treasure the times of His earthly appearing and after He left the earth. When clearly, The Lord Jesus has been present all along, from before the Old Testament and through the New Testament as Redeemer, Mediator, Saviour, and Friend. He is all we need.

People like Job experienced Him as all of that throughout the Old Testament, howbeit, in a Heavenly abode. Many others would later experience Him as all that in an earthly place through the New Testament era. Today, you and I can relate with Him in both the Old and New Testament experiences.

Revelation is the ability to see Him in the most unlikely places in all Scripture and encounters. You do yourself a great disservice by limiting yourself to the New Testament. I often wonder that in a bid to distinguish BC and AD, using "old" and "new," we may have created a programming. One that distracts many from plowing in the fields and reaping the fruits of great revelation and insight into YHVH's utmost desire for us.

God is for You, But the Judge Will Rule Righteously

Now, let's turn our attention to Job's default feeling. It is a feeling that most of us are familiar with and pretty much go through at the onset of calamity. It is that feeling God is the one afflicting us. Have you ever thought or even said out clear, at some time, "why me, God?" or, "God, why would you let this happen to me?" Well, there goes that *default* feeling that God is the one afflicting you. Job had it too.

> "*The mediator could make God stop beating me, and I would no longer live in terror of his punishment.*"

> — JOB 9:34 NLT.

Job was right about needing a mediator. He was also right about the power the Mediator had to end his affliction. However, he was not right in thinking that God was the cause of his misery; neither was to blame for it all.

Even though Job had been at the receiving end of God's love and blessings through the years, he felt God turned His back on him. Quite sad how we submit to a mindset programmed to think God is afflicting us when in reality, He is ruling as Judge. The real inflictor and accuser is Satan. God rules in justice and righteousness as akin to His nature. The accuser, as in his character, is the one tirelessly seeking grounds to afflict us. The same continues to hinder us from the truth, so we never realize we can plead our cases before the Righteous Judge.

We see in Zachariah 3:1-7, when Joshua showed up in Heaven's Courts, Satan was already there to oppose Joshua. We also understand that Satan had some dirt on Joshua because he was in filthy garments. God's verdict was a total rebuke and rejection of Satan's accusations while Joshua stood before His throne. God was delighted to see Joshua receive a righteous ruling in his favor for being present. Joshua was arrayed in a clean robe and turban. In the same manner, as Job was.

Then Zachariah instructed, "...They should also place a clean turban on his head." So they put a clean priestly turban on his head and dressed him in new clothes while the angel of the Lord stood by." (Zachariah 3:5 NLT)

> "Everything *I did was honest. Righteousness covered me like a robe, and I wore justice like a turban.*"

> — JOB 29:14 NLT.

In this statement, Job speaks of the times he received the same cleansing, and clothing Joshua received before God. Even though at the time, Job no longer felt his heavenly clothing in this way, Job would eventually feel it again. The Lord would rule in favor of His son, Job, who had now come before Him as an active participant in Heaven's Courts.

When Job realized he was in a court setting, it became clear what he needed to do. What conviction when he said, "I have prepared my case; I will be proved innocent." (Job 13:18 NLT). Even in distress, Job knew that if he prepared his case, stepped into Heaven's Court, and had it presented, he would win. Job understood that God was for him and therefore, he became convinced of having a winning case if he showed up before the Righteous Judge.

The Lord always makes way for His own. How would Job have known what steps he needed to take? How would Job have known what to do, like prepare a case?

Job had confidence in his right-standing before the Judge; above all, he had great confidence in his mediator's capability. I believe this is the bedrock of our faith. Like Job, we must hold unto the truth that God will never cast us away. His love for us should assure us that we can never lose a case we bring to Him. It gives a whole new depth of meaning to drawing near God with confidence, knowing that we have right through Jesus. (See Hebrews 4:16 & 10:23) All my years of taking cases to Court, there hasn't been any loss.

It is a great assurance to know God provides a way for us out of circumstances, even those beyond our control. Be confident that God shows you the way to victory when you stay the course like Job. With the win, we also step into a process of restoration. Job's health, family, and wealth were all restored, and then some.

I love the assurance Job ended up having in Job 42:1-14 (please read). Unlike in the previous setting, where he was still going through, Job encountered God through his trial. He had the opportunity to see and know God in a personal relationship.

"I have heard of You by the hearing *of the ear, But now my eye sees You. 6 Therefore I abhor myself, And repent in dust and ashes.*"

— JOB 42:5-6.

Job no longer had to rely on the things he heard about God; he now could see they only relegated him to a religious lifestyle, of making sure he covered all his bases in the hope of being made righteous through his sacrifices.

What Have You Heard about God or Yourself?

It is good to have people share and learn from one another how God has been good in their lives. It is even better when you have experienced God's goodness and power in your life and for yourself. The latter will sustain you better when things happen that shake you to your core. Job's reliance alone on the things he heard about God made him question God. After seeing God, he was set free from a life of sin consciousness.

Contrary to everything he heard and believed to be accurate throughout his lifetime to that very moment, He was awe-struck at who God is. He was confident of his victory even though his wife and friends told him otherwise. There is nothing like being in a personal relationship with Abba that lessens the power of external nay-voices around you.

One of Satan's many ways to accomplish his mission in a person's life is by infusing his lies into key voices around us, especially the voices of those to whom we are the most vulnerable. He also uses the people who know some of our stories that will add some sauce to it, and it comes out to hurt you in the process. Familiar spirits are what they are.

Satan is the instigator of falsehood. He is behind the lies you hear against God and yourself. He accuses you on earth even as he already is doing in the Heavenly Court. Like we have all failed to realize, Job did not know this either. Just as Job suffered from these accusations, we suffer for not perceiving we need to take up our cases beyond the earthly accusers. We go about fighting people, oblivious to who the real enemy accusing us is.

"People are not the enemy (whether they be husbands, wives, children, or parents, slaves, or bosses. They might host hostile, law-inspired thought patterns through their unbelief or ignorance but) to target one another is to engage in the wrong combat. We represent the authority of the victory of Christ in the spiritual realm. We are positioned there (in Christ); we target

the mind games and structures of darkness, religious thought patterns, governing, and conditioning human behavior."

— EPHESIANS 6:12 THE MIRROR

"For we do not wrestle against flesh and blood, but against principalities, against powers, against the rulers of the darkness of this age, against spiritual hosts of wickedness in the heavenly places."

— EPHESIANS 6:12

Instead of going at people for what they have wrongfully accused us of, we are to go into Heaven's Court. We know who accuses us and where he stands to charge us; it is the same place we get vindicated.

The good news in all this is that just like Job, we too can take our prepared cases and present them before the Lord in Court. We can have the Lord thoroughly deal with and render judgments on these beings that have tormented us for too long.

Listen to what the Lord God is saying to you: *"I am the Lord, the King of Israel! Come argue your case with me. Present your evidence."* (Isaiah 41:21 CEV)

God is Righteous. He is The Righteous Judge who will judge all things righteously. The Courts of Heaven is open for us to go and get to the root of our problems and generational issues. We ought to get in on the power of going before Heaven's Courts and winning cases. You can experience the joy of seeing cases you have won in Heaven's Courts manifest in your earthly circumstances.

PONDER POINT:

Have you tried everything, and nothing seems to be working? Does it feel like you have come to the end of yourself? The question to answer is, "are you prepared to take that situation to the Courts of Heaven? Get a piece of paper and begin to write down specific issues you need addressing in Court.

A WINNING CASE AGAINST SEX DEMONS

The following testimony is a real-life example of winning a case in Court against years of affliction from the incubus and succubus spirits – these are demonic entities that have sexual relations with people in their dreams. These sex demons disguise using human faces. Sometimes, they may bear the face of an ex who is either engaged in spiritism or has ties to the demonic realm.

People who suffer from their molestation speak of bedwetting. Married people would feel detached from their spouses and no longer desire sexual relations with their spouses. Some even lose their husbands or children if they do not undergo deliverance in the name of Jesus. Some people have an entire dream life where these sex demons communicate their desires, like displeasure with their victims' spouses, thus the term *spirit husband* or *spirit wife*. The list of their harassment goes on.

But they can be judged in the Courts of Heaven when you bring them before God as can be seen in the following testimony.

"Nadia & I spent time in worship & gradually got into a place where I was fully immersed in this spiritual arena. It seemed like an earthly court with a Judge, defendant, plaintiff, & audience. I saw myself stand in the box speaking. As Nadia continued praying, I saw the Judge rule my case as "Not guilty!" At that point, I was in tears feeling like it was never my fault. I never consciously got into any agreement with the accuser.

I had been wrongly accused & harassed for years, but I had believed it was ok, so the dreams continued. As soon as my case was ruled "Not guilty," I immediately saw these 'spirit husbands' walking out of the Court. They were angry. It seemed like their hands were handcuffed to their backs as they walked out one after the other.

(Before wrapping up the testimony, I want to add that *'spirit husbands'* are sex demons disguised with human faces. Sometimes, they may bear the face of an ex who is either engaged in spiritism or has ties to the demonic realm)

I felt a sense of freedom. I was afraid because one of the spirit husbands almost refused to leave (this man was the main element in my dreams over these years). I suppose it was a bitter breakup, but it was the most incredible feeling of deliverance I got when he finally walked out. I then saw myself walk out of the courtroom towards the entrance, standing outside with a certificate in my hand, which I believe was a divorce certificate. Here were my freedom & deliverance.

It's been nine months now; besides a couple of less intense dreams where I saw one looking at me from a distance but not having contact with me as it had been for many years prior, I have not had any of these dreams again. The fantastic thing about this deliverance is that it stopped the spiritual attacks in my dreams and ended the physical connection to my ex, too, as I broke every tie I had with the spirit husbands.

I have now learned to go to the courts with everything I struggle with, and I feel blessed to be free at last after many years of this torture."

10

WHAT IT MEANS TO BEHOLD YHVH

~ You Receive of God, in the Measure you can Trust His Word. You Fill
yourself with Him to the Degree you Empty yourself of Man's Ideologies ~

~

SEEK GOD FOR YOURSELF

I t does seem like Job could not fully articulate the description of what he saw in his revelation. Still, he did get to *'see.'* After searching all the nooks and crannies of the known realm, he eventually pressed deeper into his relationship with God, and then came the revelation he needed. In Job 42, Job's eyes were open following a series of divine truths about God revealed through young Elihu. Let's begin reading from the third verse.

> 3 *"You asked, 'Who is this that obscures my plans without knowledge?'*
>   *Surely I spoke of things I did not understand,*
>   *things too wonderful for me to know.*
>   4 *"You said, 'Listen now, and I will speak;*
>   *I will question you,*

and you shall answer me.'
5 My ears had heard of you
   but now my eyes have seen you.
6 Therefore, I despise myself
   and repent *in dust and ashes."*

— JOB 42:3-6

How gracious God the Father is? If only we seek to know and relate with Him always. A quick examination of how Job got to this powerful realization in chapter 42 is key. God would use young Elihu to draw Job back into focus in the right direction for his redemption. (see Job 32:6, 18-22; Job 33 and 34. NIV)

In all the chapters from 33 through to 41, it is amazing how much transformation comes with knowing the God he (Job, and we) have. It changes everything. It changed it all for Job. Soon after, he let himself be vulnerable and drawn into who God is and goes from counting his merits to repenting before an awesome and loving God. His eyes become opened to see the process the God-head designed all along for his vindication and, ultimately, restoration. (Job 42:7-12a)

Job stepped into Heaven's Courts and was present before the Lord God – YHVH. It changed his perspective of YHVH. The religious activities he had engaged in prior were based on his religious perception of God. His misinformation of God cleared out when he saw YHVH for himself. Sadly, many people spend an entire lifetime following differing religious rules and belief systems instead of absolute truth. Many still observe specific ordinances as ways to secure their blessings and a passage to Heaven. However, what changes you is your personal relationship with YHVH; which is beyond what anyone else has told you.

When you desire Him more than your very existence, more than anything you have, more than desire itself, you get to that point where one look at Him changes everything for you. You begin to experience an overhaul of false representations of Him you may have had or heard of from others. The perception you once had of Him immediately goes out the window.

Job's encounter with God had him in absolute shock. It was clear He didn't expect what he saw. He first acknowledged the grave misinterpretation of God. His immediate reaction said it all. In Job's words;

> *"I have heard of You by the hearing of the ear, But now my eye sees You. 6 Therefore I abhor myself. And repent in dust and ashes."*

> — JOB 42:5-6

Job despised the fallen nature in his life, inner motivations, the stench of all his actions. And all that because all he had heard could not compare to such magnanimous glory of God. The love in His eyes was so overwhelming that Job could now see that this God was not and would never be against him. He saw such a love that would sacrifice His only Son for him; The beauty of His righteousness glimmering into his very core, drawing him in bit by bit, by bit.

Like the different wavelengths of light, YHVH's glory is far beyond what any natural eye has seen or even think imaginable. The grandeur of God's majesty was one for which Job had no reference or grid. He could never have pictured this magnificent *Being* as the One he referred to as God, not in his wildest imaginations.

In that moment with your ABBA (Heavenly Father) where your soul is screaming, "I had no clue." Every fragmented part of your being desiring to return to the origins of your design. Your external being burns up in the light of His consuming fire upon your spirit.

However, in your spirit-man, it seems as though your body were returning to dust as though in Eden, back to recalibration to God's original pattern. Your utmost desire to lose that form into a new beginning as particles of creation meets Creator. Your spirit-man yearns to take on a new record. It is taking on the nature and state of the One you are beholding.

"But we all, with unveiled face, beholding as in a mirror the glory of the Lord, are being transformed into the same image from glory to glory, just as by the Spirit of the Lord."

— 2 CORINTHIANS 3:18

In such incredible light and presence, you feel dead, at least to the best of your understanding. Suddenly you realize you are so filthy; everything that meant something is no longer desirable. You want no more of that degraded nature. No pleasure in that scum of dirt, and from your depths, you cry: "Oh, change me, my Father, transform me, transfigure me into Your image. *I only want You, God. I repent in dust and ashes.*"

"Repentance" is the Hebrew term **teshuvah** (meaning "return"). It describes returning to your glory state. Notice how Job's immediate reaction when his desire met with God's glory was repentance. How quickly your spirit man recognizes it has been in a cloak of filthy slumber while looking at the possibility of becoming like the One you are beholding. His deep calls to your deep.

After Job repented, the Lord went on and took care of Job's business with His friends without Job asking. The Lord addressed Job's "so-called friends" by;
- Rebuking them for their actions towards His son, Job.
- Proving and displaying ownership over Job.
- Providing a way for their redemption from falsehood
- Allowing reconciliation and restoration.

Not only will the Lord show His displeasure towards those who submit themselves as agents to afflict you, but He will also prove to them and your accuser that you are His. God is gracious also to provide a way for those in deception to be restored.

When people are willing to respond to divine guidance and correction, they get the opportunity to be reconciled to God. There are instances where I have seen an opponent miraculously come round and even begin to seek prayers for themselves in the same way Job's friends sought for Job's blessings.

At this juncture, I will urge you, my precious reader, that if you are on the other side as the violator, there is power in repentance for you as well. This restoration can be yours, too, if you choose to believe and repent.

You may ask, what if the person or people I hurt are now dead or have no contact and unable to reach them? How can I reconcile?

Well, praise God; we are all spirit beings. You go to God and confess it all to Him. There is no barrier to our reach in God. They must have forgiven us. If they didn't then, they certainly will now. However, you must repent for being the agent through which a demon operated. You must seek cleansing from that demonic influence in your life through repentance so you no longer carry that seed to harm another.

You also do not want that seed passed on through you to your children. Take the matter to the Lord in repentance, and He will give you His lasting peace. He will also remove all legal rights of accusation as though there was never such a record of offense or sin in your life. Amen!

A Court Case Borne out of Relationship

Let us consider a case of a human being present in the Heavenly Court simultaneously as Satan. We will see here that while Joshua, the high priest, was present in the Courts of Heaven, the accuser was also there to oppose him. Unlike Job, who had no clue what was going on in the spirit realm concerning his life, Joshua took the bull by the horns. I guess those are the perks of meeting with God face to face in His Most Holy Place in a relationship rather than through religion/sacrifices.

Let's pause and emphasize that Job's prior understanding of going before God was through sacrifice offerings. Job diligently made sacrifices for himself and his family.

On the other hand, Joshua thrived at building an intimate relationship with God within the Holy of Holies. Joshua had already taken the initiative to be in Heaven's Court. Therefore, we will see how his own life turned out. Job suffered so many losses before figuring what he was going through was spiritual legalities requiring his presence in Court to answer for them.

Interestingly, the man reporting this heavenly scene, Zachariah, was no stranger to having a face-to-face relationship with God either. I want to emphasize that this degree of intimacy with Abba-Father allowed Zachariah to operate in judicial matters in the Courts of Heaven.

Zachariah was drawn (by the Angel of God) into this particular court session. Consider this an invitation to partner with God to see Joshua established in God's Kingdom as he was. From how we will see Zachariah operate, it will become apparent that this was not his first rodeo. Zachariah had a position before God and a relationship that we will explore in this chapter.

As spirit beings, God draws us by His Spirit to effect His purposes in the most supernatural ways. Could it be that you have been missing out on living more fully in God's divine plan(s)? Keep that in mind as we proceed.

Now, come with me as we engage revelation in Zechariah 3:1-7. Whenever I have walked through this scripture passage with people, I ask them specific questions. It is interesting to see their initial reaction to entering into God's word. I want to walk through this scripture with you as well.

Let's go into the verses by faith. Allow the Holy Spirit to guide you; let Him guide you, not from a place of belief systems or preconceived notions. But from a place of absolute surrender to His revelation and guidance. He will be your present help through this study.

Prayer:

Lord, thank you for the honor we have as Your sons to be guided by your Spirit, who teaches us everything. Therefore, we come in light of who You are, the reality of who we are in You. We settle into the understanding that Your Holy Spirit is leading us through your Word this very moment.

Now, consider the first verse of Zachariah 3.

*"Then he showed **me** Joshua, the high priest standing before the Angel of the Lord, and Satan standing at his right hand to oppose him."*

— ZACHARIAH 3:1

A close-up look at this verse gets you wondering what form the narrator ("*me*") had this encounter. Well, most Bible translations say it was in the form of a vision, so that may not give you much room to deliberate or think otherwise. The understanding becomes more apparent when you continue this journey through Zachariah's experience.

QUESTION 1

My first question is; *Is Zachariah having a vision - like an open vision, a dream, trance, or is he present?*

You choose which of these ways you think was the medium through which Zachariah was engaging this experience. You can even go with the interpretation proffered by your Bible. This exercise aims to take you into a walk through the scriptures. Your experiences with God will grow when you engage the Word of God as a *Living Being.*

"For the word of God is living and powerful, and sharper than any two-edged sword, piercing even to the division of soul and spirit, and of joints and marrow, and is a discerner of the thoughts and intents of the heart."

— HEBREWS 4:12

Hold on to your choice or thought for just a bit; we shall come back to it shortly.

QUESTION 2

Who is the "me" in this verse?

Someone is witnessing Joshua standing before the Angel of God. He also sees the opposition raised against Joshua.

What if you had the privilege to see this scenario play out for someone else?

Place yourself as the "me" in the verse we read and see into what "me" is seeing. Hold that view in mind.

Let's move on to Zachariah 3:2

"And the Lord said to Satan, "The Lord rebuke you, Satan! The Lord who has chosen Jerusalem rebuke you! Is this not a brand plucked from the fire?"

One minute we see the Angel of the Lord, and the next moment it is the Lord speaking.

Are you beginning to see the number of people within this setting?

Picture a scenario where the Lord is rebuking Satan. Conversations in the Heavenly Courts between God and Satan.

Notice that the Lord defends Joshua instead of condemning him. The Lord states Joshua is literal wood rescued from being burnt in the fire. Imagine there is so much evidence against you of all the times you dabbled in the wrong things. Imagine the voices of those you hurt are rising against you, imagine your sins are red like crimson (Isaiah 1:18), and everything points to your failure as a person, even as a child of God.

It gets so bad that the Lord agrees that indeed you are wood heading towards ash but by His authority, He rescued you at the nick of time - hallelujah. And because He did, that is all that matters. His verdict cancels out every demand for your condemnation as a result of your actions or sins.

At this point, the Lord – the Judge – was done listening to all the accusations Satan was bringing against Joshua. God immediately dealt with the record that gave Satan the right to oppose Joshua.

As God rebukes Satan, a question you may be asking takes us to the third question.

QUESTION 3

Why is the Lord addressing one man as Jerusalem? Why is the Lord refer-ring to Joshua as Jerusalem here?

It is one man, Joshua, the high priest of Jerusalem, standing before the Lord, and the Lord refers to a nation whom this priest has jurisdiction over. The high priest of that day was the only person with access to the Holy of Holies. He was the only man who would stand to make atonement for the sins of the people of Israel (Jerusalem) for an entire year.

When the devil comes after a man like this, he is seeking legal grounds to discredit the purpose for which God chose this person. Your authority and calling are under attack whenever your person is under threat from the enemy. We must remember that we are priests and kings unto God.

"And have made us kings and priests to our God;
  And we shall reign on the earth."

— REVELATION 5:10

As a priest before God, you can stand on behalf of your nation. In this case, God was addressing a man as a nation because he was a high priest of God over Jerusalem. God was defending the destiny of an entire people while one representation stood under accusation. When the enemy comes against you, he comes against your personhood and comes against your destiny, passion, and the people you would impact for good.

The accuser is a threat to all those the Father has given you jurisdiction over, and this is the greater purpose you must see when you go in and plead your case as a priest unto God. The Lord has chosen you and your assignment; He will protect both jealously. His heart is to release a verdict in your favor.

The Lord speaks so clearly here; He is the one who has chosen the nation Joshua stands to represent. Even if a nation or Joshua is in the fire as a brand, I am here to let you know that the Lord decrees you plucked out of that fire. As a priest, you can begin to stand for your city and nation in Heaven's Courts as you mature in dealing with your stuff. The Lord will rescue you, your city, state, and nation out of this corruption or whatever burning circumstance.

As a whole, the nation is guilty of the atrocities that Satan is accusing Joshua of committing. The devil is claiming they were no different from other countries. They were filthy, just like others; their lives are not holy or unique.

QUESTION 4

Were there grounds for Satan's accusation? How can we ascertain that Satan had facts?

Zachariah 3:3 reads,

"Now Joshua was clothed with filthy garments and was standing before the Angel."

Joshua is in soiled clothing; his life is not pure. The man who stands to represent Jerusalem is in filthy garments. The fact is that no high priest or man can be pure enough but Jesus. (See Romans 3:10)

Satan had a record of Joshua's sin as he stood before God, so Satan had legal grounds to resist him. Sin is Satan's stuff. When we are impure, we contain stuff that belongs to him.

When you show up in Court, the stuff engaging your life has no choice but to show up there with you. Note that Satan will also show up in Court, claiming you have his stuff. We know how that goes because the Lord will rebuke him. The Righteous Judge will rebuke Satan and his authority to operate in your life. But when you don't show up, the accuser has the right of way.

God wants you liberated to fulfill the purpose you agreed to when you existed as a spirit being in His Kingdom; that was before He formed you in your mother's womb. You have a unique purpose, as did Jeremiah.

> 4 *"Now the word of the Lord came to me, saying,*
>
> 5 *"Before I formed you in the womb I knew you [and approved of you as My chosen instrument],*
>
> *And before you were born I consecrated you [to Myself as My own];*
> *I have appointed you as a prophet to the nations."*

> — JEREMIAH 1:4-5 AMP.

QUESTION 5

Who was Joshua standing before? Angel or the Lord?

I want to bring your attention to where Joshua stood before the Angel, with a capital 'A' in some translations. Many Bible scholars believe that the Angel with the capital 'A' in the old testament is the pre-incarnate Jesus. In contrast, others state that he stood before the Lord.

> *"Then He answered and spoke to those who stood before Him, saying, "Take away the filthy garments from him." And to him, He said, "See, I have removed your iniquity from you, and I will clothe you with rich robes."*

— ZACHARIAH 3:4

As a follow-up to Question 5, consider the voice speaking. What Angel can act in this authority? Rebuke Satan, defend Joshua, and remove his iniquity?

Dear reader, at this point, I believe you have entirely immersed yourself in this encounter. Hold that thought as we dive deeper. We will witness a similar scenario in Job 1.

"One day, the members of the Heavenly Court came to present themselves before the Lord, and the Accuser, Satan, came with them."

— JOB 1:6 NLT.

In the above verse, God's sons or members of the Heavenly Court gathered before God. Satan, the accuser, had come along too. We understand the position of an accuser as a prominent member of the Court.

Considering Zachariah 3:4, we read earlier. The Lord asks those standing before Him to take away Joshua's filthy garments. For a man (Joshua the high priest) who was the holiest person in Israel, the only man in his day who was qualified to enter into the Holy of Holies, this was strange that his garments could be filthy.

There were rituals and a series of ceremonial cleansing procedures a high priest underwent to make himself worthy of being in the Holy of Holies back in that day. The processes were rigorous and took many months to achieve because if the high priest were not up to date with his purification process, he would die while in the Holy of Holies. All knew this in Israel.

The high priest wore bells beneath their robes. So the temple attendants could hear the bells clang as they went about their priestly activities within the Holy of Holies where no one else could see. Once the clanging bell sound ceased for a considerably long while, it meant the high priest was no longer moving and probably dead. If the high priest were found unworthy, he died while serving.

The priestly outfit also came with a rope tethered to the outside of the Holy of Holies (inner temple courts). The priests serving in the temple courts recognized this, and they would use the rope to pull the dead high priest out. I mean, it was tough business being a high priest.

If Joshua, Israel's high priest had on filthy garments, it makes me wonder how filthy anyone else must be. There is nothing we can do to be righteous enough to stand before God. It is not a thing for anyone who has accepted Jesus as their Lord and Savior to fret over because the blood of Jesus cleanses us. Jesus tore the veil and gave all who will believe in Him access to the Heavenly Holy Place, so we are worthy to stand before God through His cleansing blood.

Please do not deny yourself the privilege of going before Heaven's Courts either, as many have questioned its existence or relevance after the finished work of Jesus. Jesus Christ is the Mediator (see Hebrews 9:15) in the Courts of Heaven. Heaven's Courts have not ceased to operate because of the salvation Jesus provides us. Jesus mediated for Peter (see Luke 22:31), and He still intercedes for you and me today (see Hebrews 12:24).

QUESTION 6

Are our acts of righteousness filthy rags? What are these filthy garments?

Below is what the Prophet Isaiah had to say:

"But we are all like an unclean thing,
And all our righteousness are like filthy rags;
We all fade as a leaf,
And our iniquities, like the wind, have taken us away."

— ISAIAH 64:6

Oh, how overpowering our iniquities are that they consume us. Like the wind, they lift us and take us away as they please. No matter how many acts, works, and religious rites we perform, they are only but filthy rags. Whenever men were called righteous, it was only because their hearts were full of love and surrender to God. The Father always looked at the motives and heart even then.

PONDER POINT:

What are my filthy rags? As yourself and ... (feel free to write yours down) _____

In the Spirit realm, the filthy garments are "iniquity." It's easy to see a commonality between Joshua, the high priest, and Job here. In the natural, they both appeared to have it all together. All the t's crossed and i's dotted. But, none was genuinely righteous. Even Job's obsession with sacrifices for himself and his children was not sufficient to count as righteousness.

I love that the Lord used the cases of people whose good deeds are hard to measure up to, making it easy for us to see that we are in good company if they were filthy. God shows us that our right-standing before Him has nothing to do with our claim to (external) purity. In Adam, we all sinned; in Christ, we are made righteous (see Romans 5:12-21, Romans 3:20-22, I Corinthians 15:21-22.)

STANDING IN COURT

Having come this far, we must not lose ground to the nagging of the voice of the accuser. I can not say this enough; Satan does not like us showing up in the Courts of Heaven.

Understand that the entire Council of Heaven is in your favor. Step in as you are and receive God's righteous verdict. Whenever you are there, realize the following.

1. God Will Not Condemn You

Notice that the Lord did not condemn Joshua for his filthy garments. Joshua did not find a solution for his filthy garments in the external works of righteousness. It is a thing to ponder upon if you are in a religion that teaches you can earn enough brownie points to gain access into God's Kingdom.

We cannot be righteous by works. Only through Jesus are we not condemned (see Romans 8:1). Even though Jesus had not physically given His life to redeem us at the time of this event, Joshua went before the Court of Heaven; therefore, the Lord did not condemn him as He will not condemn you. Even then, God provided a solution for Joshua.

2. Do Not Respond To Satan In Court

Notice that Joshua said nothing to fight the allegations against him. Joshua didn't have to argue or defend himself. All he did was be present.

The enemy has intimate knowledge of your genealogy, so fighting him when he brings up accusations is fruitless. The things he accuses you of are deeds within the bloodline. It is why Jesus uses His blood to cleanse us from sin.

Let's say your ancestors committed child murder; that offense is within the genealogy. It is not a stand-alone action of a person because it opens doors for legions of demons to operate in that bloodline. Those open doors empower the devil to service the alters generations after.

Sometimes, certain things may skip a generation but show up in the next because it has a stake in the bloodline. Please do not be ignorant of this; it may subsequently appear in the form of abortions or intense hatred towards others which is as severe as murder, to mention a few (see Matthew 5:22).

Doctors use blood analysis to see what exists in their patient's genealogy, health-wise. I know a few young women who have had their breasts surgically removed even before anything is detected because they had someone in the bloodline die of breast cancer.

If the blood can physically show depth readily applicable in the natural, the same applies to the supernatural. It would be best to recognize the blood's universality and what power lies within generations of operations in the bloodline.

Some parents mark their children in yearly rituals with razor blade cuts while covenanting them to their family gods. As a result, they find themselves open to demonic influences even when they never asked for it.

For reasons like this, Scripture admonishes us to agree with the accuser without hesitation (see Matthew 5:25). He has the records of your genealogy. Why do you fight what you do not know? If you are standing before God, there is no cause to fear the outcome.

Many people are deceived into thinking that rejecting or fighting something makes it disappear. I'm sorry to let you know that it does not happen that way. There is no situation in the spiritual realm that you can wish away.

There is a real kingdom that is fighting to get access to you. If you choose to ignore, then you are doing exactly what they want. Which only strengthens their actions through to the next generation. You can choose to deal with them in Heaven's Courts, so your children have a softer landing dealing with generational issues.

Satan's kingdom is one of dog-eat-dog situation; demons are fighting for power to reign on earth. Demons do not have a body; they need a body with which to express their evil nature on the earth. They will manipulate, set traps, and seduce you into sin for the right to have relevance on earth. They will continue with their schemes to grow into a stronghold in your lineage. They crave more power as other lesser demons bow to them. They are just like their father, the devil who wanted to be like God. It's a never-ending cycle.

3. Keep Your Eyes On The Judge

The Spirit realm operates on legalities. Understand you have rights as a son of God and do not shy away from taking any situation before the Heavenly Courts. Earlier, we established that demons are associated with sinful stuff that engages you. These demons also show up when you show up in Court. The good news is that they are judged as God's judgment comes upon the things that engage you.

Show up when you feel that urge to watch pornography. Show up from your dream or night terror when you feel something touch you. Go straight into Heaven's Court when someone attacks you, and you lose your calm.

The good thing about this is, God is setting the devil up for a rebuke while delivering you from that demonic hold. But for your accuser, everyone there in Heaven's Courts is for you. They are your support system, and they rejoice in seeing you victorious.

At the end of a Courtroom session, the Judge renders His ruling. In that verdict, you will be acquitted. By the same verdict, the Judge restricts the devil from attacking you.

Every time you go to Court, you are better off than before you entered. Angels are rejoicing as God assigns them to help another son of God fulfill every word written in his destiny scroll. I must let you know that it's a great day when you step in there. Just **keep your eyes on the Judge!**

It is refreshing to know that God cares about you regardless of where you have been or the things you have done. God's standard and love are the same for everyone.

Right now, God is giving you an invitation to reason with Him, regardless of how sinful you think you are. You can come into Court and present the stained and filthy garment of your sins and iniquities.

He has ready clean robes, white like fresh snow, and wool has nothing on you!

Allow Him to reveal His passion as Judge concerning your next steps starting now.

> *"Come now,* and *let us reason together," Says the Lord, "Though your sins are like scarlet, they shall be as white as snow; though they are red like crimson, they shall be as wool."*

> — ISAIAH 1:18

Prayer:

> *Father, I come before your Courts like Joshua, and I stand. With no defense for all my wrongs. I ask that you forgive me ...* (go for it, whatever comes to mind, tell the Lord).
>
> *I ask for clean garments, my soul washed in the cleansing blood of Jesus Christ.*

PONDER POINT:

If you have hesitations because of the places you have been, here are some profound truths to internalize;

- The Father does not show favoritism.
- God sees my heart. I choose to present my heart to Him. I begin a supernatural journey with Him.
- It doesn't matter how far or how long I have strayed; the Lord will accept me.
- My past will not count against me in the Heavenly Courts. I may have more to deal with than others, but I am assured of the same results – freedom if I stay the course.

A Man Like Us

Now, let us move on to the next verse, Zechariah 3:5

"And I (Zechariah) said, "Let them put a clean turban on his head." So they put a clean turban on his head and clothed him with [rich] garments. And the Angel of the Lord stood by." (AMP)

We are experiencing a shift in this verse. Out of nowhere, someone who seemed to be having a vision, an open vision, a dream, or whatever you had guessed in the beginning suddenly begins to give directions concerning Joshua. "And I said, ..."'

Earlier on, we wondered who the spectator was in this chapter; he was Zachariah. We also asked if this scenario played out through a vision, trance, dream, or in person. It now proves that Zachariah was present in Joshua's court session.

Three key things to note in understanding Zachariah's position in this passage are;

1. Zachariah is not just a spectator or a silent member in this whole event. But also an authority. Zachariah is actively involved in this encounter. He is not on the sidelines watching events unfold or dreaming of it, as some may presume.
2. He was part of Courtroom judication. He was able to identify that Joshua needed a new turban, and he gave orders for a replacement.
3. His orders received a response, and the Lord was pleased to stand by and watch him adjudicate.

Those who stood by and removed filthy garments off of Joshua, those who put clean clothes on him, are now following Zachariah's instruction. At Zachariah's direction, they put a turban as well as rich robes on Joshua. Per the Lord and Zachariah's instructions, Joshua was now fully clothed, from head to body, in the righteousness that comes from God and not by works.

Come on now! That a man like you and I can have a voice in the Courts of Heaven, give a decree, and be followed through by Heavenly beings is mind-blowing. Zechariah probably ate fish with his breakfast earlier that day, loved to dance, and may have worn sandals, just like you and me.

Like anybody else, he walked the streets of his neighborhood— a regular guy, known within his community. Yet, we find him fully functional in the Heavenly Kingdom as a spirit being.

"And the Angel of the Lord stood by"

— ZECHARIAH 3:5 AMP

The Angel of God stood by without interrupting Zachariah. Permit me to rephrase it by saying that the Triune God (Father, Son, and Holy Spirit) enjoyed standing by and watching His son operate in the authority they gave him; Just as it gave God pleasure watching Adam name all the animals in the garden of Eden. God framed man to operate this way from the beginning.

Get this. Zachariah was functionally living out of his Kingdom mandate not only on the Earth but also in the Heavens.

God framed you in His exact likeness. God has made it a priority that you function in this way. It is why He enjoys it when you display sonship. It is a place of absolute authority, not only on earth but also in Heaven's Courts. I hope you can feel excitement swell up within you.

The Judge of all the Earth calls us judges in His Courts. He loves to watch us do what we see Him do. He loves to watch us display His ways as sons made in very likeness and nature as God.

In summary, the Lord rebuked Satan concerning Joshua, after which He and Zechariah gave instructions to adorn Joshua. Restoration decrees for one son of God (Joshua) in the Heavenly Courts involved the Lord, another of God's sons (Zechariah), as did all the angels and members of the Heavenly Courts.

Walking Among Angels

"And the Angel of the Lord [solemnly and earnestly] admonished Joshua, saying, 7 "Thus says the Lord of hosts, 'If you will walk in My ways [that is, remain faithful] and perform My service, then you will also govern My house and have charge of My courts, and I will give you free access [to My presence] among these who are standing here."

— ZECHARIAH 3:6-7 AMP

Again we find the Angel of the Lord speaking in a voice that only God would. He gives Joshua an admonition that, if observed, would enable him to operate in God's house in the way Zachariah did.

According to the dictionary, to admonish someone is to warn or reprimand them firmly or to advise and urge someone earnestly. So basically, this is the Lord telling Joshua to get his act together; and live his most authentic life as a priest and a son of God.

Zechariah was already walking in God's ways and judging in His Courts; that is why when a living priest in his day stood in the Heavenly Courts, he received a call to step in to adjudicate as a live judge on the earth.

The admonition Joshua is now receiving would enable him to have a say in the Courts, be familiar with the on-goings, and be an authority to give commands freely. Joshua's invitation to function in God's Courts depended on His willingness to walk in God's ways.

In return for Joshua's obedience, God promises to give him charge over his House and Courts, just like Zachariah had the charge of God's House and Heaven's Courts.

What this means for us is, God can assign heavenly jurisdiction to a man like you and me. We can have charge over the Courts of Heaven. Having responsibility in Heaven is within reach for us (see Ephesians 2:6)

Come to Mount Zion: The Courts of Heaven

In the earthly mount Zion, Mount Zion was a place of 24-hour worship. It was out of that glorious atmosphere of worship to God that King David would release divine decrees and judgments over the land.

What happens at Mount Zion could not be better summed up than in Isaiah 2:3

> "*Many* people *shall come and say,*
>   *"Come, and let us go up to the mountain of the Lord,*
>   *To the house of the God of Jacob;*
>   *He will teach us His ways,*
>   *And we shall walk in His paths."*
>   *For out of Zion shall go forth the law,*
>   *And the word of the Lord from Jerusalem.* "

The laws and ordinances that governed the land came out of Mount Zion. God teaches His people His ways in Mount Zion. Remember we studied earlier it was a requirement for Joshua to walk in Heavenly places (see Zachariah 3:7)

God reveals His Path upon Mount Zion. Deliverance from demonic strongholds and bondages takes place in Mount Zion.

Justice takes place on Mount Zion. Restoration of what we lost happens when justice gets served, and we have our possessions.

> "*But on Mount Zion, there shall be deliverance,*
>   *And there shall be holiness;*
>   *The house of Jacob shall possess their possessions.*"

— OBADIAH 17

Now, the earthly Mount Zion was a picture of the Heavenly Mount Zion. What took place in the Heavenly Mount Zion was mirrored upon the Earth by king David. The activities and the results were similar.

When we look at the activities, we see a setting where God is the

Judge. In studying Scripture, be attentive to how it describes God in different parts of the Holy Scriptures that reveal His function in those particular moments. Here He is portrayed as a Judge, not Father or Ancient of Days. So, you instantly know you are stepping into an arena where judgments and rulings will occur.

The Bible calls it Mount Zion, the Heavenly Jerusalem. Here we also notice the legal position in which Jesus is portrayed, not Redeemer, Savior, etc. but as Mediator. He is the Mediator in this place.

We also see witnesses here; the spirits of just men made perfect are all here. The angels of God are also here. Fascinatingly, the Blood of Jesus is here, and it has a voice. It is speaking for you. We know here that Abel's blood spoke, and God immediately judged Cain.

Now then, Jesus's Blood is saying much better things concerning your life than what Abel's blood spoke for him. How about that Jesus spilled His blood on your behalf, and so is defending you? You bet the Judge will rule in your favor. If the Judge could step into the Earth realm and judge Cain, how much more will He do for you when the devil comes at you?

It fascinates me every time I read in Hebrews 12:22-24: "*22 But you have come to Mount Zion and to the city of the living God, the heavenly Jerusalem, to an innumerable company of angels, 23 to the general assembly and church of the firstborn who are registered in heaven, to God the Judge of all, to the spirits of just men made perfect, 24 to Jesus the Mediator of the new covenant, and to the blood of sprinkling that speaks better things than that of Abel.*"

These Scripture verses tell you to come. You come and stand before a company of mighty beings that bear witness that you are a son of God. These witnesses are rooting for you, and their voices are powerful. Key into your purpose and consider the powerful company you come into when you come to the Heavenly Mount Zion. There, you have:

- God – the Judge
- Jesus – the Mediator
- The blood of sprinkling. The voice of Jesus' blood speaks in Mount Zion. It is where you, every spirit being and angel

hear the speaking blood of Jesus gushing out & speaking forth on your behalf. It declares you redeemed and all of your sins (of which the accuser levies against you) forgiven.

- An innumerable company of angels
- The General Assembly
- The Church of the Firstborn who are registered in heaven
- The spirits of just men made perfect.

Many things such as deliverance and freedom to walk in God's ways will happen for you when you come to Mount Zion. You have come to a place of God's mighty rule on your behalf. A place where Jesus sits enthroned, yet in Mediation for you. You have come to a place where so many Heavenly habitants gather to assist you. The Court of Heaven will always provide you with justice. Some may call it a rigged Court because of all the support you already have at your disposal, so do not hesitate to come. Just come!

My beloved, this promise is available to every believer in Christ Jesus today. You can also be functional in God's Court. You have access through Jesus to present yourself before God like all other members of His Courts. You can walk among the angelic beings and sons of God.

These were men like us. I believe that with this possibility, you will see that God gives His children access to function in Heaven's Courts today. He has called you to bring His justice to bear in your life and the lives of those around you. However, there is a requirement. There must be total obedience to God's ways and living a life of submission to Him.

The precursor to having that responsibility in Heaven is walking in the ways of God and keeping His laws. Like Joshua, God will give us places to walk, not on the earth but among those standing in God's presence. Hallelujah!

You can have charge of God's house and courts today if you will walk in His ways. God would later in the Gospels introduce His Son – Jesus – as the Way (see Johns 14:6). To follow the Way is to follow Jesus intimately.

It is crucial to note; this lifestyle is not after death but a life with God in His Spirit realm while also living on earth. I know this may

sound like going against the grain. It might even sound like breaking a
belief system here, but it is the sole purpose of walking in His fullness.

"These that stand here" (Zechariah 3:7). Refers to many angels, heavenly beings, and humans like Zechariah who have become familiar
with the pathway into Heaven and back into the earth. I tell you many
will be so shocked to discover later in their spiritual journey that some
of the ordinary people they knew and even hung out with were walking
in heavenly places. They will later find that these people were actively
involved in their existence in Heaven while still on earth by the Holy
Spirit's power.

It is a reality that is ours as it was for Zachariah and Joshua, and
several others. Will you enter in? Or will you remain in the earthly
belief system craftily enacted by the father of deception and lies
(Satan), placed within the religious enclave; inscribed in doctrines that
seek to manipulate people, thus shutting them out of God's Kingdom?
(see Matthew 23:13)

We must choose to break free from the limitations of this physical
realm. I urge you not to make any man's limited reality of life with God
your own reality. Choose to receive all that is available to you in the
Spirit and from your intimate relationship with God.

A Broken Belief System

Jesus addressed the religious system of His day. In Matthew 23:13, Jesus
rebukes the Pharisees, saying:

> *"What* sorrow *awaits you, teachers of religious law and you Pharisees.
> Hypocrites! For you shut the door of the Kingdom of Heaven in people's faces.
> You won't go in yourselves, and you don't let others enter either."*
>
> — MATTHEW 23:13 NLT

They knew the truth about Heaven's accessibility. They chose not to
go in because they would not commit to walking in complete obedi-

ence to God. They chose lifestyles that gratified their passions. To please their father, the devil, they taught doctrines that hindered people from understanding this truth was attainable.

If they won't go in, why not let others who want to go into God's Kingdom do so? There is a kingdom that has been actively working against your intimacy and access to God. That kingdom is active within the religious system today as it was then.

Through the ages, many religious circles have played a significant role in restricting access to Scripture. Some religious systems still rely on only a priest reading the Bible to them. When you read historical accounts of the many lives lost for us to have access to God's word, you will understand the enemy's battle for your soul is real. Lives sacrificed, so we have the opportunity of holding that Bible in our hands.

It's incredible how blessed we are today. How can we neglect such a blessing to have this knowledge of God's Word in our day? It is luxury we now have access even on phones.

I hope you are beginning to have a glimpse of the strength of the opposition against anyone accessing the Kingdom of God. It is still happening all around us. Whereas this example I make is with regards to religious systems denying people access to the Scriptures they had, what Jesus was talking about was having access to go in and be present in God's Kingdom realm.

Just like in that day, Jesus, your Redeemer, is not happy about religious lies/ belief systems that have oppressed you. Be wise and know that your walk with God should not be impeded by belief systems that aim to stop you from entering and operating from within God's Kingdom as sons and daughters of the Most High God.

What do you want framed around your life? Which of these do you desire? True revelation stemming from an intimate relationship with Abba-Father? Or barriers and boxes set in place by the enemy to restrict and cause you to live a lower nature that does not align with the truth of who you are?

God gives us free will. We choose how far we want to go with Him (see James 4:8).

Prayer:

Father, I pray for this amazing brother/sister to receive clarity into this truth, this mystery stored up in Your Word for ages. I pray that as many as read through these pages will realize the truth of who they are in You. The entrance of Your Word brings light; Your Word is a light unto our path, so right this moment, let the light be released. Clean them of belief systems that are against embracing Your truth. Cause them to see clearly and walk through this brightened passage into Heaven and back out into the earth in Jesus' mighty name!

Lately, the Lord has been reminding me that we are in the fulfillment of Habakkuk 2:14. And I am here making sure to declare it to you. Let it be so in your life and mine, In Jesus's mighty name. Amen!

"But [the time is coming when] the earth shall be filled
With the knowledge of the glory of the Lord,
As the waters cover the sea."

— HABAKKUK 2:14 AMP

11

JESUS REVEALS OUR SPIRIT REALM ENGAGEMENTS

~ We Desire that the Devil goes out of Business with Every Generation from now on ~

~

THE DATA

Earthly operations are pretty similar to spiritual operations, so I will use an earthly depiction to reveal spiritual truth. In this instance, a business model will work to explain how the devil goes about his business.

Having a business is a gift from God. Joseph, Solomon, and many people of God were successful businessmen. Satan's spiritual business is different from having a business. I am only giving you a picture to facilitate your understanding of how business happens in the spirit realm. Make no mistake that God also pulls out all the stops for your success in your spiritual journey.

I desire that you are empowered to be vigilant as you go about your walk as a spirit being on earth.

Earlier, at the beginning of Chapter 7, we discussed *the merchant*.

We saw that successful merchants rely on how well they know their target market. For a business to succeed, a company carries out statistics on people based on geographical region, age, race, finances, places they shop, their likes, spending power, etc.

They gather relevant information on the target demographics, which they analyze into data for staging an effective marketing campaign. I would love to reiterate that the data is the most valuable tool for a merchant's cause and success.

With the data, the merchant creates marketing strategies. Sales teams can create an enticing and convincing pitch for their product. Their plan centered on making the target audience feel like they need the offered product or service to satisfy their appetite or need.

As a spirit being, notice that the merchant operates in this way towards you. Whenever you feel coercion towards the things God protects you from by saying not to do, know that you are a target market for this merchant - Satan, in that area.

The data received enables a company to streamline its product and services to their target market's interest – the things they will likely fall for; it reveals an area of weakness. At the height of intelligent marketing are the most susceptible temptations spawn from the data analysis; it guarantees transactions happen.

Like with marketing courses, *the merchant* (Satan) always has a motive or agenda. It is to get as many to fall in love with his product ideas, whatever the cost, and give money/value in exchange for the product offering.

The more persuasive the sales agents are in getting results, the better the incentives they get. And make no mistake, Satan has his agents all out and about. I call these agents of Satan, Satan's sales team.

Fundamental Truths of Satan's Attempts at Your Spirit Life

Without the necessary evidence (papers) to prove you are a willing party for the repercussions you receive, Satan cannot win any case against you. Satan seeks ways for legal rights to prevail when he comes against you with his accusations. It is the same old trick, the same old methods all over Scripture and today.

Balaam and Balak's interaction gives us further insight into how the enemy gets a person to break YHVH's hedge of protection. It is the only way that gives him legal rights to afflict. It is similar to his approach towards Job.

To get a full picture, Numbers 22-25 are three chapters worth reading. Balak saw the incredible feats the people of Israel had done in destroying the nations around them. He was scared of the Israelites and sought a spiritual way to attack them.

Spiritual attacks are a designated way to catch you off guard. It is a covert way people can send destructive weaponry against you, which you may not know exists. These sorts of attacks can bring confusion to the life of the victim. It can also bring sickness, pain, dullness, poverty, shame, and stagnation to an unsuspecting victim's life.

~

CURSES

When an evil person feels threatened, they may seek avenues to attack the perceived threat. Those with diabolic tendencies turn to cowardly undetectable ways – usually involving the use of a curse. Typically, a spiritual attack is more often the performance or outcome of a curse.

Curses can come by way of an evil person releasing demonic entities to work against another. They may do so by speaking evil words against a person.

Another commonly used method evil people use to send curses at their victim includes occultic instruments/practices, like casting spells, calling the victim up in a mirror, and some diabolical concoctions on personal items like clothing or hair of their victim.

It may be that they have a vendetta against you for something you may have done or said to them. Sometimes you may not even be aware of what you did or said to offend anyone, much less intended to have caused any offense.

That said, there are cases where someone is out to witch-hunt a person for no reason at all. Some have presented me with instances of waking up with nicely cut circles on their scalp or scars that appear like they had suffered beatings, all from a dream. These are common when there is a curse in effect against someone.

There was this case of a lady. This lady had gone to live with a friend to assist her during childbirth. However, not long after having her baby, she presented bruises on her body and nicely cut circles on her head - her hair cut in those places. She reported she was unable to sleep since having her baby. She went on to lose subsequent babies till the Lord delivered her from the curse.

If you find yourself in such a situation, quickly seek deliverance from those curses. Present it before The Righteous Judge of all by going to the Courts of Heaven.

A person who places curses or seeks to put a curse on you is in a deal with your ultimate enemy – Satan. God's people are to partner with God's Kingdom at all times. We are to bless people and not to curse them. The bible states that as God's people, we are never to curse people even in persecution.

Apostle Paul, writing to the believers in Rome, admonished them, saying, "Bless those who persecute you; bless and do not curse." (Romans 12:14)

Unfortunately, when done, curses often are released on groups of people, e.g., a family, nation, race, or a religious group. Those kinds of curses can go undetected for generations. These curses keep flying around and landing on unsuspecting lives for ages until a person chooses to go before God and have Him deliver them from its stronghold.

> "Like a flitting sparrow, like a flying swallow, So a curse without cause shall not alight."

> — PROVERBS 26:2)

Let me pause and emphasize that to overcome spiritual attacks that come at you, you need to:

- Go before the Courts of Heaven and plead your case to God. As the righteous Judge, it is His great pleasure to rule in your favor.

- Live a life of surrender to God. It also helps deter the enemy's plans,

- Walk by faith; When a person chooses faith in the Lord God, they walk in His pleasure, making it very difficult for *flying curses* (those without cause) to rest on them.

In previous chapters (of this book), we saw that Job and Joshua did everything externally right, but that didn't stop the devil from coming after them. However, when they stood before God, it was a game-changer for them.

When a person's life threatens Satan, he finds ways to cut them short. When your life threatens someone evil, they will seek ways to attack you via any evil and dark means they know. In doing this, they choose to partner with the devil to come at you. Demons are always willing to do the bidding of the devil big time. A curse is one of such spiritual weaponry an enemy uses.

In Numbers 21, Balak wanted to enact a curse on the Israelites and disarm them militarily so he could triumph over them. Balak feared his defeat would come if he faced the Israelites in battle. So, Balak came to Balaam to help him execute this wicked scheme. It is the same way Satan fears his defeat will come from the sons of God.

Barak goes seeking someone who he thought could curse or put a spell on the Israelites. He went ahead to lure Balaam with several gifts. He even sent dignitaries to entice Balaam into executing his plan. These presentations enticed Balaam; I call them *spiritual business product offerings*. People of God, beware of the devils product offerings!

However, Balaam's attempt at cursing the Israelites ended up in him blessing them instead.

As a people who remained in their Godly hedge and covenant, they were under God's blessings. Balaam couldn't curse what God had blessed. And so, Balak dismisses Balaam without a reward.

Years ago, a man got delivered from the occult by the power of God. This man would later confess to how they would go inside a person's life to corrupt them by sowing demonic seeds and desires while being agents of Satan, whom they referred to as Lucifer. He recounted the experience that began his freedom.

Once, when they attempted spiritually accessing a certain man of God, he said they saw fire within him that would not consume him. However, they got burnt; and ran out of the man of God.

Out of fear and shock, he recounted how he had expressed his concerns to Lucifer. He recalled asking Lucifer, their evil master, "why is this man in a fire that does not consume him?" Lucifer told him not to worry.

Typical of a deflecting devil; instead of answering him with the truth, Lucifer said they should keep watch and continue making attempts to corrupt the man's life until they sense the fire dwindle. Lucifer then went ahead to advise they should make a significant attack on the man of God at the decrease of this spiritual fire.

It also helps answer questions of how mighty men of God fall. It is hard for demons to function if they can't access that person standing in the way of their assignment. A raging army of frustrated demons waiting to attack, but all watching out for a launch window.

It always reminds me of this story in Jeremiah 20:9 about how Jeremiah, the prophet, had a fire in his bones (see Jeremiah 20:9). God's throne is encased in burning fire (see Daniel 7:9-10). Your physical body can feel His fires whenever you get into intensive prayers. God's praying ministers are a mighty fire. Imagine this, God "...makes his angels spirits, his ministers a flaming fire," (Psalm 104:4 JUB)

Balak is a picture of the unrelenting nature of the devil, seeking to do evil at any cost. Balak was relentless in his pursuit; he again returned to Balaam with opportunities that fulfilled Balaam's fleshly desires.

Balaam became spurred into fulfilling Balak's desire due to the transaction Balaam had begun making. Balaam already entangled his soul in a spiritual trade by receiving gifts in exchange for information that would favor the curse. But God then sends His people angelic intervention.

In Numbers 22:23, an angel stands in Balaam's way with a sword to prevent his journey. The Lord also made Balaam's donkey speak to protect Balaam from being killed by the angel whose assignment was to protect the people of God (see Numbers 22:21-39).

Since Balaam failed in every effort to uphold his end of the bargain (with Balak) against God's people, he figured a way that ensured he saw through with his contract. It became the case of the enticed seeking to entice.

You see, Balaam had a clear picture of how the spiritual realm operates as we all should. Be not fooled; even Satan can disguise as an angel of light (see 2 Corinthians 11:14). So it is not surprising what Balaam does next;

- Balaam knew how to tune his *spiritual antenna* to hear God because false prophets can also hear God. However, their motives are what we have to consider. The gift of prophecy is from God, but false prophets will also lend their *antennas* to the devil to do his biddings. We can also read of a similar instance in 1 Kings 13:11-25.
- Balaam knew God's unchangeability in His stand concerning His people.
- Balaam was aware of how God's justice system operates. He knew that a man's partnership with Satan, to sin against God, can remove God's hedge and blessings from that man.
- Balaam knew that God does not force His ways upon a man. And so, if a man willingly sins, it breaks the hedge, and the Lord's covering will no longer shield them against enemy attacks. He could see how willful sin raises the accuser's chance at winning that case in court.

Actions Can Attract Curses

Our actions can attract curses, sinful ones especially. Balaam thought one way this curse could alight on the Israelites would be by creating opportunities that would appeal to the young men with high-flying passions. He figured, why not trap them to sin by presenting them with a chance to satisfy their innate desires? The hedge of protection breaks, and the serpent, Satan, can strike. (see Ecclesiastes 10:8)

He hatches an *evil* plan. They got Moabite women to invite some Israeli men to dinner, satisfy their food cravings; and with some wine intoxication, get these women to have ungodly sexual relations with these Israeli men. That was the plan. Sex outside of marriage breaks your hedge. For generations, Satan continues to present sexual enticement as bait to pull great men and women out of their Godly hedge and blessings.

Once the Israeli men willfully exchanged their covering on this demonic alter, Balaam was confident they would no longer be under God's protection. His plan would ensure they became exposed and vulnerable to a spiritual attack.

By knowingly engaging in sexual and spiritual harlotry, they naturally attracted a curse. The devil could then have legal grounds of accusations against them; the Righteous Judge being a God of justice, would, unfortunately, rule in favor of the devil.

"If the foundations are destroyed,
  What can the righteous do?"

— PSALM 11:3

The curse of Balak and Balaam came into effect. The Israelites will receive the consequences of their choice via a plague, and Balak would have won. The demonic world triumphed in that case.

"Look, these women caused the children of Israel, through the counsel of Balaam, to trespass against the Lord in the incident of Peor, and there was a plague among the congregation of the Lord."

— NUMBERS 31:16

Many curses are successful against people when they are in business with the devil. I love how my spiritual mommy often refers to such a curse as being "self-acquired."

But Balaam and Balak were not free from God's judgment for their part in leading God's people to sin. However, even when someone else is the cause of our demonic trade, we still suffer the consequences of our choices and (or) actions.

The Lord was not pleased with the human agents that led to Israel's failure either. Jesus would later address His displeasure over these sorts of demonically inclined churches in Pergamos many years later, in Revelation 2.

"Nevertheless, I have a few things against you. There are some among you who hold to the teachings of Balaam, who taught Balak to entice the Israelites to eat things that were sacrificed to idols and to commit sexual immorality."

— REVELATION 2:14 TPT

If you are someone who the devil has used to bring others to fall, you must recognize the gravity of your sin. You have to understand that you have allowed yourself to sit in Satan's seat. You must repent and seek deliverance from making such evil trade that hurts God's people.

There is no mystery about Satan's strategies. Balaam advised Balak to get the Israelites to sin, knowing their sin will turn them away from God. This false prophet, Balaam, knew something about how to create legal evidence against God's people. Satan's kingdom was now turned towards them, trusting that the Israeli men's choices and actions will make them succeed in enacting a curse. It works well for Satan when we choose his ways, as this gives him legal grounds to afflict us. Sadly, the Israelites played right into his alley, and many of them perished as a result.

In Numbers 23, the Lord did everything to bless His people in the face of demonic plots against them. God will go to great lengths to protect you from the assault of the devil; however, He is helpless when instead of partnering with God for our continual blessings, we smear ourselves by our choices.

Maybe, if Israeli men had prior information that Balak instigated the demonic setup with the Moabite women, they would not have engaged in the feast, let alone have ungodly sex with them.

The truth we must know is that we may never get a prior warning or any information about the things the demonic kingdom is setting up against us. They are counting on our responses to the daily temptations before us.

We may never have information on the people who did or attempted to curse us either; however, those curses become effective when we break our hedge.

My prayer is that you will realize that the devil is always plotting against us. That one fornication, that one drink, that one drug, one act of disobedience, one careless moment, one seemingly innocent act of letting your guard down are all the setups it takes to get you hooked. It will take you down in the end if you choose not to repent and return to God.

A compromise here and another there, to what extent? No one ever imagines they would deteriorate to the degree they eventually end up. That is why it is common to hear people, once held in high esteem, speaking of their unfortunate fall, say things like;

"I don't know how it happened,"

"I don't know what came over me."

While some still bewildered would say,

"I would never do that in a million years,'"

"I can't explain how I got here."

Yet again, others will go like,

"It is not in my character because I wasn't raised this way," or

"I didn't see that coming."

Our life on earth is a constant battle in the Spirit realm (see Ephesians 6:12). The Spirit realm is active concerning your life. The Lord calls us to live a sober life and never assume that any one of us is above temptation (1 Peter 5:8-9). Only Jesus overcame all temptation.

> **18** Because He Himself [in His humanity] has suffered in being tempted, He is able to help *and* provide immediate assistance to those who are being tempted *and* exposed to suffering.
>
> — HEBREWS 2:18

All of Heaven is rooting for us to succeed. It is only through Jesus that we can overcome. He cautions us to understand that our journey on earth is not an easy one. We could easily fall into sin by assuming we are above sin.

> *"Therefore let the one who thinks he stands firm [immune to temptation, being overconfident and self-righteous], take care that he does not fall [into sin and condemnation]."*
>
> — 1 CORINTHIANS 10:12 AMP

Prayer:

If you have gotten to this point and feel condemnation,

> *I pray Satan's lies be broken off your life right now. I release the love of God over your life in Jesus' name.*

You need to know that Lord does not condemn you. So, as you turn your heart, in repentance, away from the ways that brought condemnation upon you, let the power of His love clean you today.

Therefore, we loosen every stronghold of condemnation against you in your new walk with God. We silence every whisper of darkness against you. We decree that you are victorious in Jesus' name!

"There is therefore now no condemnation to them which are in Christ Jesus, who walk not after the flesh, but after the Spirit."

— ROMANS 8:1 KJV

Understand that condemnation thrives in a lifestyle that enjoys sinning. The moment you turn towards God in repentance, the blood of Jesus blots that sin out of your life. Again, your choice is the determining factor.

Through time, we have known that God is never one to impose. We have free will, and the Lord would love that we choose His love any day over carnality, but He knows we will be in situations we may not always choose Him. Through the sacrifice of Jesus, God has made way for us to deal with that seed of sin that makes us vulnerable to worldly, and demonic seductions.

God is not happy when we fall, and He never condemns us forever. God continues to love us regardless of our failings and choices. He gives us several chances every time. All of Heaven expects you to win. The angels assigned to our lives do not get reassigned to others because we haven't responded to God's call. They continue with you, ministering to you and working tirelessly to see you fulfill your great call (see Hebrews 1:14).

Whenever you feel condemnation, understand that God knows it is not the end. We read about David, Paul, and Peter, and we see how these people became more successful in their destiny in spite of a fall.

These are examples of the lives that await us; after a fall, we must get up, repent daily, and receive God's empowerment for each day.

A consistent pattern in Scripture is that God loves to turn the tables against the devil. It is one of God's great ways that encourage us to stay the course in resisting sin and the devil.

By the mercies of God, He turns curses into blessings. There are many accusations Satan has presented against you that God, the Righteous Judge, has thrown out of His Court. In His loving-kindness, He showers you with His blessings to the shame of your accuser.

Now, read the following Scripture verses carefully and note how the Lord suffered the accuser to get nothing against His people.

> *"An Ammonite or Moabite shall not enter the assembly of the Lord; even to the tenth generation none of his descendants shall enter the assembly of the Lord forever, 4 because they did not meet you with bread and water on the road when you came out of Egypt, and because they hired against you Balaam the son of Beor from Pethor of Mesopotamia, to curse you. 5 Nevertheless the Lord your God would not listen to Balaam, but the Lord your God turned the curse into a blessing for you, because the Lord your God loves you."*

— DEUTERONOMY 23:3-5

Jesus is against the deceiver and the lies showing up within his people. Inspired by the Holy Spirit, Apostle John writes: "But I have a few things against you because you have there those who hold the doctrine of Balaam, who taught Balak to put a stumbling block before the children of Israel, to eat things sacrificed to idols, and to commit sexual immorality." (Revelations 2:14)

Recall in Chapters 6 and 7; we discussed extensively on *Trades* and *The Merchant*, respectively. Well, now you see how Balak made the Israelites buy his merchandise by enticing them with sexual sins, a typical bait for man.

All they needed to do was make a trade and break the hedge around them. Satan had legal rights to afflict them. The serpent will strike every time we break our hedge (see Ecclesiastes 10:8).

Similarly, the devil will devise ways to lure people into breaking the hedge by bringing them into sin covenants. The devil will present the glittering aspects of sin. A spiritual transaction occurs when we fall for his merchandise by engaging in his trade (refer to Ch.6). He will then pay us with accusations leading to spiritual death & destruction. Again,

I recall, my sweet mentor calls the results of willful sinning "self-acquired."

When you deliberately sin against God, you begin to feel dead in your spirit; you become an easy target for the enemy. You expose yourself to shame, brokenness, curses, and in some instances, sicknesses.

The devil will also provide significant incentives and rewards to all his agents and demons who will go out to close these deals for him. The more they execute, the more the tips, and the more they gain ground over human territory.

This hideous cycle can go on for generations. Until one stands up within the Courts of Heaven to repent of it and deal with the desire that first gave room for the devil to succeed with his product offerings.

Based on the strategy we have seen in operation in the case of Balaam against God's people, the Israelites, and that of Satan against Job in the previous chapters, we can establish some fundamental truths of Satan's attempts at every child of God.

The consistent search for grounds to pick apart in all the cases mentioned proves beyond reasonable doubt that;

1. The Devil will Seek out Loopholes.

If the enemy fails to succeed in having you break your (God's) hedge, and because you are so pleasing unto the Lord, the enemy will find legal grounds to accuse you. He does this so he can seek permission to have you tried or sifted.

> "Peter, my dear friend, listen to what I'm about to tell you. Satan has demanded to come and sift you like wheat and test your faith."
>
> — LUKE 22:31 TPT

There is nothing that the devil can bring against us without seeking permission from God. In Job's case, he had legal grounds based on Job's motives for serving God.

2. People Partner with Satan to Effect Evil Intents.

When a person goes out in pursuit of a way to bring a curse on another, they are actually going into partnership with Satan. But as a child of the most high God, when such persons come against your life, they fail if you stay within your hedge.

So, beware of the rising passions within you. Some friendships will surface based on your lustful desires. Satan and his agents will set you up with a way to fulfill those passions to your detriment.

BE INTENTIONAL WITH PARTNERSHIPS

The more you seek the Lord with all your heart, the more you grow in your partnership with God and His kingdom. You will also begin to attract kingdom-minded friendships that will blow your socks off. You will find similar people in the same partnership with you that will enhance your spiritual journey.

It is a beautiful thing to see that people who trade into the same kingdom build long-lasting partnerships. You are a family of God, born by the Spirit of God. God - the Abba Father - is your Daddy and will bring His children into His purpose. It is how God sets you up to fulfill your destiny; you are within a partnership that God already designed in His kingdom before He formed you in your mother's womb. See Jeremiah 1:5.

Seek for God's Kingdom realm partnerships, Holy Spirit born and not natural born. You can also have a natural-born as your Holy Spirit-born partnership in life, but there is safety in pursuing a Holy Spirit-born relationship in all your dealings.

I do not say this lightly, but I have seen many natural-born relationships open doors to manipulations, curses, and deep darkness because we are more vulnerable to people with whom we share family ties. Familiar spirits thrive within your acquaintances to access you. We shall discuss more on this in the sequel.

Families not committed to a partnership with God's Kingdom can bring in unnecessary hardships and open demonic doors of pain, sickness, and disease. While God has placed you there for a reason and a calling to pray for them and walk with them in love, you must seek to see them drawn to Christ Jesus and not the other way round.

However, when you recognize who your Heavenly Father is, you begin to see your heart and mind change regarding the true meaning of *family*. You will, in turn, strengthen your hedge and grow your spirit-man to attract your Heavenly Father's Kingdom children and partnerships.

What we want to happen is to have Satan's seed and root cut off. We want to experience the cleansing power of Jesus' blood by freedom from the desire for Satan's business. We are no longer likely to buy when he presents it or dangles that sin carrot in our faces. That is absolute freedom!

What we want is to ensure that we no longer tick the boxes as his target market. We desire that the devil goes out of business with every generation from now on because nothing he has will entice us. We want him to fail, with nothing he can use against us, for he no longer has a hold on us.

Like Jesus declared, "I won't speak with you much longer, for the ruler of this dark world is coming. But he has no power over me, for he has nothing to use against me." (John 14:30 TPT). We want to experience the power of being a new creation because we can then say these words about ourselves like Jesus.

∾

THE NEW CREATION

"Therefore, if anyone is in Christ, he is a new creation; old things have passed away; behold, all things have become new."

— 2 CORINTHIANS 5:17

What does this new creation look like? The world should see him. This new creation is not like the former; he's an entirely different being.

1. A Carrier of the Spirit of God

> *"13 But when the Spirit of truth comes, he will ·lead [guide] you into all truth. He will not speak ·his own words [from his own authority; from himself], but he will speak only what he hears [from the Father], and he will tell [announce/declare to] you what is to come. 14 The Spirit of truth will ·bring glory to [glorify; honor] me, because he will take what ·I have to say [is mine] and tell [announce; declare] it to you. 15 All that the Father has is mine. That is why I said that the Spirit will take what I have to say [what is mine] and tell [announce; declare] it to you."*

> — JOHN 16:13-15 EXB

For that reason, he is constantly tuned to the Holy Spirit and will hear Him speak what Jesus is saying. He has a personal communicator empowering His spirit man and keeping him aligned with the voice of Him who sits at God's right hand. What created being has made it that close?

This new creation will have access to all that the Father has because Jesus has all the Father has, and He has given it all to you through the Spirit of God. You will speak in the voice of Jesus as you listen carefully to the exact words of Jesus speaking to you by the Holy Spirit.

2. A Bearer of The Name

> *"12 "Most assuredly, I say to you, he who believes in Me, the works that I do he will do also; and greater works than these he will do, because I go to My Father. 13 And whatever you ask in My name, that I will do, that the Father may be glorified in the Son. 14 If you ask anything in My name, I will do it."*

> — JOHN 14:12-14

The name of Jesus is weighty. No other name measures anywhere near to His. In *the name* of Jesus, demons flee. As bearers of His Name, this new creation walks in the highest authority. Jesus is committed to doing what the new creation asks in His Name. Not only that but God the Father receives glory when this new creation asks for anything in *the name* of *Jesus.*

Jesus is with the Father, assured that He has these new creation beings (for whom he died) who will do more extraordinary things from their heavenly sited position, right beside Jesus. Yes! From the highest throne in the universe, His new creation people would operate and do greater works than He (Jesus) did.

He does not make Himself less than them. Instead, He lays His life for them so He can have *duplicity* (the deposit) of Himself in them all. Not only is there His throne, but now thrones beside His. There are thrones for all He has adopted through rebirth (accept Jesus and have become born of the Holy Spirit).

Thrones of new creations He proudly displays and presents to His Father as sons - many sons. He speaks boldly of these new creations, which will believe Him and live in the way He has made for them.

3. Jesus Calls Us His Brothers and Sisters

"11 For both He Who sanctifies [making men holy] and those who are sancti-fied all have one [Father]. For this reason, He is not ashamed to call them brethren;

12 For He says I will declare Your [the Father's] name to My brethren; in the midst of the [worshiping] congregation I will sing hymns of praise to You.

13 And again He says, My trust and assured reliance and confident hope shall be fixed in Him. And yet again, Here I am, I and the children whom God has given Me."

— HEBREWS 2:11-13 AMPC

As a brother and sister to Jesus, Jesus promises His Father that He will teach us who our Daddy is. As His children, we are seeded in ABBA and born of God. You and I are made holy and in the same family as our Purifier – Jesus Christ.

> "*Everyone who is truly God's child will refuse to keep sinning because God's seed remains within him, and he is unable to continue sinning because he has been fathered by God himself.*"
>
> — 1 JOHN 3:9 TPT

So instead of attracting demons and their merchandise, our desires are on a dimension of holiness, drawing the angelic. We grow and foster our Abba-Father's business generations after us here on earth.

PONDER POINT:

Are you able to recognize the times you have compromised and made an ungodly trade because you wanted to please someone close to you? Would you have done it if that person wasn't a relative or friend?

The devil will use the people that appeal to your natural senses to get you to break your spiritual covering. No one is worth the pain of getting your spirit-man entangled with the devil. You are borne of God and will not think of yourself as a flesh-borne being anymore.

You must guard your spirit against the flesh's influences because they have a tremendous spiritual impact on you. If only you saw how vulnerable you become without your hedge, you would trust God more with your life choices.

The Pattern to Pray: Engage The Righteous Judge

There is a prayer pattern where we must pray without losing heart. Jesus clearly illustrated that pattern. It is to seek justice persistently. Due to our accuser's practice in the Courts of Heaven, it becomes a responsibility for us to assume a comfortable position in Heaven's Court. There is no question about what we need to do.

In Luke 18, Jesus showed us another dimension to our spirit-life privilege as sons of God. Through His teachings and parables, Jesus showed us many facets of the nature of God. As the One who reconciles us to God, He shows us God's nature as Father, Creator, Friend, Ancient of days, you name it.

In the same Luke 18, Jesus introduces us to the facet of our God as the Righteous Judge. Within this passage, He shows us how we must approach God as our righteous Judge in Heaven's Courts. Finally, with all focus on God's commitment to the foundations of His throne - righteousness, and justice - we can always trust Him to move within these key pillars.

"Righteousness and justice are the foundation of Your throne;
Mercy and truth go before Your face."

(Psalm 89:14)

Therefore, Jesus shows us how to position ourselves to expect rulings from His throne. Jesus shows us a surer path to seek out God's righteousness and justice when faced with calamity, injustice, and troubles that do not reflect God's heart for us.

Many of us read Luke 18 and think it is merely a teaching of Jesus on persistence in prayer. More than that, Jesus draws us to the higher place of operations in the Courts of Heaven, where justice is always rendered. The key here is calling for "justice."

"Then He spoke a parable to them, that men always ought to pray and not lose heart, 2 saying: "There was in a certain city a judge who did not fear God nor regard man. 3 Now there was a widow in that city, and she came to him, saying, 'Get justice for me from my adversary.' 4 And he would not for a while; but afterward he said within himself, 'Though I do not fear God nor regard man, 5 yet because this widow troubles me I will avenge her, lest by her continual coming she weary me.'" 6 Then the Lord said, "Hear what the unjust Judge said. 7 And shall God not avenge His own elect who cry out day

and night to Him, though He bears long with them? 8 I tell you that He will
avenge them speedily. Nevertheless, when the Son of Man comes, will He
really find faith on the earth?"

— LUKE 18:1-8

In the first verse, we see Jesus giving a powerful insight into how
we **ought** *to pray and not give up.* The word "ought" is used to indicate
correctness, a pattern of doing something. The Webster's dictionary
describes it as a duty, a natural expectation, a moral obligation. Jesus
shows us that seeking justice in Heaven's Courts is our moral obligation. It is a responsibility, people!

You and I have judicially mandated duties. And creation expects us
to live up to our responsibility to establish justice, God's way, in our
lives and our world.

It important to note that Jesus chooses to use a court setting to
demonstrate how we ought to pray and not give up; A bit of insight into
how operations go in the Heavens.

Everything Jesus Did and Said was Intentional

A widow depicts a vulnerable person who has lost a loved one. It
describes someone with known pain, trauma, loneliness, sadness, and
all kinds of things. You see a picture of someone just trying to get by or
in search of a way to put their lives back together. She knew not to
engage with her adversary over the troubles he was causing her.

She had an enemy, an adversary, she needed to be free from, and so
she took it upon herself to come before the court to plead her case. In
the Luke 18 case, the judge was unrighteous, so he didn't pay much
attention to her. But the bottom line is (and this where persistence
comes in) that her persistence caused even an unrighteous judge to rule
in her favor.

Jesus emphasized the difference between an earthly judge and our
heavenly Judge as well. Whereas a lay judge may act based on their
beliefs and unrighteous predisposition, God the Righteous Judge is

constant in His position for us. We are His chosen ones, and His verdict will favor us. Therefore, we should expect that His ruling in our favor is righteous and speedy. As we fulfill our moral obligation in this manner, we must place this sort of expectation on the Righteous Judge alone.

We have continued to establish that Jesus came to teach us about life as spirit beings who should impact both the Spirit and physical realm. Therefore, Jesus used parables - which are earthly stories with heavenly/spiritual meanings. He used illustrations of the spiritual world and paralleled them to the natural world to enable us grasp His teachings. To help us comprehend greater spiritual truths.

He was already taking them from earthly ways of operating to spiritual realities. These truths we engage with in our spirit ultimately fashion our lives on earth. He would consciously make sure these spiritual truths were hidden from others but reserved for only His disciples.

> *10 And the disciples came and said to Him, "Why do You speak to them in parables?"*
>
> *11 He answered and said to them, "Because it has been given to you to know the mysteries of the kingdom of heaven, but to them it has not been given.*

— MATTHEW 13:10, 11

Jesus establishes to us who God the Father is. He also shows what His nature is as Father and as Judge. Finally, Jesus reveals how we can receive from Him every provision we need - be it a need only a Father can meet or a need for justice that only a Judge can give.

LIKE FATHER

Jesus gave us a parable of the lost son in Luke 15:11-32 in a situation where it had to do with a son of God who had lost his identity.

Unlike the scenario of a widow who knew she had the right to go to her Judge in light of her adversary's torment, it is different for a son who has lost all rights of sonship. Jesus showed us how a loving father would still restore the lost son, who returned to sonship.

> *"But the father wasn't listening. He was calling to the servants, 'Quick. Bring a clean set of clothes and dress him. Put the family ring on his finger and sandals on his feet. Then get a grain-fed heifer and roast it. We're going to feast! We're going to have a wonderful time! My son is here—given up for dead and now alive! Given up for lost and now found!' And they began to have a wonderful time."*

> — LUKE 15:22-24 MSG

Jesus's parable shows us God's nature as a Father who waits in expectation for His son's restoration. God is a Father who will run towards you, my beloved reader, and to anyone who will choose to return to Him no matter what they have done or how far they have been.

Another vital point to realize is that your place as a son of God is positional. You can see that with the father's reaction. The father's first action is to restore his son to his position by having him in new royal robes. Again, in Zechariah 3:4-5, isn't this just like our God to also order clean robes for Joshua when Joshua stood before God in Heaven's Courts?

The father also ordered a family ring and sandals on the feet of his prodigal son. All of these are symbols of acceptance and authority. Thus, the father restored his son to his rightful position. It was as though the son never relinquished it.

Your Heavenly Father desires to bring you into your position as His son. Therefore, it is all about your authority to exercise your calling. You are unmistakably recognizable with that robe as God's son before all spirit beings.

The ring you wear bears His name; therefore, His seal is upon your life forever. With the family ring, you can make decrees. An heir wears the sandal; you can walk in His authority, walk into Heavenly places, and exercise dominion.

Again, in Luke 11:10-12, we see Jesus liken God to the earthly father who would not give a stone when his son asks for fish.

> "Yes, [For; Because] everyone who asks will receive. The one who searches [seeks] will find. And everyone who knocks will have the door opened. 11 If your children ask [or son asks] for a fish, which of you fathers would give them a snake instead? 12 Or, if your children ask [or he asks] for an egg, would you give them a scorpion? 13 Even though you are bad [sinful; evil], you know how to give good things [gifts] to your children. How much more your heavenly Father will give the Holy Spirit to those who ask him!"

> — LUKE 11:10-13 EXB

Even though an earthly father gives good gifts, Jesus reveals God's nature to provide us with gifts, talents, and skills beyond the earthly realm. God will unreservedly provide us with the blessing and assistance of Himself, which will empower our spirit to operate beyond the cares and needs of this earthly realm. He will give us gifts that will authorize such a supply into our spirit, such that our physical being will overflow in the benefits.

God is the Father who gives good gifts, blessings, and abilities at the level of God. We must step into a heavenly mindset to ask. We are not to sell ourselves short but receive the fullness of God in the Spirit.

We are welcome to make requests that match His position. Make demands of God that do not just keep him at par with what your earthly father can do for you. It is His good pleasure to give us the Kingdom. See Luke 12:32.

We can see that God the Father is so willing to release all His fullness into us. God the Father desires to put all of Himself into His sons to be like Him - that we can lack nothing and indeed reign like Him. The question is, will the sons of God enter in to receive all of their Father? Are the sons willing to become all their Father wants to give?

Invariably, asking for all of God's personhood is what God our Abba Father wants us to do. How better can you explain what Jesus was clearly showing us here? You must understand that the gift of Jesus

Christ to us was on a whole other level gift. As is written: "He who did not spare His own Son, but delivered Him up for us all, how shall He not with Him also freely give us all things?" (Romans 8:32)

He is a Father who gives us all things. Yet, all things pale in comparison to His son. What further proof does humanity need? God, our Father, spares nothing/no one for us. Yet, He withholds nothing from us.

Therefore, we must come away from all deception and embrace our Father in His reality; only then can we be in authentic existence, just like Daddy.

As Judge

Chapter 8 identified Satan's propensity to stay true to his nature as Ha'satan – the accuser.

All through Scripture, we see God remain faithful to His role as "Judge." He will not go against the foundation of His Kingdom. It would be a skewed Kingdom and will no longer stand.

In very nature, He (God) is the God of justice, just as the enemy is, in very nature, the accuser. Again, Scripture declares that "righteousness and justice are the foundation of God's throne" (Psalm 89:14).

The laws of the Spirit realm include that the penalty for sin is death. See Ezekiel 18:20. We best believe that God made way for us through the sacrifice of His son so we would no longer be victims of sin.

We cannot break the laws that determine which kingdom we belong to and expect the God of justice to be unjust. However, we can repent, and the blood of Jesus will clean us out from the consequences of sin. See 1 Corinthians 6:20.

Now that you can see from Scripture a baseline for where God's fatherly heart stands, we do well to understand how He rules in the seat of justice.

In Luke 18, where we read, Jesus stated that if an unrighteous judge would grant justice following the persistence of a widow with rights, we must know that God, who is the righteous Judge, would give us justice without question. Our part is always clearly defined in all the Court scenarios we have seen.

It is a choice we make to go to Heaven's Courts. We must get used to going there! The decision to go before the Judge has always guaranteed a verdict that favors God's people. We are to ask, seek, and knock (see Matthew 7:7).

For everyone who would go before the righteous Judge (the widow in Luke 18:1-8, Joshua the high priest in Zachariah 3, and Job in the book of Job), one thing stood out; they all received justice.

Using an earthly pattern, Jesus teaches us how we should go before God as the Judge in Heaven's Court in search of justice. He did not advocate going to argue with the adversary, as many do when they feel attacked by the devil. He is not a proponent for accepting abuse or oppression from your enemy - Satan. On the contrary, Jesus reveals that we have a right to correct the situation.

Jesus shows us how to defeat the devil when he comes to steal, kill, and destroy us. So it is in preparing our case and heading into Heaven's Court by faith. Just like the widow had the rights as a human being with a lawsuit against her adversary, we also have rights as spirit beings to go into Heaven's Courts in the Spirit realm.

Even an unrighteous judge on earth world rule righteously. Thus the widow received a verdict that favored her and stopped the enemy from harassing her. In other words, she received restraining orders against her adversary.

Since this is a depiction of the Courts in Heaven, Jesus is telling us that when we have an adversary coming at us, we ought to step into the realm of Heaven. We cannot succeed by exchanging words with the enemy. There was none of that in all those cases. We must recognize that the Righteous Judge will give our adversary restraining orders. Then, we will indeed walk out free from his ongoing attacks against us.

As spirit beings who have access to Heaven's Courts, Jesus provides us with a way out amid our painful circumstances. It is a pattern of praying in Heaven's Courts, and it works. He gives us justice for all our losses, justice for the hopeless, and our world.

In the places where the enemy has relentlessly accused us and stolen from us, Jesus assures us of receiving full justice and restoration. Therefore, we ought to step up and assume our responsibility in Court.

The Lord is God of justice. And being our faithful, loving Father and righteous Judge, He will not hesitate but will rule in our favor speedily when we step into His courts as we ought.

Right after that parable, Jesus tells a story about the Pharisee and the tax collector. In Luke 18: 9-14, the Pharisee felt righteous because he kept all the laws. He believed his righteous acts were his ticket of approval. In a way, the Pharisee reminds us of Job and Joshua, whom we have spoken about extensively. But only with regards to being religious in their actions.

Jesus was specific in identifying that the Pharisee was prideful. His actions and words displayed his lack of humility. The tax collector, on the other hand, admitted guilt and repented of his partnership with sin.

We see two individuals each engage a separate kingdom in their quiet place, but not so quiet as they are visible before an audience in the Spirit realm. Within the same story, Jesus reveals the superiority of repentance and humility. Both of which draws on the favor of the One who sits as Judge of all.

12

THE POWER OF REPENTANCE

~ A Force that Pulls you Closer to your Source ~

∾

THE GLORY STATE

The way to breaking free from ungodly trades is by repenting. John the Baptist lived and died heralding the soon coming Kingdom of God with no other than the powerful message of turning to God in true repentance. The power of repentance transcends both time and the physical. It is a spiritual exercise seen through Scripture where a human being can step beyond his fleshly limitations into his spiritual standing. It is God's provision and man's opportunity for return to his glory state.

Repentance from a life of sin is not only that one particular moment when a person turns away from walking in darkness. It is at the fore of choice to walk in the light of Christ Jesus. As powerful as that is, repentance is a lifelong arsenal in winning spiritual battles and establishing God's Kingdom in our lives as believers. We will always need to apply the cleansing blood of Jesus over our failures from daily engagements on this side of Heaven.

Please do not take for granted the value that Jesus Christ Himself placed on the power of repentance. It is all wrapped up in the purpose of being in Christ. He put the same necessity on sacrificing himself and his resurrection as He did on repentance and remission of sins.

> "Then He said to them, "Thus it is written, and thus it was necessary for the Christ to suffer and to rise from the dead the third day, 47 and that repentance and remission of sins should be preached in His name to all nations, beginning at Jerusalem. 48 And you are witnesses of these things."

> — LUKE 24:46-48

Repentance activates the purpose of His death and resurrection. His death and resurrection brought and consolidated the forgiveness of our sins. Jesus did for us what we could not do for ourselves; however, we can take His blood and apply it in times of our weaknesses. We can also engage the Holy Spirit, Whose groans help us in our weakness. See Romans 8:26-27.

In repentance, we agree to partake in what He has done. Every time we repent, we agree to His death and resurrection and His shed blood wiping away the sin we partook in.

Repentance – A Chain Breaker

Being forgiven breaks Satan's power over our lives. Jesus' sacrifice has given us a way out of hopelessness that would have clouded our lives. By that singular action, His name has brought us all manner of rewards.

The power to have your sins forgiven is in living a life of repentance. The power that destroys the strength of sin, addictions, and its consequences is enjoyed/received in a life of repentance. I describe it as the power of winning spiritual battles. Satan's wicked schemes cannot thrive in a life of repentance. Through repentance, we receive the reward of sins forgiven.

I pray the principle of repentance is stirred back into the body of Christ; because the enemy has found a way to remove one of the most potent spiritual exercises a person in the flesh can achieve for himself, lineage, nation, and the world at large.

With no redemptive place for the devil and his demons, they are furious, restless, and vicious. "8 Be careful—watch out for attacks from Satan, your great enemy. He prowls around like a hungry, roaring lion, looking for some victim to tear apart." (1 Peter 5:8 TLB). Resolving that since they can't win, everyone loses; they'd rather ruin it for everyone else.

Even if the devil were to desire repentance, he would be unable to. There is no remedy for him and his fallen angels (demons). No way can they right their wrongs or make things right for themselves. Their case is a downward spiral, whereas God has given us the power to choose.

We can choose to turn our lives around and go back to the perfect state of God's design. We can engage in a powerful spiritual exercise that rights our wrongs and makes the latter part of our existence more incredible than the former because we conform to God's image! (See Haggai 2:9)

A great thing to note in Scripture is having an in-depth look at the things God the Father, Jesus, and the Holy Spirit majored in; if we also major in, those would make a spiritual impact. And will ultimately impact our existence in this physical world.

Life-Changing Outcomes

In 2 Samuel 24:10, when David disobeyed God's instruction never to count the Israelites, David was faced with the punishment choice. God asked David to suffer by man or by God. In repentance, David chose punishment from God's hands rather than by the hands of man. God would bring forth a way of delivering an entire nation from death because David humbled himself before God in repentance.

The prophets of old knew this principle, preached about it, practiced it. (see 2 Chronicles 7:14, 30:9b, Psalm 38:18, and Joel 2:13) They knew it was a key that changed the course of events.

When you change your ways in repentance towards God, you also change the trajectory of the events or challenges that the devil sets to come to you. The issues you dealt with in your spirit, soul, and body also change. The changes that begin to occur around your kingdom and your temple include freedom from shame, guilt, low self-esteem, etc., and all the things the accuser throws at you as one who is messing around with his stuff (sin).

Other changes include walking in wisdom, discernment, and overall wellness, joy. You will need to pay attention to see the tremendous changes you begin to experience.

Write them down so you can remember them. Have records of your spiritual activities because they are more tangible than you have ever been drawn to see. We can identify the feelings of changes in our natural circumstances, such as when you have a child, when you bought a car, when you came out of debt, fell in love, etc.

When you make a wise financial decision and begin to reap the benefits, you naturally stick to that decision. You even start to teach other people how to live the good life you now have based on your choices and how those decisions changed your previous path.

Now, recognize that your spiritual decisions also have a more significant impact on your life. We have placed the activities in our spiritual life on the back burner for all our lives, so we cannot see the impact our decisions make on our spiritual well-being.

All hope is not lost, it's a new day, and you can begin to practice walking in the Spirit. Begin to practice observing the changes you feel within you; observe how you interact with the world around you when you make good spiritual choices. Begin to notice how you see people and how people act around you when you make a powerful spiritual choice like repenting.

Notice how much lighter you feel. Note the songs you sing, even unconsciously humming a tune (sounds of freedom), and things you have not done in a while. See that desire to love more, give more, etc., the list is endless, but you must take action when the godly desires come.

You know how you feel that pain in your body, and then the first thought you have is, oh, it may be cancer or some serious ailment. Oh, the google searches you make. By the time you speak to someone about it, you already sound like a doctor. Apply that level of awareness, focus, and cultivate the habit of researching and getting to know what's going on with your spirit like you do your body.

If you make this your new culture, you will never again underestimate the powerful spirit-being you are ever again. You must practice your sonship and no longer live your life only for the here and now. You are a spirit being with a soul, and you only live in the body. Live your life in your authentic original form. Do the things that speak to your primary existence and nature as a spirit being.

In the book of Jonah chapters 1-4, Jonah ran away from God, knowing the power that was within the message of repentance. He knew that no matter the lifestyle of sin a man lived and the extent a people group go in an attempt at defying God, God would forgive once they return to Him in repentance (see Jonah 4:1-2).

Even though there is no way to run and hide from God, Jonah would rather believe he could run than see God deliver people through repentance. Again, it proved the power in repentance as Jonah feared because that is all God needs to set His people free from Satan's damning accusations. It is beneficial to remember that there are legalities and protocols in the Spirit realm governing operations, just as there are legalities in the earth realm.

Jesus gave a parable about the prodigal son. He likened this parable to how God's love waits on us. In Luke 15:11–32, when the prodigal son asked for his inheritance, his father could not convince him otherwise. How do you convince a person whose heart has been captivated by sin? However, the Father waited.

The Father is always expecting you to return. After the prodigal son lost all, he came round to a love he had experienced – his father's love and provision.

Scripture says the son came to himself: "But when he came to himself, he said, 'How many of my father's hired servants have more than enough bread, but I perish here with hunger!" (Luke 15:17 ESV)

That is a fantastic description. When a person's life is on a trajectory of sin, he has lost himself. He is not himself due to his agreement/trade with a lifestyle that has removed him from his glory state. Such a person cannot remember who he is. He is not in a state of upholding his nature in God. After the prodigal son comes to himself (as he did eventually), he recognizes his failures and repents.

> *"And the son said to him, 'Father, I have sinned against Heaven and before you. I am no longer worthy to be called your son."*
>
> — LUKE 15:21 ESV

Thus the prodigal son shows a picture of a man returning to his glory state after coming to himself. It was pretty much the only lifetime message John the Baptist (the forerunner of Jesus Christ) preached (see Matthew 3:1-2). Repent!

BENEFITS OF REPENTANCE

In Acts 2:38, Peter preached on the power of repentance. God would show the power of repentance through generations to prove to you and me today that there is nowhere we have been, no evil thing done on earth that God will not forgive when we turn over to Jesus Christ in repentance. He will deliver; He will set free. He will save! Provision is made for us today through an even greater covenant in the body and blood of His son Jesus Christ!

1. It opens the doors for times of refreshing to come into your life. (see Acts 3:19). It brings you peace and balance. It gives you relief from anxiety.

2. We place ourselves at a vantage point to draw on God.

> *"Therefore tell the people: This is what the Lord Almighty says: 'Return to me,' declares the Lord Almighty, 'and I will return to you,' says the Lord Almighty."*
>
> — ZECHARIAH 1:3 NIV

Repentance is an action. A life of repentance calls for a change in our lifestyles. We have to make decisions that are consistent with repentance actively. By choosing to turn away from sin, a person is continuously aligning himself with God's ways.

> *"Do the things [Produce the fruit] that show you really have changed your hearts and lives [that prove your repentance; of repentance]."*
>
> — MATTHEW 3:8 EXB

3. It also repairs your hedge of protection when you break it knowingly or unknowingly.

God does not require that you operate from a work-based salvation mentality. You cannot earn salvation; therefore, do not allow the devil's lies, which tell you to work hard for salvation. When you say "yes" to God, you are transferred from the Kingdom in darkness to the Kingdom of Light.

4. You simply begin desiring to know God and operate in the new ways of His Kingdom. A fundamental change begins to happen as the Holy Spirit lives inside you. He helps you overcome your weakness and susceptivity to temptations.

The Holy Spirit trains you in the ways of God's Kingdom. God chastises those he loves (Hebrews 12:6-11), and so, when you fall, you will feel His conviction and subsequent discipline. You can call out to Him in repentance, and He will answer you. You will quickly rise from your fall, and it will be for you as though you never fell.

This is the way God's Kingdom operates. He wipes out your sins as though they never existed in you. You are the one who needs to erase those sin patterns from your memory and walk free from them. Even when the devil accuses you of them, you step into the Courts of Heaven and repent of them. You make it clear to the devil that he has no legal rights to bring you shame and condemnation for sins you have repented.

Now that God has got you back into His arms, He does not want the devil's ways operational in your life anymore. God is also very patient, and He will walk with you to see you mature in His ways.

As a son and daughter of God, repentance is one of God's Kingdom fruits you begin to have an affinity towards. It is the process of your restoration from sin. Make pleasing God your motive, and don't just seek to earn brownie points. The Lord sees your heart every time you come to Him. He will reward the fruit of repentance that you bear.

Indeed Jesus's sacrifice was once and for all. However, there is no record where *repentance from sins* is ever limited to a one-time event and should no longer be a practice after the initial repentance at conversion to a life in Jesus.

Satan will conjure up and twist the truth, and it will continue for generations until a person rises to stop it. He is the authority on twisting God's truth. That is why he is also known as Leviathan, which means "the twister."

"For Christ also suffered once for sins, the just for the unjust, that He might bring us to God, being put to death in the flesh but made alive by the Spirit."

— 1 PETER 3:18

"For the death that He died, He died to sin once for all; but the life that He lives, He lives to God."

— ROMANS *6:10*

So, whenever you hear the "once and for all" doctrine on repentance whereby people say, you do it once when you come to Christ, and that's it, please flee from that deception for it is destructive to you, and it seeks to steal your godly heritage! Our salvation is by faith alone, but an aptness to repent is vital for intimacy with the Godhead.

That Jesus died to/for sin once for all does not translate as repentance "once and for all." It is the price He paid for sin "once and for all" for humanity. It is a covenant made in His blood to redeem us from all sin every time we repent. He gives the repentant one the power to live above sin if they ask for it.

Jesus' sacrifice (of Himself) was a one-time event. It ended all other sacrifices offered to atone for sin, and it was a sacrifice that extended and covered all humanity.

On the other hand, repentance is ongoing for as long as we live in this bodily estate. You never get to a point within this estate where you are above repentance. Repentance is birthed from humility and surrender to the Lordship of Jesus Christ.

As people of God's Kingdom, we are in pursuit of the ways of His Kingdom and His righteousness. Like, genuine patriotic citizens of any earthly kingdom would. When self-righteousness and pride are in rule, it hinders true repentance.

We must be honest with ourselves that we sin even after accepting Jesus into our lives. To go on in our sin, without repenting, and assume that Grace covers us is not different from a life that enjoys their sins. It is the contrary; Grace teaches us to live above sin.

Grace empowers you to rise above temptations and sins' enslavement.

"For the Grace of God that brings salvation has appeared to all men, 12 teaching us that, denying ungodliness and worldly lusts, we should live soberly, righteously, and godly in the present age, 13 looking for the blessed hope and glorious appearing of our great God and Savior Jesus Christ, 14

who gave Himself for us, that He might redeem us from every lawless deed
and purify for Himself His own special people, zealous for good works."

— TITUS 2:11-14

We must detest sin and actively choose to end it in our lives. Grace has appeared to us all. Those who are willing will learn the ways of God. They will not only repent with their words, but their actions will prove their consistency.

Certain principles like repentance cannot be done away with as though there was an upgrade in our spirit. In our quest for knowledge, we have embraced along with it some complexity that has not done us any favors. Human knowledge puffs up, and that is the tool the devil promotes to make people think they know it all, that they have it all figured out.

But to draw closer to God in a relationship, one will quickly realize that spiritual principles are simple. They are the basics you've always known. Sometimes they may be twisted or altered by man, but you'll soon detect those through personal intimacy with Abba - Father.

There is no twist or manipulation of God's word that an intimate relationship with God in His Kingdom cannot fix. Abba will draw you into His name and refresh you by His Holy Spirit, whose abode is within you. Within the basics, such as cultivating a daily walk with Him, repentance, and humility, you'll find spiritual growth.

Repentance is Taking Responsibility as a Son of God

Ever thought about a force that pulls you closer to your Source? I mean, consider that Satan is the opposite of a draw to God. You must know that everything that attracts Satan is repellent to God. The refusal to repent is a repellant to God and an attraction to Satan.

Repentance is what the enemy can never do. He lost his place as the anointed cherub and never repented. In his nature is no inkling towards admitting wrong. It is the same with one who turns towards Satan and refuses to repent - exact nature. They fail to see that Satan likes to keep them bound in sin. Satan fears he will no longer have a hold on a repentant son of God.

We must have encountered a few people with such an unrepentant nature in them. You may even be that person that blames everyone else and takes no responsibility for the wrong action. We must understand the need to be delivered and set free from such a stronghold.

The good news is that we can step into the Courts of Heaven and repent of partnering with that prideful unrepentant spirit. The Lord will judge it, and we can step out free from all its claims to us.

You and I are powerful spirit beings made in God's image. However, we have been infringed upon by the devil. We need justice. Our world needs justice, the same protocol, but we must start with us.

A significant misconception (perpetuated by the devil) about repentance is that certain circles perceive it as a weakness. I can promise you that many of the things we think are weaknesses are the complete opposite in the Spirit realm. The ability to summon the courage and admit guilt is seen only in men of great integrity. To take responsibility for willfully engaging with sin and returning to God is the wisdom that keeps a king winning battles against his dreaded enemy.

PONDER POINT:

Have you ever wondered what would have happened if (instead of allocating blames) Adam and Eve took responsibility for their actions and repented? See Genesis 3:12-13.

Repentance is Spiritual Integrity - A New Way of Life

Our lives are to reflect repentance. Our lives must reveal the glory of God, which only happens when we repent.

> *"Prove by the way you live that you have repented of your sins and turned to God."*

— MATTHEW 3:8 NLT

The Lord gave me a vision of a lovely gem of light with a string rounded up into a ball around it. I just sat down and watched because it didn't look like there was anything to a bunch of strings at first.

As it unraveled, it revealed the most breathtaking gem with all its glory bursting out. At the same time, I saw layers of filth separating out. It got brighter and brighter as He finished pulling off the layers. After He got done, He said, "this is what you become when you repent. What do you say to that?"

Why would you hold onto the things that hinder you from revealing your glory? Indeed, it is a sight if you could see what you are becoming right now as you repent.

When you step into the Kingdom Realm of our God, you will know that repentance is heavenly power seen only by men of integrity who stretch out their soul (through desire) and reach out for it. It takes much courage to grab hold of it. It unravels with the person. As it unravels, so does all the stain of sin as the enemy looses his grip on the person. It's truly a fantastic sight to behold.

So, in reality, it is only attained by the spiritually brave. Repentance is a powerful key in aligning us with ABBA as His sons in a bond that frees us of every pre-existing counterfeit nature. See 1 John 1:9

Throughout Scripture, when anyone repents, it's as though they never sinned before. Their slates become wholly wiped off. Like they, our slates are wiped clean by the blood of Jesus. See Isaiah 1:18. Thus, we can have a fresh start - an empowered beginning by/in the power of the One who makes everything new.

Restores Intimacy – Repentance is a Magnet to the Father's Heart

Allow yourself to have comfort from God's word revealed in this verse; "As many as I love, I rebuke and chasten. Therefore be zealous and repent." (Revelation 3:19)

Sometimes, when you feel God chastise you for your actions, He is guiding you towards repentance. See God's discipline as a gift to you because you are His son and act immediately. It is the force that gives God the legal right to absolve you of all sin and accusations levelled against you.

As many as were David's sins (he used his power to take a man's wife and murder her husband, see 2 Samuel 11-12), so was he quick to acknowledge his failings and repent. He was willing to own up to his sin and accept all of what he deserved when Nathan confronted him.

God called him a man after his heart (see Acts 13:22) because of his humility and swiftness to repent. Psalm 51, written by David, is a great place to learn how to repent.

After realizing they hurt their parent, a child's genuine reaction is priceless—no matter the severity of the offense, the parent forgives and becomes naturally more endeared to them.

Before YHVH, we are always that repentant child, and the enemy is still that loser who will never comprehend the Father's love for us. It only draws you closer to God; it never pulls you away from Him. However, resisting repentance draws you closer to the devil's nature and further away from God. The accuser is pained to see what power we have when we repent because he loses his cases every time.

You must break through the resistance and see this treasure within, drawing you nearer to the nature of your Source once the whole unraveling occurs.

PONDER POINT:

What if Judas Iscariot, who constantly stole from the ministry purse and later betrayed Jesus, repented?

Now ask yourself, "what if I got on my knees and repented before God for my ungodly choices?" What if you took responsibility and placed yourself in the Hands of the One who delivers you?

Be honest with yourself; thus, I chose to watch that porn. I chose to fantasize about that thought. I chose to go there with that relationship. I chose to take resources that aren't mine. I chose to hate that person that hurt me. I chose to walk away from God. The list could go on and on;

however, this is your moment to be neither Adam nor Judas. The Spirit realm witnessed it all. Now, they will witness your return to your glory state. Seize this moment, my beloved. Repent!

HUMILITY – THE POSTURE IN REPENTANCE

There is a posture in repentance. It is not one of feeling self-accomplished, not of arrogance but one of humility. As an outward expression of the state of their hearts before God, men of God and the Israelites would put on sackcloth and ashes. (See Jonah 3:3-8, Job 42:6)

Sackcloth and ashes were a public sign of repentance and humility before God. This repentance posture was a practical way of aligning the body with what was in one's heart. They denied their bodies comfort.

The sackcloth was a coarse material usually made of black goat's hair. It was uncomfortable to the skin and had no aesthetic appeal. They abstained from anything that could trigger a sense of pride or anything that would puff up the flesh.

They put on sackcloth to show an acknowledgment of their frailty and devotion to God as Lord over their lives. They acknowledged that their bodies came from dust, hence putting dust or ashes on their heads and bodies.

The posture of sitting in ashes was thus declaring they are only subject to the Creator who took on the dust they were made of and made it into a being worth something. Therefore Job's immediate reaction to the sight of God in Job 42:6.

Recall at first; Job continually offered sacrifices to God all his life in the hopes of being justified by his actions. He, however, came to a shocking realization of his unfounded belief system by just one humbling encounter and quickly expressed his repentant heart outwardly - in dust and ashes before God. This action would generate a phenomenal response.

It was not this outward action that caused God to move. But God would intervene because of the humility that their activity demonstrated.

We also see a similar situation with Esther and Mordecai in Esther 3 and 4. With Nineveh in Jonah 3:5-7, King Hezekiah in Isaiah 37:1, Eliakim (2 Kings 19:2), King Ahab (1 Kings 21:27). The elders of Jerusalem (Lamentations 2:10), Daniel (Daniel 9:3), and the two witness (Revelation 11:3)

When these people repented with sackcloth and ashes (a symbol of humility), a consistent response through Scripture is that God delivered them from impending judgment. In some cases, the Lord healed and restored them.

"if My people who are called by My name will humble themselves, and pray and seek My face, and turn from their wicked ways, then I will hear from Heaven and will forgive their sins and heal their land."

— 2 CHRONICLES 7:14

As with repentance, humility is dissimilar to Satan's nature. Satan fell as a result of pride. He wants to be God; therefore, this posture of being humble before God is something he cannot attain. We can turn to God in humility. Not him though.

Humility is a powerful virtue to grow in. It is the virtue Jesus walked in. Jesus Christ was God but humbled himself before God and became man. He submitted His will to God by enduring the highest pain and the lowest abasement (See Philippians 2:5-11). He made this choice to see God have many children and see you and I come into our godly inheritance as sons of God.

God the Father would reward and exalt Jesus for being humble to bring forth God's desire for all of humanity. He would pay the costliest price and go low for God's children to go high.

You and I are sons of God due to Christ Jesus humbling himself to come as man, die, and rise into His exalted position. A position we can have by making Him our Lord and Saviour. We died with Him, arose with Him by the power of the Holy Spirit. We are seated in heavenly places with Him.

I love how the Expanded Bible version puts it, "But God's mercy is great [God is rich in mercy], and he loved us very much. 5 Though we were spiritually dead because of the things we did against God [our transgressions], he gave us new life [brought us to life] with Christ. You have been saved by God's Grace. 6 And he raised us up with Christ and gave us a seat with him in the heavens [heavenly places/realms]. He did this for those in Christ Jesus." (Ephesians 2:4-6 EXB)

The spirit world knows this; it's time we also fully understand who we are. Jesus's humility birthed us into sonship. It should be the powerful principle that keeps us within the confines of the rewards we have in Him. From this virtue of humility, Jesus got the name above all names (see Philippians 2:9). A name that every knee on earth and in Heaven must bow to when mentioned. A name demons tremble at, and Satan flees to his shame. Hallelujah!

Many of us have witnessed demons struggle to leave people's bodies while screaming at the mention of Jesus. These victories we experience come about because Jesus Christ, being God in very nature, would humble Himself and become a victorious man so we can be victorious men against the darkness in our lives.

Further, the Apostle Paul urges, "Have this same attitude in yourselves which was in Christ Jesus [look to Him as your example in self-less humility], 6 who, although He existed in the form *and* unchanging essence of God [as One with Him, possessing the fullness of all the divine attributes—the entire nature of deity], did not regard equality with God a thing to be grasped *or* asserted [as if He did not already possess it, or was afraid of losing it];" (Philippians 2:5-6 AMP)

Jesus would resist the temptation to grasp onto His exalted position (and rightfully so), a thing Satan could not do as an anointed cherub (a lesser being). Read Ezekiel 28:15-17 for reference.

There is a lot of history in the grand scheme that we need to understand.

Like Jesus Christ, God will exalt the humble person (see 1Peter 5:5-6).

Jesus Taught on Humility

> *"And the tax collector, standing afar off, would not so much as raise his eyes to Heaven but beat his breast, saying, 'God, be merciful to me a sinner!' 14 I tell you, this man went down to his house justified rather than the other; for everyone who exalts himself will be humbled, and he who humbles himself will be exalted."*

> — LUKE 18:13-14

Consider what Jesus said in this of a humble and repentant tax collector. This man received justification and exaltation for his humility and repentance. Talk about the benefits of repentance.

A humble heart is what attracts God. It was not so for the religious and proud. Trying to attain perfection by engaging in religious activities to reach God is not what attracts Him. But what attracts Him is our humility, a heart that is not puffed up but broken before Him (see Psalm 34:18-20, and 51:17).

Please make no mistake; the nature you exhibit will attract the realm of its Source. Every realm has its characteristic traits, and each realm will draw unto its kind as a magnet to metal. Either kingdom will begin to pick interest in you if you play by its rules.

Cornelius attracted God and received the benefit of a son of God by his choices even though he was not a Jew. Acts 10:2. If you desire intimacy with God and humble yourself, Heaven will turn its face toward you.

Humility is the nature of Heaven. Even angels rejected worship from every man they visited (see Revelation 22:9). It's a characteristic trait modeled by Jesus.

We became a part of God's kingdom due to Jesus humbling himself to become one of us. Humility is where the real power lies. It is where the scales tip and change happens beyond any opposition. The good news is that it is our inheritance (see 1Peter 5:6).

On the contrary, Lucifer, master of pride, was cast out of Heaven to the earth realm. And all he has been doing ever since is breed his kind. God resists the proud. God's Grace is sufficient to deliver anyone from pride and all sin; however, He is completely turned off by a nature that reeks of Satan (see James 4:6-7).

Humility is a virtue we can choose to walk in consciously. It may not be second nature to us. But we must understand that God always turns His face towards a humble person. Watch out for your soul.

Again, I would love to strengthen you against the "once for all" teaching of repenting once and done - this time regarding the devil's prideful nature. This type of doctrine only hypes up people already absorbed by an exaggerated sense of self. It creates prideful people. A proud person will always fall as Satan did.

"Pride *leads to destruction [comes before a disaster];*
a proud attitude brings ruin [pride comes before a fall]."

— *PROVERBS* 16:18 EXB

Remember that the twister will twist things by creating a belief system of puffing up the flesh. Thereby short-changing the body of Christ of great power and influence before God. What you get with this is a people that Heaven is disinterested in; you get a people where demons quickly flock around. And Satan has legal grounds to accuse, attack, and subvert God's Kingdom in them.

Persons who buy into the devil's lies begin by accept the grey areas as okay. They may not even notice how they compromise. They are the same ones that say God is too loving to send anyone to hell. They are the ones who say "God wants me to be happy, so if this makes me happy, then God supports me." These are the many ways of spiritual failure. It is how many gradually lose their place in God and end up as hell's candidates.

It does not happen overnight. One proud attitude after another gets your soul entangled in all kinds of spiritual agreements that you fail to see how far you have fallen.

On the contrary, a humble heart is always quick to repent of sin;

they recognize which Kingdom they belong, trade into, and make it a point to choose God regardless of their challenges.

Here is a good insight for a daily walk with the Lord;

- The closer you draw to God, you no longer desire to sin, which is one thing, but again, it becomes easier for you to walk in humility. Another thing is, you don't feel that strong sense of resistance towards repentance anymore - that's humility taking over your heart.
- Satan's core weaknesses are evident. Where Satan's weaknesses lie, we will also see, lies power that is ours if we walk in opposition to Satan's ways. His weaknesses are the things he is unable to do. Notice they are also the very graces Jesus excelled at in redeeming us. It was humility that brought Jesus to earth in the form of a man. In humility, being God, He underwent the cross.
- God, the Father, exalted God, the Son; because of His humility (See Philippians 2:6-11), you best believe He will exalt you too.

"He who did not spare his own Son but gave him up for us all—how will he not also, along with him, graciously give us all things?" (Romans 8:32 NIV)

- Jesus uses these powerful virtues that Satan cannot have to save us. He then gives us the ability to walk in these virtues to destroy Satan's powers further. As Jesus is, so are we in this world; therefore, Satan's weaknesses are our strength because we have embraced Jesus Christ. (See 1 John 4:17)

YOUR WINNING STRATEGY - THE MIND TO HAVE

Do not use limited reasoning to rationalize spiritual principles. As a believer and spirit being, you can think in Kingdom terms. When a kingdom is at war, it positions itself at a vantage point so it can win. You have to think in these terms. God wants you to begin to have this mind.

A powerful nugget of truth that unlocks great spiritual rewards is to have this same mind as Jesus.

"Let this same attitude and purpose and [humble] mind be in you which was in Christ Jesus: [Let Him be your example in humility:]"

— PHILIPPIANS 2:5 AMPC

Ask yourself, what are the things that will bring about restoration in my life? How can I get God's attention? Humility is your first winning battle strategy.

"Then, if my people who are called by my name will humble themselves and pray and seek my face and turn from their wicked ways, I will hear from heaven and will forgive their sins and restore their land."

— 2 CHRONICLES 7:14 NLT

Position yourself as a kingdom that wins. You will be more successful in life when you understand how to receive victories in the Spirit realm. That trickles down to your physical life too.

We read about the spiritual exaltation Jesus received from God, the Father, in Philippians 2:5-11. How would one ever think there could be a more excellent position (humility) for God the Son, for He is God. A position that gave Him the name above all names, for all eternity. When a son or daughter of God calls upon the name "Jesus," every opposition succumbs.

The authority in the name of Jesus was birth in humility. Positioned in this unique virtue, Jesus saved all humanity, triumphed over darkness, and now is building up a people to walk in divine authority. Imagine what you become when you begin having this mind. Imagine the reward you receive from God, knowing the reward Jesus received positioned in humility.

God has called you to a spiritual awareness that will bring forth exponential growth in your spiritual authority. You will be victorious and blessed to walk in it and be it.

Pack a New Bag, Label It; My Spirit Journey Begins

"Therefore if anyone is in Christ [that is, grafted in, joined to Him by faith in Him as Savior], he is a new creature [reborn and renewed by the Holy Spirit]; the old things [the previous moral and spiritual condition] have passed away. Behold, new things have come [because spiritual awakening brings a new life]."

— 2 CORINTHIANS 5:17

Now, begin to purpose to change the dynamics of your life. What are you passionate about? The hard work and excellence you put into your regular earthly jobs, business, working out, making it in life, etc., begin to put that same energy to establish this new way of life.

Just like you eat healthy to keep well, begin to put heavenly nourishment into your spirit-man. Boldly declare your freedom from old ways and consciously decree the things God has said concerning you.

Pull out the junk by looking deeply into your life and identify the triggers that have made you self-sabotage. Repent and begin to pull them out from your life, physically and spiritually. Tell the Lord you are breaking free of them and entering into a covenant with Him.

Jesus paid the price for you to walk in His authority. Take that authority and enforce God's Kingdom in your life. You cannot continue with the former ways of thinking and doing things and expect different results. You must become God's new creation. You will effectively define who this new creation is by the power of the Holy Spirit. Nobody can do it for you but you. How badly do you want it? How long do you want to sit and watch your life pass without you getting the things God said are yours?

If you got here and still feel passive about your spiritual stance, there is a stronghold over your life that you must be free from; reach out to us for prayer and counsel. It is a plot of Satan to overcome you if you will still sit and complain about the shame of 20 years ago when you can change it now. It is the plan of God for you to have stayed on till now. Daily choose to partner with God. Use your voice and speak God's plans over your life the things you have learned. Your voice is powerful in the entire universe. The kingdoms of this world must know that the Kingdom of God is speaking when you talk. Your spirit journey begins.

A Prayer to Consciously Engage Your Spirit in New Patterns

Think of all the covenants you may have made with the demonic spirit realm that has limited you from a life of total devotion to God and begin to pray.

In the name of Jesus, I break free from these (list them) covenants. I cut them off from their roots in the name of Jesus. I will not feed into it anymore. Depression, oppression, I cut off the source of your power in me in Jesus' name. Pornography, sexual addictions, drug addictions, masturbation, (and name all the things you struggle with) hear the voice of the Lord right now; I cut off every attraction towards these strongholds. Every desire and propensities towards satisfying my flesh, I uproot from my life right now. I declare that I am removing everything God has not planted in my life now.

Today, I uproot every plant of wickedness, addictions, poverty, curses, and I command them out. All of these strongholds, both spiritual, mental, and physical, I command you to be uprooted from my life in Jesus' name.

I uproot the patterns of operations the demonic realm has had in my decision-making processes. I clean out the pathways these sins and heartbreaks have made inside me that keep me returning back to the old ways of living. I command every demon that sat upon my brokenness to break off now in Jesus' name. I uproot the seed of fear that keeps holding me in a lie of bondage, thinking that I will never survive without this thing (name it...).

I command every demon that sat upon my areas of brokenness to break off now, in Jesus' name. I uproot the seed of fear. I look you in the eyes, and I cast you out! Get out of my life for good in Jesus' name.

I decree that my body, God's temple, and kingdom will no longer partici-pate in Satan's filthy ways. I declare that I can sense ungodly triggers and immediately rise to pray and cut off its support system in my life in Jesus' name.

I begin to establish new desires of love, power, and a sound mind in Jesus' name. "For God has not given us a spirit of fear, but of power and of love and of a sound mind." (2 Timothy 1:7).

I declare that this new creation will live with the Father, Son, and the Holy Spirit. I declare that they alone have the final say in my life.

I have turned away from the former ways; I have thrown away the old bag and that old, fruitless journey I was on. My bags are packed. I proceed with You into the new life, new ways, new patterns, and new hope.

May all that flows from Heaven find their place within my life moving forward. I will consciously entertain God's word in my daily walk. I will make it the standard for all my operations. I will commune with You, God, always. Seeking You every day will be the delight of my life. I decree this in the most victorious name of Jesus. Amen!

I decree that the blood of Jesus flushes out every part of my being that has harbored ungodly influences. I apply the blood of Jesus to every ungodly altars I have raised in my temple. I break down the foundations of demonic triggers and the source of their looming presence over me. Whether they stem from my childhood, I step out of their shadow and that evil cast they have placed over me. I decree that I no longer reside under their covering anymore. But as a son of God, I come under the shadow of the Most High God.

> "He who dwells in the secret place of the Most High
>   Shall abide under the shadow of the Almighty."

— PSALM 91:1

> "You will also declare a thing,
>   And it will be established for you;
>   So light will shine on your ways."

— JOB 22:28

Now, *declare* the following with me, speaking out loud, if you can:

El Shaddai, I come underneath Your shadow. I sit underneath You, and I feel the covering protection of Your wings around me. I sit and begin to dream afresh about the new journeys that await me.

An adventure of a lifetime opens up before me, and I choose to go on ahead and be everything you have called and fashioned me to be on the face of the earth. I do all of these through Your mighty Spirit living within me.

The Spirit of God will now trigger me to righteousness. Activate me for heavenly triggers. I do all things by the Holy Spirit's leading. I win all battles. I am victorious.

I choose to enjoy relationship with my Father in His Kingdom today. I desire face-to-face encounters with Him.

I come reintroducing myself to my world: Look, here I come, a son of God, fulfilling the will of my Father alone. I come to flesh out every word You wrote concerning me in my destiny scroll.

> *"Then I said, 'Behold, I have come—*
> *In the volume of the book it is written of Me—*
> *To do Your will, O God.'"*

> — HEBREWS 10:7

I come as one bought by the blood of Jesus. Lord, I stand before Your Throne, decreeing to all the kingdoms of this world that I will not be touched. I will not be harmed, for I bear upon my body the marks of the Lord Jesus Christ.

> *"From now on let no one trouble me, for I bear in my body the marks of the Lord Jesus."*

> — GALATIANS 6:17

The Godhead has placed a beautiful robe upon you. You have a lovely crown on your head. You wear it well, my beloved. See, Your Abba Father clothes you in the power of the Holy Spirit. God displays you as His whatever messes with you is messing with the apple of God's eyes. (See Deuteronomy 32:10, Psalm 17:8). Your invitation remains, Spirit, Spirit, Spirit!

By God's Grace, I will be with you again in the sequel "***Spirit Spirit Spirit: Restoring the God-Image.***"

Now, go, live as a spirit being, borne by the Spirit of God and living a victorious life in God's Kingdom realm. Your spirit-man ready and yearning to walk in the Spirit. (See Galatians 5:16-18)

Win all your cases in the Courts of Heaven and bring that victory into your life here on earth. Rule and Reign!

ABOUT THE AUTHOR

Nadia is the founder of "*Spirit Talks with Nadia.*" She leads "*Power with God Prayers*" live on Facebook every Saturday on her "*Spirit Talks with Nadia*" Page, from where testimonies abound of the miraculous healings, restoration, and deliverances through God's loving touch. Nadia has been in ministry for over 20 years, upholding God's Word and Truth and seeing many delivered.

One day, in prayer with her husband, Nadia bursts into Heaven right out of her living room. That would be the start of a unique relationship with God that she never knew existed on this side of eternity.

Nadia reveals Wisdom and Truth embedded in Scripture that breaks spiritual bondages and establishes God's great plans in many lives. With revelation knowledge of the Bible and Heaven, she equips, trains, and empowers people towards intimacy with God in Heaven.

Nadia and her husband, Ime, are blessed with two lovely daughters.

Connect with Nadia at Spirit Talks with Nadia on Facebook, Instagram, YouTube, Podcasts – available on most platforms. Also, visit Nadia's website for amazing testimonies and more resources at spirittalkswithnadia.com.

facebook.com/spirittalkswithnadia

instagram.com/spirittalkswithnadia

Made in the USA
Middletown, DE
10 September 2022

10117205R00157